# PASSPORT
# TO
# DISCOUNT TRAVEL

by Christopher Allen

**World View Press**
**Orlando, Florida**

# PASSPORT TO DISCOUNT TRAVEL

Although the author and publisher have exhaustively researched all sources to ensure the accuracy and completeness of the information contained in the book, we assume no responsibility for errors, inaccuracies, omissions or any other inconsistency herein. Any slights against people or organizations are unintentional.

**Passport to Discount Travel.**
Copyright © 1992 by Christopher Allen.
Printed and bound in the United States of America.

First Edition

Book Design by Jean Naumann and Debra Tate

HERMAN copyright 1990 Jim Unger. Reprinted with permission of Universal Press Syndicate.

Published by World View Press,
P. O. Box 620821
Orlando, FL 32862-0821.

Allen, Christopher, 1947–
    Passport to discount travel/by Christopher Allen.
        p.  cm.
    Includes bibliographical references.
    ISBN 0-9629048–0–5 : $14.95
    1.  Travel.    I. Title.
G151.A45  1991
910.2'02—dc20                                        91–40853
                                                      CIP

Dedicated
to my loving parents,
Christine and Al

# ACKNOWLEDGEMENTS

I owe much to many people for their tremendous contributions in behalf of this book. Although too numerous to mention individually, I nonetheless wish to convey my gratitude to all of them. I would like to thank specifically six incredibly energetic spirits responsible for bringing me into the world of travel and for expanding my horizons to unimagined limits: Bob and Barbara Rogers, and Gwen Morrisette of Richmond, Virginia, and Cal Simmons and Dan and Gloria Bohan of Washington DC. They all run successful travel agencies, and are the most knowledgeable, wonderful folks to know.

For vital assistance in producing this book, I wish to thank: Jill Lai, copy-editing; Alice and Jack Mahnke proofreading; Jean Naumann, cover design; David Herman, graphic art; and Phyllis Herman, editing and typography.

My heartfelt gratitude goes to two individuals who contributed the most in creating the clarity and logic between these covers: Christine Ferrari for insightful suggestions, and Debra, my wife and co-editor, for her abundant input, unflagging patience, and ultimate wisdom in giving me the original inspiration to write this book.

# PASSPORT TO
# DISCOUNT TRAVEL

# TABLE OF CONTENTS

## INTRODUCTION

## CHAPTER 1: DO YOUR RESEARCH

## CHAPTER 2: LAST-MINUTE BARGAINS

## CHAPTER 3: AIRLINES

# TABLE OF CONTENTS

# PASSPORT TO
# DISCOUNT TRAVEL

## CHAPTER 4: HOTELS

## CHAPTER 5: RENTAL CARS

# TABLE OF CONTENTS

## CHAPTER 6: CRUISES

# PASSPORT TO
# DISCOUNT TRAVEL

## CHAPTER 7: TOURS

## CHAPTER 8: TRAINS

# TABLE OF CONTENTS

## CHAPTER 9: INSURE YOUR TRIP

# PASSPORT TO
# DISCOUNT TRAVEL

## CHAPTER 10: BEWARE OF TRAVEL RIP-OFFS

## CHAPTER 11: SAFETY TIPS

## CHAPTER 12: PACKING POINTERS

## CHAPTER 13: WHAT ABOUT MONEY?

# TABLE OF CONTENTS

## CHAPTER 14: WORK IN THE WORLD OF TRAVEL

## CHAPTER 15: REMINDERS

## APPENDIXES

# INTRODUCTION

**"To be able to fill leisure intelligently
is the last product of civilization."**
Arnold Toynbee

Here is the first consumer guide designed to show you how to save money on all your travel expenses. It will help cut costs whenever and wherever you journey. It is dedicated to the principle that most people love to travel ... they just don't like to pay so much for it!

One key to success in acquiring travel bargains is knowing your options. Discounts of all kinds abound in the travel world. Last-minute specials, new service promotions, and off-season rates are just a few examples. Also, trips planned well in advance often result in good prices. However, in order to realize these savings and many others, you must first learn where and how to look for them, and when to arrange your schedule to meet their restrictions. This book will help you accomplish these goals.

Researching your options, keeping a flexible schedule, and traveling "off-peak" are big pluses in receiving the lowest rates. But what if you have to leave in a hurry? Can you still save

# INTRODUCTION

money? Yes. We will show you how.

We will also present and explain some old and new methods of finding and obtaining travel discounts not only on airfares, but also on hotels, car rentals, cruises, tours, and trains. Most of the money-saving techniques will work successfully for anyone. Others, however, work best only for certain kinds of individuals such as students, senior citizens, business travelers, military personnel, and the truly adventurous.

Much of the information in this book pertains to travel in North America, the Caribbean and Europe; however, most of the discount-producing suggestions can be applied in a variety of countries around the world.

Included are chapters on protecting your trip with travel insurance, and safeguarding your home and yourself while you're away; traveling safely with your pet; getting the most out of foreign exchange rates, and obtaining foreign tax refunds on purchases.

Experts will tell you that the one constant in the travel industry is change. Because of the highly competitive nature of business, all prices, policies and procedures may change at any time without notice. Therefore, play it safe. When planning your trip, check with the travel operators you'll be using to verify their current policies. Typically, the more you prepare for your trip, the fewer unpleasant surprises you'll encounter on your journey.

Travel is a growing, multi-billion dollar business with many operators wanting a piece of the pie. Reputable transportation and travel companies operate under government regulations and conduct business according to clearly defined industry guidelines. Unfortunately, even in such a closely regulated industry, some companies operate on shaky legal and financial ground. Can you tell if your travel service is reputable and solvent? We'll show you how to assess travel vendor legitimacy,

# PASSPORT TO
# DISCOUNT TRAVEL

determine provider credibility, and avoid costly rip-offs.

Our aim is to give you the most bang for your travel buck. After reading this book, it is hoped that if you are careful and wise when planning and taking your trip, you will have little cause to repeat Richard Armour's lament ...

"That money talks,
I'll not deny.
I heard it once:
It said, 'Goodbye.' "

**Passport to Discount Travel** contains knowledge gleaned from nearly 15 years in the business, and from countless miles, days, and nights on the go. May it help you plan your future trips wisely and economically so they are filled with joyous adventure. Bon voyage!

# PASSPORT TO DISCOUNT TRAVEL

**HERMAN**®

"What have you got within walking distance?"

# Chapter 1

# DO YOUR RESEARCH

**"Idleness is the holiday of fools."**
Chinese proverb

Living in this miraculous age of unlimited travel, we can visit almost anywhere in the world. Some people travel for business, others for fun. Some enjoy vacations at a frantic pace; others like to slow it down a little, agreeing with J. B. Priestley that, "a good holiday is one spent among people whose notions of time are vaguer than yours."

Travel is the most rewarding way to explore the world's amazing diversity of people, places, countries, and cultures. Only through first-hand experience can you truly appreciate the beauty of a languid Caribbean sunset, the thrill of an aerial cable-car ride up the Swiss Alps, the serenity of a Japanese flower garden, the adventure of an African safari, the bustle of a Parisian shopping district, the fertility of an Amazon rain forest, or the majesty of the Grand Canyon.

As Erma Bombeck, who prefers getting away from it all when she travels, says: "Escaping to a civilization that has never seen raisins dance on TV or a Liz Claiborne label fascinates me. If I wanted to drink tap water, speak English and eat Italian, I'd stay home."

Yet all these experiences will mean different things to different people, because wherever you go, whatever you do, you

**1**

# PASSPORT TO
# DISCOUNT TRAVEL

perceive the world through your own experiences. That's what makes travel so fascinating... it enables you to see and feel the world, "up close and personal."

The Boy Scouts' motto is, "Be prepared," and it works here, too. Planning your trip carefully is not only part of the fun of any vacation, it also enhances the degree of enjoyment and savings you'll receive, especially if you keep an eye on the bottom line. If you shop wisely for good values, you'll enjoy more savings from the start and have fewer mishaps while traveling, resulting in more fun on your trip.

Now don't misunderstand. There is nothing wrong with spontaneity—some terrific jaunts begin on sheer impulse—but you're likely to increase your trip's economy and pleasure by doing your homework first. Besides looking for good prices, you should become familiar with the history and customs of your destinations.

Start by reading up on where you want to go. At your public library or local bookstore, you'll find guidebooks on travel to the four corners of the world, for all budgets, and all types of trips—from "bed and breakfast" weekends to "big spender" expeditions.

Magazines such as TRAVEL AND LEISURE, Conde Nast's TRAVELER, and National Geographic's TRAVEL, publish articles about upscale ventures to many places in the world. They also report travel news, money-saving ideas and programs. INTERNATIONAL TRAVEL NEWS, 201 Lathrop Way, Suite D, Sacramento, CA 95815 (916-457-3643) publishes tips on economical travel outside the United States.

Read your newspaper's Travel section each week. The articles and ads provide useful information on trendy travel spots and current bargains. Check out the in-depth reports on destinations, cruises and late-breaking travel news in the Sunday supplements of

# DO YOUR RESEARCH

newspapers such as THE NEW YORK TIMES, THE WASHINGTON POST or THE LOS ANGELES TIMES. No matter where you live, make an effort to obtain a copy of at least one of them. They carry timely articles and advertisements which may not be listed in your local paper.

Well-known travel guides, such as THOMAS COOK, FIELD-ING, FODOR, and MICHELIN (available in libraries and bookstores), describe numerous countries and cities, and rate many restaurants and lodgings by price and service. For those on a tight budget, Harvard's LET'S GO! series is favored, as are several books published yearly on how to travel for a set amount each day, such as Frommer's EUROPE ON A BUDGET. Those who need to pare their expense account items may be interested in THE WALL STREET JOURNAL GUIDES TO BUSINESS TRAVEL, at libraries, bookstores or direct from the publisher: (800-733-3000). Volumes cover U.S. and Canada, Europe, the Pacific Rim, and International cities (about $20).

You can even catch highlights of your destination before leaving home on cable TV travel programs (see Appendix I), or on videos available at bookstores, travel agencies and videotape rental outlets. FODOR'S VIDEO TRAVEL GUIDES preview such exciting places as Hawaii, Singapore, Bangkok, Great Britain and Mexico. They are produced by the same Fodor family famous for their fine guidebooks. The tapes (approximately $25 to $30) present a travelogue on each location, and include a map and a booklet filled with information. These tapes are distributed by the INTERNATIONAL VIDEO NETWORK, 2242 Camino Ramon, San Ramon, CA 94583 (800-443-0100). IVN also produces tapes for travelers called VIDEO VISITS, focusing on the history and culture of various cities and countries.

Take advantage of the booking and information services provided free of charge by travel agencies. They supply numerous brochures describing vacations, tours and cruises, and recommend special bargains based on first-hand knowledge. They guide you through the complicated maze of fares and travel packages, and help select good values. As competitive and confusing as the travel market is today, you would be wise to use a travel agent.

Automobile clubs such as the American Automobile Association (AAA), and those sponsored by some oil companies, department stores, and credit card issuers, provide members with excellent routing guides and road maps of the U.S. and foreign countries, as well as information on hotels, restaurants, tours, and points of interest.

Tourist boards representing the states or countries you plan to visit are extremely helpful and provide brochures, maps and other information. See the Appendix at the back of this book for a complete list of phone numbers for the tourist boards of all the states. Most foreign tourist information offices can be found in at least one major city in North America such as New York, Washington, Los Angeles or Toronto. Check your phone directory, or call information in one of those cities for the tourist board.

Embassies and consulates provide details about major hotel and tourist attractions in their countries. Most foreign embassies are located in Washington, DC, and can supply information concerning visas, vaccines, entry requirements, and customs duties.

Contact your local post office or the U.S. State Department for passport information. The State Department can also inform you about any restrictions or advisories concerning countries considered dangerous for American visitors.

The State Department publishes a free guide for overseas travelers called, WHAT YOU SHOULD KNOW BEFORE YOU GO. Write: Americans Abroad, Consumer Information Center,

# DO YOUR RESEARCH

Pueblo, CO 81009. It covers a wide range of important subjects including traveling safely and securely; contacting local authorities, consulates or embassies in case of emergency; plus tips on medical matters, travel insurance, and visa and passport requirements. The State Department also publishes TIPS FOR TRAVELERS TO CENTRAL AND SOUTH AMERICA ($1.00).

If you are concerned about conditions ranging from civil unrest to natural disasters, a call on a touch-tone phone to the U.S. STATE DEPARTMENT CITIZENS EMERGENCY CENTER (202-647-5225) will give you information about problems in all parts of the world. The C.E.C. hotline, operating 24 hours a day, updates recorded travel advisories on dangerous and potentially risky countries, and explains how to get help when in trouble overseas. Advisories, by the way, are not restrictions, nor do they mean you should not visit the area. They are presented simply to make travelers aware of certain situations—if there are no problem in a particular country, no advisory is given.

For a list of U.S. Embassies, Consulates General, Consulates and Missions obtain a copy of KEY OFFICERS OF FOREIGN SERVICE POSTS, available for $1.75 from the Superintendent of Documents, U.S. Government Printing Office, Washington, DC 20402.

## VISA REQUIREMENTS

Most countries allow Americans to visit for less than three months with only a valid U.S. passport; others, however, require visas or passport stamps. A visa is an endorsement made on a passport allowing entry into a country, and shows that the

# PASSPORT TO
# DISCOUNT TRAVEL

passport has been examined and found in order. This permits visits to that country for a specific length of time and purpose.

Canada, Mexico, England, Japan, Hong Kong, much of the Caribbean and Western Europe do not require entry visas. Many other countries do, including Australia, Brazil, China, India, Kenya, and the former Eastern Bloc countries, although. visa restrictions in most former Communist countries are easing. Within unified East and West Germany, all visa requirements have been dropped. Czechoslovakia, Bulgaria and Hungary have also abolished visa requirements for American passport holders. Visits to Bulgaria and Czechoslovakia of less than 30 days, and visits to Hungary, up to 90 days, are visa-free. As of presstime, Poland and Romania still require visas. For more information, call their embassies or obtain a copy of EASTERN EUROPE: A TRAVELER'S COMPANION, (Houghton Mifflin, $14.95).

Some nations require visas to be obtained in the United States before departure; others issue them upon arrival in their country. To acquire a visa in advance, each traveler must submit an application, accompanied by a photograph, his or her passport, and a copy of a round trip airline ticket or other proof of transportation out of the country.

Visa application processing for many countries can take anywhere from a few days to two weeks or more. Visa handling can take up to a month, and sometimes even longer during the busy summer season, so allow plenty of time to apply for one. Business travelers to countries requiring visas may have to complete a separate business visa, and present a letter of reference from their employers vouching for the travelers' "moral and financial responsibility" while he or she is visiting the country.

Some visas are free while others cost anywhere from a few dollars to about $25. Applications may be obtained in person, or by mail, from each country's embassy or consulate. When

# DO YOUR RESEARCH

applying by mail, be sure to send your passport by **Registered Mail** and allow at least two weeks for processing. Professional visa services, usually located in major cities, will handle the paperwork for a fee starting at about $20, plus any applicable charges and postage. Because of their regular interaction with governmental agencies, these companies normally provide rush service.

A helpful booklet, FOREIGN ENTRY REQUIREMENTS, reviews passport and visa documents needed for travel to more than 150 countries, and lists addresses and phone numbers of the embassies and consulates. It can be obtained for 50 cents from the Consumer Information Center, Box 100, Pueblo, CO 81002.

If you need passport and visa information quickly, ask your travel agent, or call the U.S. State Department Citizen Emergency Center, open 24 hours a day in Washington, DC (202-647-5225).

## CUSTOMS AND IMPORT DUTIES

Import duties are government-assessed fees, on all items exceeding allowable free limits, which travelers bring into a country. "Customs" refers to the government agency empowered to enforce import restrictions and collect import duties.

American citizens returning from abroad, after at least 48 hours out of the country, may bring in $400 worth of non-prohibited merchandise and 2 quarts of liquor duty-free. Americans returning home from the countries and islands of the Caribbean are allowed to bring back $600 in goods without

# PASSPORT TO DISCOUNT TRAVEL

duty. Travelers returning from the U.S. Virgin Islands, Samoa or Guam enjoy exemptions up to $1,200, including 10 quarts of liquor. Other rules exist if you return in less than 2 days, or have used up the exemption during the previous 30 days. Products in excess of these limits are subject to Customs fees.

Families may combine exemptions, but minors may not import tobacco or alcoholic products. Since allowances are subject to change, check with an American embassy or customs office before purchasing products to bring home with you, or contact United States Customs, Department of the Treasury, Washington, DC 20229.

Knowing about import duties can help you save money since they are often low enough to make it more economical to buy certain products abroad and pay the import fees, than it is to buy the same items in the United States. Keep receipts handy to show value, especially on expensive merchandise. If purchases exceed exemptions, 10% is charged on the next $1,000 worth of goods, or 5% when returning from the U.S Virgin Islands, Samoa or Guam. Thereafter, individual items are charged variable fees set by the U.S. Customs Service and are subject to change.

When in doubt, call the nearest American embassy for advice, or refer to these booklets explaining customs regulations: KNOW BEFORE YOU GO gives detailed Customs information, and POCKET HINTS covers Customs exemptions. Both are available from United States Customs Service, Box 7407, Washington, DC 20044.

Duty free allowances for citizens of the United States returning from most countries applies only to items carried with you. Items mailed home are subject to duty, however, packages mailed home marked "unsolicited gift" with an indicated value of $50 or less are **not**, as of press-time, subject to duty. Appropriate mailing forms are available at foreign post offices.

# DO YOUR RESEARCH

Some articles brought into the United States are closely controlled. Most medicines and drug-administering paraphernalia must be accompanied by valid prescriptions. Firearms and ammunition require special permits. Certain foods, seeds, cuttings, and rooted plants are not allowed. Some other prohibited items include illegal drugs, products made from endangered species, ceramics with lead-based glaze, and automobiles not modified to meet current Environmental Protection Agency pollution control standards.

The United States Department of Agriculture publishes TRAVELERS' TIPS, a guide listing agricultural items banned from the country, and contains information on bringing back food, plants, and animals from abroad. For your free copy, write to: U.S. Dept. of Agriculture, Print and Distribution Branch, Room G-110, 6505 Belcrest Road, Hyattsville, MD 20782.

## HOW TO OBTAIN A PASSPORT

To acquire a U.S. passport, you will need proof of United States citizenship, such as an original birth certificate or notarized copy of your birth certificate, plus two recent 2" x 2" color photographs, a completed official passport application form, and the application fee. If your town doesn't have a U.S. State Department Passport Agency, you can pick up an application at most post offices, and federal or state courthouses. For recorded passport information, 24 hours a day, call 202-647-0518. For additional assistance, dial 202-326-6060 during normal business hours.

9

# PASSPORT TO DISCOUNT TRAVEL

When going abroad, make sure your passport is current. Some places, such as Bermuda and the Bahamas, accept expired passports from American citizens, but most other countries **do not**. If you don't have a passport, it's a good idea to get one, even if you don't plan to travel overseas any time soon. (After reading this book, you may be inspired to visit foreign countries sooner than you think!) Newly issued passports are valid for 10 years. Apply for your passport early, so you'll have it when you need it. Allow at least four to six weeks for processing, especially if you are planning to travel during the busy summer season.

## THE TRAVEL PLANNER

An excellent reference to help organize a trip is the TRAVEL PLANNER which contains a wealth of important data, including the addresses and toll-free phone numbers of practically every major airline, hotel chain, tourist board, tour operator, cruise line and car rental company in the world. It publishes maps of airports in major cities, lists ground transportation and air taxi services, supplies city and hotel information, and pinpoints colleges, universities, and military installations. For foreign countries, it presents facts on currency, language, weather, entry requirements, and major holidays and festivals. You can find the TRAVEL PLANNER at most travel agencies and public libraries. For subscription information, call 800-323-3537.

For complete schedules of all domestic and international airlines, check the OFFICIAL AIRLINE GUIDE (OAG). This large,

# DO YOUR RESEARCH

phone book-size version of the OAG is available at every travel agency. However, you may want a copy of the handy POCKET FLIGHT GUIDE for personal use. Four geographic editions are published: North America; Europe/Middle East/Africa; Pacific/Asia; and Latin America/Caribbean. Subscribers receive copies of FREQUENT FLYER MAGAZINE (800-342-5624). An electronic flight guide called THE OAG ELECTRONIC EDITION is also available on disks for personal computers and permits you to access over 20 travel related databases. It lets you check sched-ules, choose fares, and make reservations using your own com-puter. Specify IBM or Mac version when ordering.

A new executive-travel handbook, called ON-TIME, from East/West Network, publisher of in-flight magazines, lists 65,000 flight schedules in a compact 4x9 inch format. Updated monthly, the guide contains information on hotels, restaurants and executive services in a score of American cities and a half-dozen foreign destinations. European editions are also available. The cost is $10 per issue; annual subscription is $69, plus $6 for shipping (800-765-8453).

## THE WEATHER

After you've reviewed travel brochures, researched options, and decided on destinations, don't stop there—consider the climate where you're going. Don't let your hopes for good weather blind you to the possibility of poor weather such as severe storms or unusually hot or cold spells.

"Off-season" rates may mean a bargain, and although the weather may not be ideal during your stay, fewer tourists may

# PASSPORT TO
# DISCOUNT TRAVEL

result in less hassles and more fun. Skiing the Rockies in Spring, for example, may not be considered "in-season" by powder snow purists, but the skiing is still good, the lift lines are shorter, and the prices are normally lower. Decide which is more important to you ... ideal weather or off-season rates.

Be savvy about conditions which could affect your trip. When staying in high mountains such as the Rockies or Alps, allow time for your body to adjust to the thin air. For some people, this could take several days. Fortunately, the common symptoms of oxygen deprivation such as headaches, shortness of breath, nausea and lack of energy are temporary and normally disappear after you become acclimated to the altitude. Anticipate these potential effects by easing into high elevations and avoiding extensive physical activity or over-exertion immediately.

When taking a cruise, or traveling in the tropics, beware of possible skin damage from intense equatorial sun. The "CRUISE" chapter of this book discusses sunscreens, clothing and other tips to protect you from sunburn.

Up-to-the-minute weather information for various locations can be obtained in several ways. Most newspapers publish temperatures, current conditions, and forecasts for cities worldwide. Cable television's WEATHER CHANNEL updates travelers' advisories twice an hour. WEATHERTRAK provides telephone weather reports for more than 750 cities around the globe (900-370-8728). A special feature of WEATHERTRAK is its selection of information, including extended forecasts, weather and road conditions, foreign currency exchange rates, and entry requirements. The cost is about a dollar for the first minute and 50 cents for each additional minute.

900-WEATHER provides extended forecasts, road conditions, ski reports, and other travel tips for more than 600

# DO YOUR RESEARCH

cities in the U.S. and 225 cities overseas. Using a touch-tone phone, press: 1 for U.S. cities; 2 for foreign cities; 3 for specific conditions (boating, skiing, etc.). The cost, 95 cents per minute, will appear on your phone bill or may be charged to your American Express Card.

To receive a list of all cities covered under the service, send a self-addressed, stamped envelope to 900-WEATHER, 100 Church St., 14th Floor, New York, NY 10007.

The American Automobile Association (AAA) offers a similar worldwide weather service to its customers. By dialing 1-900-884-AAA1, the caller receives weather reports for cities around the world, plus detailed road conditions and other pertinent information. The charge is 75 cents for the first minute and 50 cents for each additional minute. Non-members can also use this service.

## PROTECT YOUR HEALTH

**Never run when you can walk, never stand when you can sit, never sit when you can lie down, and never pass up a chance to use the bathroom.**

Following this advice will help you conserve energy and avoid fatigue. Prevent illness by taking a few, common sense precautions. Get plenty of rest before starting a long journey. Although this is difficult to do sometimes in the frenzied days leading up to a much-anticipated trip, get as much sleep as possible several days before departure.

# PASSPORT TO
# DISCOUNT TRAVEL

You may wish to offset the effects of jet lag, caused when crossing too many time zones, by trying the ANTI-JET LAG DIET developed by the Argonne Laboratory, a U.S. Department of Energy research center. This laminated credit card-size guide explains the correct combination of feasting and fasting which will help acclimate your body to new time zones. For a free copy, send a stamped, self-addressed envelope to Argonne National Laboratory, 9700 South Cass Ave., Argonne, IL 60439.

When planning you trip, consider how to find, and pay for, emergency medical help if needed. Check your insurance policy for overseas medical coverage and exemptions. Purchase any additional medical travel insurance needed before you go. (See the chapter, INSURE YOUR TRIP for more details.) Get copies of your prescriptions from your doctor before departure, and ask for any recommendations or medical contacts in the areas you'll be visiting.

When traveling abroad, call the appropriate tourist boards or U.S. embassies or consulates for medical references. Embassies are your safe haven in an emergency overseas. They will assist you by providing names of doctors who speak English, and hospitals with English-speaking staff. For that matter, if you ever encounter an emergency you cannot handle, the U.S. embassy is there to both help and protect you.

The INTERNATIONAL ASSOCIATION FOR MEDICAL ASSISTANCE TO TRAVELERS (IAMAT) has organized a network of English and French-speaking physicians in over 500 cities worldwide who have post-graduate training in either North America or Britain, make housecalls and charge reasonable pre-set fees.

With your free membership, you receive a booklet listing IAMAT centers, participating hospitals and doctors providing competent medical care on a 24-hour basis. They also supply helpful materials such as the World Immunization Chart, World

# DO YOUR RESEARCH

Climate Chart, How to Protect Yourself Against Malaria, and more.

IAMAT is a non-profit organization dependent on grants and individual contributions which are tax-deductible. For more information or to request membership, contact: IAMAT, 417 Center Street, Lewiston, NY 14092-3633.

Before going abroad, be sure to get all necessary inoculations. Ask your personal physician, tour operator, or the State Department which shots are required or recommended for a specific area, and get them well in advance in case of a reaction to the injections.

To avoid diarrhea and other intestinal problems common to travelers, exercise caution with local food and drink. Refrigeration in some countries is spotty at best, so avoid foods which should be kept cool but may have been left at room temperature. In certain areas, it is wise **not** to drink the water, or any beverage with ice in it. Steer clear of salads containing uncooked vegetables which may have been rinsed in local tap water. **Boil it, cook it, peel it or forget it!**

Here are some other ways to safeguard your health while traveling:

• **Drink bottled water or soda, and eat fresh citrus fruit which you peel yourself**. Eat foods which have been cooked thoroughly to destroy bacteria. Some places where this precaution applies are: Mexico, Central America, parts of South America, Africa, and the Orient, outside of Japan.

You can purify water several ways:

(1) **Boiling**. This is the most common and effective way of reducing potentially harmful germs. Since many hotel rooms do **not** come equipped with a hotplate or a pot, resourceful

# PASSPORT TO DISCOUNT TRAVEL

travelers heat small amounts of water with "heating coils". These electric heating elements are placed in a cup or jar to produce boiling water in about five minutes. These can be purchased at department stores and travel-specialty shops. Be sure to get the correct electrical adaptors required in the countries you are visiting.

(2) **Chemical Treatment**. Water may be sanitized with a few drops of tincture of iodine or commercial water purification tablets available at many pharmacies and camping-supply stores.

(3) **Ultra-Violet Light**. Compact, portable sterilizers utilize ultra-violet light to purify up to a quart of water in minutes without changing the temperature. Use the proper electrical outlet adaptor overseas. Call a travel merchandise shop for prices and details about UV sterilizers such as the "Aqua Light" which weighs just 2 pounds and measures 9x7x3 inches.

• **Be smart and avoid fatigue**. Pace yourself. Don't try to do everything right away. You'll knock yourself out if you attempt to do too much. Prioritize what you want to see most, and start at the top of the list allowing time for spontaneous side-trips, exploration, and adventure. Afford yourself the leisure to browse in a fascinating shop, or relax in a hidden cafe.

Don't program yourself too strictly, and don't frustrate yourself by poor planning. Always check museum times and store hours before you go. Avoid the disappointment of finding an important site closed, especially near the end of your trip when you may not have a chance to revisit it. Double check the performance times of shows or special events you hope to see. Plan ahead, and adjust your schedule accordingly.

# DO YOUR RESEARCH

In some hot countries, everything stops in the middle of the day for a leisurely break or siesta. Shops and banks close, commerce ceases, and life slows to a crawl. A late dinner hour is typical as life returns to normal in the cooler evening.

• **Keep up your strength by eating normally**. Try not to skip meals. Sightseeing and traveling take energy, so treat your body well. If you don't have a sit-down meal, economize by having a picnic! Buy some wine or cold drinks, your favorite cheese, bread, fruit, and anything else you'd like, then enjoy a picnic in a park, or along the way to your next destination.

• **Get your health questions answered before you go**. The State Department Citizen Emergency Center will tell you if health advisories have been issued for any of your destinations. If you need information about inoculations required for any country, contact the U.S. Department of Health and Human Services in Washington, DC (202-619-0257), or read the guide entitled HEALTH INFORMATION FOR INTERNATIONAL TRAVEL published by the Center for Disease Control in Atlanta (404-639-3311).

For practical advice concerning medical problems or illness abroad, consult, TRAVEL MEDICAL HELPER by Dr. George Landis. Subtitled A MEDICAL HOW-TO WHEN YOU ARE AWAY FROM HOME, this 61-page guide covers common problems affecting the head, chest, abdomen, urinary tract, and skin as well as motion and altitude sickness. It is available for $5.00 plus $1.50 for postage from Lowell Press, P.O. Box 411877, 115 E. 31st St., Kansas City, MO 64141.

For an in-depth look at travel and health, read FIELDING'S TRAVELER'S MEDICAL COMPANION (William Morrow), available at book stores and libraries.

17

# PASSPORT TO
# DISCOUNT TRAVEL

## TRAVEL FOR HANDICAPPED PERSONS

Disabled or handicapped passengers can receive information about accessible places to stay and visit in the U.S. and abroad from the TRAVEL INFORMATION SERVICE OF MOSS REHABILITATION HOSPITAL, 1200 West Tabor Rd., Philadelphia, PA 19141-3099 (215-456-9600) or (215-456-9602) (tdd).

Information on up to three locations worldwide is provided; requests take about one month to process and costs $5 (payable to Moss Rehabilitation Hospital) to the address listed above.

Travel for the disabled can be arranged by SPROUT, INC., a non-profit organization located in New York City, specializing in foreign and domestic tours for teenagers and adults with developmental disabilities. Contact SPROUT, INC., 893 Amsterdam Ave., New York, NY 10025. (212-222-9575).

Travelers requiring medical assistance can be accompanied by trained nurses practically anywhere in the world through the TRAVELING NURSES NETWORK (206-694-2462). These nurses can obtain oxygen, respiratory or medical equipment, or specially equipped vans. The nurses assist travelers suffering from diabetes, dialysis and cardiac problems, as well as spinal cord injuries, psychiatric disorders, vision and hearing impairment or loss.

For information about facilities, services and accessible design features at over 500 airport terminals, write for a free copy of ACCESS TRAVEL:AIRPORTS, from Consumer Information Center, Pueblo, CO, 81009.

For details on renting cars in Europe with manual controls, controls for quadriplegic drivers, left-side accelerator pedals and steering knobs contact AUTO EUROPE (800-223-5555).

# Chapter 2

# LAST-MINUTE BARGAINS

**"One of the most common disruptions of
marital bliss is the choice of where to spend a
vacation. What this country needs is an ocean
in the mountains."**
Paul Sweeney

Deciding where to go on vacation can be vexing. Personal preferences, individual schedules, and available finances must be considered. Yet, a destination may practically choose itself when an excellent last-minute travel bargain comes along.

For some people, it's timing, not price, which makes a trip attractive. Two-career couples juggling conflicting schedules might like to sneak away for a weekend—with or without the kids. Unfortunately, because of the difficulty in planning a quick getaway, they may feel victimized by the high prices usually associated with short-notice travel.

The fact is travelers **do not** always have to spend more money to keep a flexible itinerary. In fact, they may even spend less because some companies buy unsold space on airlines, cruises, and tours, and pass them on at savings of 25% to 40% — **without** advance purchase requirements for discounts.

We will list some of these discount travel brokers and clubs below, but first let's see how they work.

# PASSPORT TO
# DISCOUNT TRAVEL

## TRAVEL WHOLESALERS

Travel wholesalers take unsold airplane seats, hotel rooms, and cruise cabins, then sell them at bargain rates, sometimes as much as 70% off retail. Essentially, they convert what would be a total loss into revenue.

Discount travel clubs are constantly on the lookout for "specials", not only to popular destinations, but less visited places such as Eastern Europe. Responding rapidly to bargains when they become available throughout the world, wholesale vendors look for customers who can quickly take advantage of these discounts. To get last-minute specials, you may have to travel on short notice, sometimes as little as a few days, and be flexible in your dates of departure, because bargains may not always be available on the dates you want to go.

Some "last minute clubs" specialize in international airline discounts, exotic cruises, or off-beat tours; others deal in domestic flights, standard cruises and popular tours. Some clubs offer discounts only at certain times between specific cities and destinations, while others offer discounts to many destinations year round.

When evaluating a last minute travel club, request a list of recent trips and prices, so you have an idea of their selections. Before joining, make sure the club features trips departing from nearby cities to desired destinations. Paying for expensive connecting flights from your hometown to a "gateway" airport could eliminate any savings you hoped to achieve by taking the discount package in the first place.

For an annual fee beginning at about $40, members usually receive newsletters reporting bargain travel, hotline phone numbers featuring recorded information on late-breaking specials, and of course, the service of the club as their agent.

Although some wholesalers and travel clubs are affiliated with full-service travel agencies, they generally do not plan trips nor customize vacations specifically for you. Normally, they supply little detailed advice or information about destinations or transportation companies.

Send money for a trip only when certain you intend to take it; if you do not go, you may not be able to get a refund. Full payment is usually required to reserve space, and once confirmation is made, you are virtually locked into the journey.

There are two things you can do to protect your investment:

• **Pay with a credit card.** If something goes drastically wrong during your vacation, such as your tour operator declaring bankruptcy and ceasing operations, you can challenge the charge through the credit card company. In most cases, you are not expected to pay for services not received.

• **Buy trip interruption/cancellation insurance.** You won't lose your money in case an accident or illness prevents you, or your travel companions, from starting or completing the trip or the tour operator fails to complete it obligations. Virtually all discounters sell travel insurance; some even include it automatically in the price. Ask about this coverage before paying for your trip.

A more thorough presentation of travel-related insurance is found in the subsequent chapters entitled, TOURS and INSURE YOUR TRIP.

# PASSPORT TO
# DISCOUNT TRAVEL

## DISCOUNT TRAVEL CLUBS

Some well-known wholesalers and last-minute discount travel clubs are listed below. (The companies are listed alphabetically, implying neither preference nor recommendation. Fees and services are subject to change.)

• DISCOUNT TRAVEL INTERNATIONAL, Narbeth, PA (800-334-9294) is one of the country's largest.

• ENTERTAINMENT/HOTLINE TRAVEL CLUB, Troy, MI (800-828-0826) or (313-637-9780) has a 30-day money-back satisfaction guarantee.

• LAST MINUTE TRAVEL CLUB, Boston, MA (617-267-9800) or (800-527-8646) has a score of travel consultants with a reputation for personalized service.

• MOMENTS NOTICE, New York, NY (212-486-0503) specializes in international trips. Companions travel at 30% to 60% discounts. Telephone recordings mention trips as much as a month or two ahead. Annual dues, around $50.

• R&R TRAVEL CLUB, Schaumberg, IL (800-621-5505) rebates regular travel services and provides discounts of up to 40% at more than 12,000 hotels worldwide.

# LAST MINUTE BARGAINS

• STANDBUYS, Aurora, CO (800-255-0200) lists trips discounted 5% to 50%, three days to eight weeks in advance. Membership includes a 60-day free trial.

• TRAVELERS ADVANTAGE, CITITRAVEL AND SEARS DISCOUNT TRAVEL CLUBS (800-548-1116) are credit card-related wholesalers offering a full range of club advantages: discounts, rebates, hot-lines, and travel services.

• TRAVELERS PLUS TRAVEL CLUB, San Diego, CA (800-843-0265) features low annual dues, 5% rebates on airfares, and savings on hotels and condos at over 2000 locations.

• UP 'N GO TRAVEL, Worcester, MA (800-888-8190) offers inexpensive family memberships and 50% savings on trips, primarily from New England to Florida or the Caribbean.

• VACATIONS TO GO, Houston, TX (800-338-4962) specializes in cruises and tours offering one to two-weeks' notice. Yearly fee entitles the whole family or accompanying guests to travel at discounts.

• WORLDWIDE DISCOUNT TRAVEL CLUB, Miami, FL (305-534-2082) has promoted trips to Bali, China and Southeast Asia. They sell space on flights, cruises and tours at savings of 15-50%. Annual membership is about $40; listings are mailed every three weeks.

# PASSPORT TO DISCOUNT TRAVEL

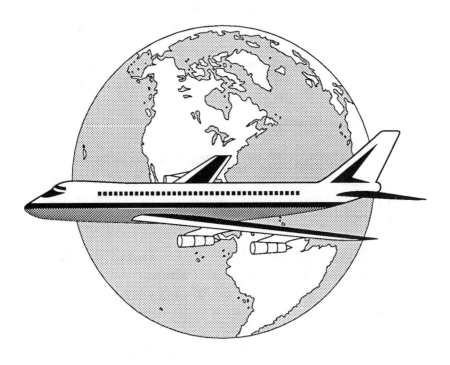

# Chapter 3

# AIRLINES

**"Manned flight is an extravagant feat of technological exhibitionism."**
Lewis Mumford

## THE MIRACLE OF FLIGHT

One of man's most remarkable achievements is his ability to fly. Throughout history, humans have looked to the skies, dreaming of soaring like birds in the heavens. For thousands of years, man has walked upon the earth; only recently has he been able to leave it. The pioneer balloonists of 18th Century France first broke the bonds of gravity when they took to the air in gas-filled balloons. At the dawn of the 20th Century, the Wright Brothers' premier powered flight in Kitty Hawk opened the skies to all mankind.

Ever since Orville and Wilbur's historic accomplishment, the pace of aviation's progress has rocketed forward at mach speed. Few fields of human endeavor have evolved as rapidly, and as radically, as flight.

In just a few generations air travel has developed from hot-air balloons to space shuttles. Aircraft have changed from

# PASSPORT TO
# DISCOUNT TRAVEL

paper and wire bi-planes, lofting one or two intrepid souls into the ether, to titanium and steel behemoths hurling up to 400 people across vast stretches of the planet. On the drawing boards for the 21st century are rocket-propelled passenger ships which can zoom through sub-orbital space, crossing oceans and continents in minutes.

Aircraft design has undergone revolutionary changes in a relative blur of time compared to the basic design changes of the automobile. In fewer years than it has taken for the car to evolve from the Ford Tin Lizzie to the Ferrari Testarosa, aircraft have evolved from man's imagination to space ships.

The basic design of the automobile, invented in Germany in 1880, has remained relatively the same over the years: an internal combustion engine, a steering wheel, four tires, two axles and a drive train. Put an antique automobile next to a sleek modern sports car, and anyone can tell they are both autos. Put a cloth-bodied, hand-stitched Wright Brothers airplane next to a huge jumbo jet, and one might wonder not only whether they were both airplanes, but whether either could actually fly at all. The "motorized-kite" of the early 1900's surely seems too flimsy to take off and land safely in one piece. The jumbo jet certainly seems too heavy to leave the ground even for one second, let alone for hours, flying higher than one can see with the naked eye.

Beyond the miracle of flight, modern aviation's most amazing feat is its mastery of both time and space. Air travel defeats distance and conquers the clock. Jet planes are nothing less than time machines. The early explorers needed one hundred hazardous days to cross the Atlantic Ocean from the Old World to the New; the fearless solo flyer, Charles Lindbergh, fought the elements for nearly forty frightening hours to cross the same ocean. Today's commercial jetliners take about eight to ten hours

# AIRLINES

for the same trip, and the faster-than-sound Concorde, a little more than four hours. Soon, the 21st Century trans-space plane will "hop the pond" in a brisk hour and a half. It will probably take longer to drive to the spaceport, park a car, and check in for the blast-off than it will to whiz from one continent to another. Aviation has come a long way, baby. And so have airfares.

## AIRFARES

Deregulation of the airline industry has created a buyer's market for discount airfares. Price wars have resulted in smaller profits for the airlines and lower prices for flyers. Over the years, air travelers have saved millions of dollars as a result of free-market competition which has kept some fares consistently low compared to the steady rise in cost for just about everything else. In general, airfares have risen at a much slower pace than the rate of inflation, but some fares, in fact, are extremely high.

The confusion lies in the pricing structure set up by the airlines themselves. In each market there are a number of different fares, some high, some low. From New York to Miami, for instance, there might be a fare of $600 roundtrip, and also one for $200. The question is, how to get the low one, and still be able to fly when you want to, and not when the airline tells you? It's relatively easy, once you know the rules of the game.

Fares change like the wind. They fluctuate depending on ever-shifting factors, such as competition in the marketplace, demand for seats, fuel and labor costs, and the financial condition of the airline and of the national economy. Cut-rate fares are attainable only if you know how to find them, but, you

# PASSPORT TO
# DISCOUNT TRAVEL

have to act fast to get them.

Exceptionally low fares are available periodically between certain cities. Normally, they last for a limited time and carry certain travel and purchase restrictions. It's impossible to predict when airlines will offer discount fares, to which cities, and for how long.

Vigilance is required to find the best prices. Check newspapers for airline advertisements. Newspapers are the chief medium used by the carriers to communicate bargain fares to the public. These fares may feature savings of 50% or more off regular coach.

When one airline starts price-cutting, others usually follow. As soon as you read about fare reductions, contact several carriers to compare prices. See if they match each others' advertised specials. If you find similar, but not necessarily identical rates on several carriers, make your selection based not only on price, but also on the value of the service you will receive. Some items to consider before choosing an airline are convenient flight schedules, non-stop or direct service, and on-time performance.

To learn an airline's recent on-time performance, simply ask the reservationist, or your travel agent, for the carrier's track record of its flights for the past 30 days. The Federal Aviation Administration (FAA) requires domestic airlines to compile statistics showing the actual times that their flights departed and arrived every day. After the data is compiled, it is passed on to reservation computers throughout the country.

A code appears in the computer indicating how often a flight is late. "Late" is defined as more than 15 minutes behind schedule. Thus, a flight with the performance code of "6" operated on time 60% to 70% during the previous month. A code of "9" means the flight was on time an average of 90% to 100%. A code "10" means perfection, something rarely seen in any human endeavor, including air travel. Knowing the history of a flight's on-time performance enhances the probability of punctual arrival by helping select flights operating on schedule more often than not.

## WHERE DO ALL THE FARES COME FROM?

Why are there so many different fares? All airlines have a multitude of prices for the destinations on their route system. Between any two cities an airline may have dozens of fares. One recent survey of several competing airlines found 63 different fares offered between New York City and Los Angeles! According to the WALL STREET JOURNAL, U.S. airlines altogether make thousands of fare changes every day!

How can you be sure of getting the lowest fare? We'll review traditional methods of finding low prices, and illustrate some new techniques and technologies used to hunt for the latest, lowest fares. But first, let's discover where all those fares come from.

The rampant profusion of fares and confusion in prices are the result of the federal government's deregulation of the airline industry. Deregulation has eliminated time-consuming governmental scrutiny over each and every fare adjustment, and has allowed unhindered competition among domestic carriers of fares and schedules, which is one reason why they change so frequently.

# PASSPORT TO DISCOUNT TRAVEL

## Yield Management

The plethora of fares is the product of a complex mathematical/marketing formula used by the airlines to maximize profits. Called yield management, this sophisticated, computer-assisted program enables airlines to juggle the availability of different fares, flight by flight, and seat by seat. Since the airlines strive to sell all of their coach seats at the highest possible amount, carriers adjust the price of unsold seats higher or lower depending on how many are still available as departure time approaches. They desperately try to sell all their remaining space, at discount prices, if necessary, so there are no empty seats when their planes take off.

Under yield management, airlines allocate certain fares to a specific number of coach seats on a given flight based on past booking patterns. As reservations come in for that flight, the computer, and a yield manager, track how the various fares are selling and make adjustments to increase revenue. The idea is to control the number of seats offered at a certain fare by revising the inventory of those seats on the basis of demand and expected no-shows. If the flight's higher-priced seats, usually bought by business travelers, seem to be selling faster than normal, the number of lower-priced seats available is reduced; if high-priced seats are not selling, then more seats will be discounted.

In other words, airlines adjust their prices based on the number of seats sold and the number of seats expected to be sold. It's a fact that an airline makes more money on a given flight by selling fewer seats at higher prices than by selling more seats at lower prices. For example, an airplane holds 150 seats. An airline will net more cash selling only 100 seats at the full coach fare of $200 ($20,000 gross income), than it would by selling out the entire plane at half-price discount fares of $100 ($15,000 gross

# AIRLINES

income). The airline that sells fewer seats for more money, makes more profit than the airline that sells all its seats for less money.

## Time Is Money

Yield management is a balancing act, and its effect is simple: The fewer people traveling on a given flight, the more seats available at reduced prices. Thus, if you are willing to travel on less popular flights, at less convenient times, or with longer flying times, you will generally find bargain seats.

Airlines usually attach restrictions to their lowest fares preventing most business travelers from using them. This forces anyone needing flexibility, convenience or immediate departures to pay more. The limited number of discount seats disappears quickly on the busiest flights; the remaining seats sell at a higher price because the airlines are banking on a greater demand for them. With such diverse requirements, it's no surprise passengers on any given flights pay various prices for their tickets.

## FINDING THE LOWEST FARES

If you follow a few basic guidelines, you can use yield management to your advantage.

• **Know the rules.** Bargain fares sound great, but they won't do you any good if you don't qualify for them. Be sure to

# PASSPORT TO
# DISCOUNT TRAVEL

ask the ariline reservationist or travel agent, "What day or times do I have to fly in order to qualify for that bargain fare?" If you know the rules of the game, and play by them, you can get the best rates.

• Nearly all reduced fares commonly known as "super-saver," "max-saver," or "super coach" come with certain booking, purchase and travel restrictions.

• The least expensive domestic fares usually require 7, 14, or 21-day advance reservations.

• You may have to purchase your ticket within 24 hours after making your reservation.

• Be prepared to stay over a Friday or Saturday night, since this is a requirement on virtually all of the lower fares.

More expensive fares have fewer restrictions concerning advance reservations, ticketing deadlines, and change/cancellation penalties. These short notice tickets are more costly because you're paying extra for rush service and the option to change or cancel without penalty.

• **Make your reservations in advance.** When shopping for fares, let your fingers do the walking. Pick up the phone and call the airlines or your travel agent for information on the lowest prices. Ask for special rates such as weekend discounts, off-season promotions, limited-time bargains, or new introductory fares.

Deeply discounted fares are limited, so if you want them,

# AIRLINES

plan ahead. For instance, if you wish to travel inexpensively over Thanksgiving or Christmas, you should reserve your seats at least four to six months in advance. For busy travel periods some people even book a year ahead to secure a good rate, however, keep an eye on changing fares and special offers, and rebook if the opportunity arises.

For general travel you should try to make your reservations about one to three months prior to departure. Booking more than three months ahead may result in your paying too much, since airline fares could just as easily go down as go up. Booking less than a month in advance may be too late to obtain discount fares for the flights you want.

Because the supply of seats in the airline industry exceeds the number of passengers demanding them, competition for those customers is keen. Consequently, carriers frequently introduce low fares to attract passengers in markets where flights are going out with empty seats.

Ticket prices are dependent on how full a flight is, so if you think a plane may not fill up, wait a while before departure to see if the fares come down. But don't wait too long, especially for peak travel— you might get shut out.

• **Be adaptable in your travel plans.** Adjust your departure and return times to the hours or days when the lowest fares are offered. Generally, midweek travel —Tuesday, Wednesday, and Thursday— provides the best chance to get the lowest fares. (The busiest days for business travel are Mondays and Fridays. The busiest days for general travel are Fridays and Sundays). If you don't mind an extra hour or two added to your travel time, consider taking a one-stop or a connecting flight instead of a non-stop. These flights may have cheaper fares because they take longer, are less convenient, and typically less in demand

# PASSPORT TO
# DISCOUNT TRAVEL

than non-stops. If the lowest fares are sold out on the flight you want, try an earlier or later departure, or call another airline.

Depending on the destination, off-peak days that feature more low fares may be "directionally determined," as in going to Florida at the beginning of the week to avoid busy weekends when most people travel there, and returning from Florida at the end of the week, but not on Sunday or on Monday morning when the majority of people return home.

During major holidays and other peak travel periods, such as ski season and summer vacation, hundreds of thousands of people fly. Because flights are crowded and discount fares are hard to get, bargains are more likely to be found on less desirable flights, or on times and days that aren't the most popular. Try to remain flexible, and, if possible, fly when it's not so busy. Most people don't like to travel on a holiday itself, but bargain seats are usually available then, and the flying is usually smoother because of fewer flights and crowds.

Some airlines slash their holiday travel rates up to 65% when you fly on a specific holiday or on less busy days around it. The only hitch is that the airlines may not make super-low, off-peak holiday fares available until a month or so prior to the holiday period, if at all. This might be too late for you to make definite plans for your trip, and by that time seats may not be open when you need them. If getting home for the holidays is important to you, and if your travel dates aren't flexible, you are wiser to plan ahead rather than wait and hope for a last minute special to come along.

• **Travel at odd times.** Buy a ticket on the less expensive "red-eye," or overnight, flight. Ask in advance to see whether you can go standby with your type of fare. Then, if you wish, try stand-by on an earlier, more desirable flight. Arrive at the airport with your discounted ticket about 45 minutes prior to the departure of your preferred flight. Tell the gate agent you would like standby. If seats are available, the agent may let you go, even though the restrictions of your discounted fare states that standby is not permitted.

• **Book a tentative reservation.** When you find a low fare to your destination, make a reservation even if you're not sure you'll be using it. Why? Since the majority of discount seats are limited in number, they sell out first. If you wait until you are absolutely certain about your travel plans, the bargain fare you want may be gone. Don't take a chance. Play it smart and make a tentative reservation. This gives you some time to consider your options while still holding a seat for the price you want. Of course, some airlines may hold your reservation only for 24 hours or until midnight of the following day, but even so, it is better to have it even for a short time. You can always call the airline again and ask them to extend your ticketing deadline one more day. As a courtesy, if you decide you don't need your reservation, cancel it with the airline.

• **Don't pay for your ticket right away.** Use the maximum allowable time given by the airline so you don't pay for a ticket you won't be using, especially if it's non-refundable or incurs charges for any changes. Hold on to your money until the deadline, or until you are absolutely sure you want the ticket, otherwise you might have difficulty changing it or getting a refund. As the cancellation deadline approaches, if you are still not certain about your plans, call the airline to rebook your reservation, and hold it until the next deadline.

# PASSPORT TO
# DISCOUNT TRAVEL

• **Remember your reservation.** Unlike hotels and assorted other travel services, airlines do not require you to "guarantee" your reservation with a credit card, but insist you purchase discount reservations shortly after booking, or else they will be canceled.

Airlines hold tentative reservations without obligation for a specific period of time. (Usually 24 hours for the most restrictive fares; seven to 14 days for other types.) The more expensive, least restrictive fares typically allow airport pick-up 30 minutes before departure. If you don't purchase your ticket by the deadline, your reservation will automatically be canceled. When that happens, you can lose your bargain fare because by the time you call back to rebook your flight, the discount seats could be gone.

If you make a reservation, and the fare you were quoted has increased before you purchase your ticket, you may have to pay the new higher price. Sometimes fares go up and down without notice—the only constant is change. Although there are trends one may use to predict changes in airfares, no one can precisely estimate what the new fares will be, or exactly when they will go into effect. During the usually slow travel periods from September to November, April through May and January to mid-February bargain rates are traditionally available.

As long as you have not paid, you can always change or cancel your reservation without penalty. You are subject to the penalty charge for changing or canceling a restricted fare only after you have actually purchased the ticket.

• **Charge your ticket on a credit card.** Should you have a dispute with the airline, you can enlist the credit card company's help in withholding payment for services not rendered.

36

• **Once you pay for your ticket, don't change your travel dates.** Most deep-discount tickets cost money to change, and are non-refundable, so it's **not** advisable to alter your travel dates once you've paid for your ticket.

Sometimes you may change the return flight on a non-refundable roundtrip "excursion" ticket, either by going standby on a different flight, or by paying a small service charge. Ask your airline representative if your particular fare allows this **before** you pay, so you don't waste time and money. Some airlines charge a flat fee for any ticket changes, regardless of reason, others allow changes at no charge if due to an emergency, illness, or jury duty. Most carriers allow you to fly standby if you miss your flight because you were late getting to the airport.

• **Find a conscientious travel agent.** As in any profession, some practitioners are better than others. You would be well-served to establish a working relationship with a travel agent who is willing to go the extra mile for you by diligently searching his or her computer network for the best fares available. If you don't already have a travel agent in whom you have confidence, ask your friends and co-workers for references, or contact the local Chamber of Commerce or Better Business Bureau.

• **Use an on-line reservation system to research your own fares.** There are several reservations programs that can be accessed via your personal computer. Two of the most detailed are EAASY, a consumer version of Sabre, American Airlines' travel-industry reservations system, and the ELECTRONIC EDITION OF THE OFFICIAL AIRLINE GUIDE (OAG). The EAASY program is available through Prodigy® — a partnership between IBM and Sears—and also through CompuServe®. The OAG system can be accessed through CompuServe as well as other public data-base networks.

Know what you need before you log on because when using on-line services, time is money. The monthly rate for Prodigy, subject to change, is about $10, and includes unlimited access to EAASY. The OAG user fee is approximately 50¢ per minute.

To access through CompuServe, you pay about $1.50 per month, plus a small connect fee and the 50¢ a minute user charge for the OAG which also lets you print out fares and schedules; EAASY does not provide this option. Some individuals may find the OAG system faster and easier to use than EAASY.

If you don't have a computer, current issues of the OAG POCKET FLIGHT GUIDE can be purchased at newsstands, or you can order 12 monthly issues by calling 1-800-323-3537.

• **Get the name of the agent who makes your reservation.** Knowing the name of your reservationist enhances your credibility if you have a dispute with the airline over inaccurate service information or a misquoted fare. Before hanging up, have the reservation agent recap your itinerary, stating clearly your specific flight numbers, dates, times, and the total fare. It's smarter to be safe than sorry.

## PROFITING FROM THE RULES

Understanding the rules governing discount prices will be to your advantage in your quest to save money. In practically every market there are a number of discount fares. On flights in the United States, Canada, Mexico and parts of the Caribbean, they are called supersaver, max-saver, and super coach. On international flights, the lowest fares are called apex, and super apex. Don't let the terminology confuse you, these are just names for different levels of bargain fares, each controlled by their own set of restrictions. Max-saver is usually the least expensive (and most restrictive) roundtrip excursion fare on domestic flights; super apex is usually the most affordable, restrictive international fare.

The following tips will illustrate how to use fare rules to your advantage:

• **Buy a roundtrip ticket but use it one way**. Because of the airline industry's pricing structure, which to any objective observer defies all logic, sometimes you can fly roundtrip for less money than one way. How is this possible?

The roundtrip max-savers are normally less expensive than unrestricted, one way fares. Call some carriers and ask for their lowest one way, and roundtrip prices. You may find that a roundtrip ticket costs a lot less than a one way. As crazy as it sounds, if you are only going one way, and you have enough advance notice to qualify for a max-saver—usually about one or two weeks—buy the roundtrip ticket and use it one way. After all, no one can force you to fly back on that ticket if you don't want to.

The max-saver saves you the most money. For example, Boston to New Orleans might cost you about $500 one way, but the max-saver, only about $350 roundtrip. (All prices quoted are approximations, and are not actual fares.)

If you buy a max-saver and use it only one way, you will not receive a refund for the unused return portion of your ticket. Do not expect the airline to repay half of your roundtrip fare if

# PASSPORT TO
# DISCOUNT TRAVEL

you only use half of the ticket. According to the rules, most max-savers are non-refundable, period. Rather than discarding your return flight coupon, hold on to it in case you decide to use it within one year after the purchase date, or wish to sell it to someone else. (Technically, tickets are non-transferable, however they are occasionally sold to others.)

Some airlines allow changing the return date of discount tickets without penalty, when flying standby on any open flight back to the city of origin. Others, however, do not permit flying standby. They may, however, permit changes to a ticket for a service charge. In general, you are not permitted to change originating or destination cities under any circumstances, and in most cases, any changes made to your flight reservations must be done prior to your scheduled departure. For specifics, check with the airlines involved.

• **Buy overlapping tickets**. How can you save money if you want to fly roundtrip, but don't want to stay over a Saturday night? Normally, fares for flying between Monday and Friday of the same week cost much more than excursion fares, which typically require staying over at least one Saturday night at your destination. You can cut the cost of midweek travel by buying two overlapping roundtrip discount tickets, each with a Saturday overnight in the itinerary. Use the first coupon of the first ticket for your originating flight and use the first coupon of the second ticket for your return.

Suppose, for example, you plan to fly from San Francisco to Dallas on Monday and return Wednesday of the same week. Assuming you have enough time to qualify for a seven or 14-day advance notice discount fare, book a roundtrip departing San Francisco on Monday, and returning any time after the first Saturday night. Then book a roundtrip flight from Dallas to San

# AIRLINES

Francisco departing Dallas on Wednesday, and returning at least a week or more later. Use your first ticket on Monday, and your second ticket on Wednesday. To avoid the airline reservation agent's suspicions, book these two reservations with two separate agents and remove the unused flight coupons from the ticket.

For weekday travel, buying two roundtrip tickets at the least expensive fare, instead of one roundtrip ticket at the unrestricted full coach fare, will save about 20%. As mentioned previously, compare the price of the roundtrip excursion fares versus normal coach fares to see how the math works out for you. If there is a chance the airline will go out of business before you fly, pay with a credit card. Then you can pursue receiving credit for any unused portions of your ticket.

**• Buy non-refundable tickets through the newspaper.** Some people who have purchased non-refundable tickets get stuck with them if their plans change. Unless they fly as ticketed, people with "use-'em-or-lose-'em" tickets generally can't get their money back from the airlines. To recoup some of the cost, they try to sell their tickets through classified ads in the newspapers. Since they will lose all their money unless they sell them, you can often get excellent bargains. Be prepared to negotiate, because you are in the driver's seat.

If you'd like to fly somewhere, but aren't too particular about the date or time, put an ad in the classifieds offering to buy non-refundable tickets. Similarly, if you are ever stuck with unused non-refundable tickets of your own, place an ad yourself to try to sell them.

Two warnings: Since most non-refundable tickets are non-changeable, or are changeable only with cash penalties, you must use the ticket you buy exactly as written, or incur additional expense. And since most tickets are non-transferable, if the airline suspects you are not the person whose name is on the ticket, it could confiscate the ticket and refuse to board you. In most cases, this happens infrequently, unless the airlines are operating under heightened security procedures. Airlines normally do not check passenger identification except on international flights when passports are required, or if they have some reason to suspect fraud.

Make sure the ticket you buy doesn't have a woman's name printed on it if you're a man, or vice versa. While it is not illegal to use a ticket with someone else's name on it, the airlines discourage the practice for several valid reasons. One is to prevent someone from attempting to use a stolen ticket. Another is the airlines' obligation to know exactly who is on their flights for insurance purposes.

## MORE STRATEGIES TO CUT FARES

• **Fly to alternate cities**. Shop airfares. Sometimes you can save a lot of money by flying to a city near your intended destination, and then driving a rental car or taking a bus to it. A flight to an alternate city might be less expensive than one to your final destination. For example, if you want to fly from Baltimore, Maryland to South Bend, Indiana, you might pay approximately $350 for a roundtrip supersaver. But if you fly to Chicago and take ground transportation to South Bend, your roundtrip airfare might run only about $250.

Another example of saving money by flying to an alternate location would be from Miami to Mobile. Flying on Delta to Alabama would involve going north to Atlanta, changing planes and then heading south to Mobile. You might pay about $350 roundtrip, and take about three to four hours to get there. However, you can fly from Miami to a close-by city — in this case Pensacola, Florida — and save both time and money. USAir has a direct flight to Pensacola, 60 miles from Mobile. The flight is much quicker, just two hours, and costs much less.

• **Fly through hub cities.** Very often flights with connections through hub cities are more affordable than non-stop flights. For example, an airline's non-stop flight from Newark, New Jersey, to Houston may cost more than a competitor's connecting flight through a hub city, such as Atlanta (Delta); Charlotte/Pittsburgh (USAir); Chicago (United); Dallas (American); and Detroit (Northwest)

Like the hub of a bicycle wheel, an airline's airport hub serves as the central connecting point for many flights which continue to other places. Before booking, check the prices for connecting flights to see if they cost less. The departure times may not be as convenient, and the flights may take longer because you will have to change planes, but it may be worth it in terms of dollars, if not time, saved.

Oddly enough, domestic airlines typically charge higher fares to fly to their hub cities, than to fly through them to other destinations. This may defy logic, but who said airfares are logical? The primary reason non-stop flights to hub cities sometimes cost more than one would expect is that the airline using a particular hub airport dominates that location and therefore, controls the market share and pricing of flights to and from that city.

# PASSPORT TO
# DISCOUNT TRAVEL

• **Search for bartered tickets.** Some airlines provide their suppliers with "travel credits," which result in airline tickets that are much less expensive than normal. These tickets are often found in newspaper classified ads under "barter" or "trade exchanges." The ads are run by individuals or organizations, such as TRAVEL WORLD LEISURE CLUB in New York (212-244-3562), whose members pay an annual fee of about $50. Like frequent flyer passes purchased through the newspaper, these tickets will have someone else's name on them, not yours. Consequently, if an airline agent checks I.D.'s, they may not let you on the plane.

Before buying a bartered ticket, check with the seller to be sure you can get a refund if the airline does not accept your ticket for passage. You should **not** use bartered tickets for overseas travel since customs officials examine your ticket to see that it matches your passport.

• **Fly to "hidden cities."** This technique is most successful on one way flights, and can yield big savings only for passengers with carry-on luggage. It's quite simple. Suppose you want to go from New York to Chicago. One airline charges $300 for a non-stop flight from New York to Chicago, but another airline charges only $225 for a flight from New York to St. Louis which connects in Chicago. Buy the less expensive fare to St. Louis and get off the plane in Chicago. Since you intend to deplane before reaching the final destination on your ticket, take only carry-on luggage with you, otherwise while you get off in Chicago your checked bags will go on to St. Louis, where they do you no good. BEST FARES, P.O. Box 171212, Arlington, TX 76003 is a monthly travel magazine listing dozens of hidden city fares and other discounts.

NOTE: The airline can refuse to accept you if you try to

board a flight at a city other than the one printed on your ticket. That's why this technique should only be used for one way travel. In the example above, for instance, if you bought a roundtrip New York-St. Louis ticket, and tried to use the return leg of the ticket by getting on the plane in Chicago where you got off earlier, you could run into trouble if the boarding agent sees you did not start your return trip from St. Louis as shown on the ticket.

• **Buy unused frequent flyer awards**. Some travelers buy frequent-flyer award certificates which are not going to be used by the frequent flyer members who earned them. Airlines frown upon the sale of non-transferable frequent-flyer bonus certificates and tickets. Be aware that some brokers marketing unused frequent flyer awards have been sued for this practice. However, several are still in business because of the demand for these items.

If you buy a frequent-flyer award ticket from a broker, charge your purchase to a credit card, and make sure you can get a refund from the broker if you are denied passage. A more thorough discussion about buying and selling bonus award certificates and tickets appears later in this chapter under the heading "Frequent Flyer Programs."

## WHAT IF THE FARE GOES DOWN?

Generally, it's best to buy your tickets as soon as you're certain about your plans. This guarantees your fare and guards

# PASSPORT TO
# DISCOUNT TRAVEL

against price increases, although prices can also decrease.

What happens if you've already purchased a non-changeable, non-refundable ticket, and the price goes down? Will you get your money back for the difference between what you paid for your ticket and the new, lower price? Policies differ among the airlines on refunding tickets when a lower fare is introduced. Under certain conditions some carriers will reimburse the difference, others won't.

Assuming you discover the price reduction in time, you may get a refund if: 1) seats are still available at the new fare on your particular flight and 2) you make no changes to your itinerary and travel dates. Take your ticket back to the airline or travel agency where you purchased it, and seek a refund. They may accept the old ticket, issue you a new one, and process a refund for the difference—then again, they may not. You'll never know until you ask.

Why isn't the refund automatic? Three reasons: 1) Many airlines believe that it is neither wise, nor smart business to reimburse customers for the difference in price of a ticket purchased prior to the introduction of a lower fare; 2) All the new low-fare seats may be sold out on your flight, meaning there are no more discount seats available for anyone; 3) Changes to most discount tickets carry a service charge, which could cost more than the refund you are trying to get.

To summarize, you do have a chance to get a refund for the difference between the fare you paid and a new lower fare if you:

• Learn about the new fare in time to meet all its restrictions.
• Keep your itinerary unchanged—same flights, same dates, same cities.

# AIRLINES

• Ascertain whether seats are available on your flights at the new low fare.
• Change your ticket within the deadline dictated by the new fare rules.

If you do all this, you may receive reimbursement. Finally, ask the airline reservationist or your travel agent to explain all your options. If you are satisfied with what they tell you, fine; if not, speak to a supervisor. Remember, the squeaky wheel gets the grease.


## HIGH-TECH TO THE RESCUE


If you have made an airline reservation recently, you know how frustrating shopping for low fares can be. With all the rules about advance reservations, instant purchases, refund penalties, and minimum stay requirements, you have to come armed with a good pen and plenty of paper just to take notes!

Avoid these headaches and enter the hi-tech age! Use a travel agent whose computer is programmed to scan airline lists for the lowest fares. Since most travel agencies do not have this capability, you'll have to hunt for one. Here's how it will pay off.

Airlines spend thousands of dollars advertising reduced fares to fill empty seats and to match competition. It is up to the consumer and the travel agencies to find out about them. For competitive reasons, most U.S. airlines make hundreds of schedule and fare adjustments every day, often without any advance notice! No, that's not a typo. That's hundreds of daily changes per carrier!

# PASSPORT TO
# DISCOUNT TRAVEL

Unfortunately, many people do not discover these new low fares in time to use them, either because they do not see the ads, or because their travel agency is unaware of the reduced rates. Unless travel agents have state-of-the-art computer systems constantly updating fares, the agents may not learn about these lower rates in time to be of use for some of their clients.

Without advanced computers, a time lag occurs between the moment the changes go into effect, and when they appear on the travel agent's screen. This programming delay could run into several days, during which the travel agent may be ignorant of the new fares and schedule changes.

Innovative automated computer programs help travel agents bring some order to the confusion of finding the lowest fares. These remarkable programs scan thousands of prices and hundreds of passenger records to find the best rate for each itinerary booked in the agency's computers. They save thousands of dollars for their clients and countless man-hours for their agents. On the downside, because these computer enhancements are expensive, not all agencies have them.

One fare-search program helping agents to spot new low fares is called FARE ASSURANCE, developed by System One Corporation, in Atlanta, GA. FARE ASSURANCE and similar programs automatically double-check every customer's ticketing records each night to determine whether they qualify for any fare reductions posted during the day. It also searches for seats on flights with low fares which may have more convenient times or better connections—then compiles the information for the travel agents' use next morning.

A similar program called AQUA, developed by Travel-Tron, a travel agency in California, is an in-house system which continuously monitors airline fares to determine if any discounted seats suddenly open up on flights their customers may

# AIRLINES

want. When they do, TravelTron located at 1241 E. Dyer Rd, Santa Ana, CA 92705 (714-644-8766) acts quickly to reserve them. If you purchase a ticket from them, the cost of your phone call is reimbursed

Garber Travel Service of Brookline, Massachusetts (800-225-4570 or 800-562-2143 in NY) is one of several other large travel agencies which have invested in low-fare-finder programs. Several times a day, up to the day before departure, Garber's computers check for the availability of better fares. You may charge your tickets over the phone and receive them by mail at no additional cost.

These valuable fare search programs benefit business and pleasure travelers alike by saving time and money. When a new, low fare is announced, wait a day or two to see whether other airlines, perhaps with better schedules or connections, come up with similar prices. But don't wait too long, or you may miss out.

For the latest fares, use a travel agency with one of these advanced fare-search systems. Call several agencies and ask about their computer capabilities. If you can't find an agency with the low-fare finder, don't worry—most conscientious travel agents will conduct the comparison shopping necessary to find the best schedules and fares. They may even know of some additional specials!

## AIRFARE DISCOUNTERS

There are a number of organizations which buy unused space on airplanes, cruises and tours, and sell them below regular rates to members:

**49**

# PASSPORT TO
# DISCOUNT TRAVEL

American Express operates EXPRESS WEEKEND for members departing from Chicago, New York and Boston (800-722-5669). Memberships start at under $100 a year. Newsletters list specials on a number of domestic and international airlines, hotels and rental cars with savings of up to 50%.

Trans World Airways has the BREAKAWAY CLUB (800-872-8364). Its bi-monthly newsletter describes TWA air fares and tour packages available at discounts up to 80% off regular price. Memberships cost about $50 a year for individuals, and about $100 for two person (the second person can be anyone accompanying the member).

Naturally, airlines, tour operators, and travel agencies want you to think that high-priced tickets are all that are available for short notice travel, since they make more money by selling you non-discounted tickets. However, you can usually find reasonably priced, last-minute values if you are willing to do most of the work yourself. Persistence on your part often pays off in obtaining low fares.

Here's how:

If possible, take last minute trips on lower-priced, lesser-known carriers, via lesser-flown routes. Avoid flights to the most heavily visited spots during peak periods. For example, traveling to Hawaii, Rome, and the French Riviera all cost more in-season, yet are still very delightful to visit when the rates and the crowds are down in the off-season,

Seek out smaller carriers for domestic flights, or larger carriers matching the smaller airline's discount fares. Sometimes a smaller airline's short notice fares are lower than those of larger competitors. The same is true for international carriers.

# AIRLINES

Some smaller airlines such as Icelandair, Air India, and Poland's LOT, often run specials costing hundreds of dollars less than the more well-known carriers. Britain's Virgin Atlantic Airways has advertised flights from New York or Miami to London for around $100 each way. Shop around because larger airlines with perhaps better schedules and more flights may be willing to match their smaller competitors' prices.

Some airlines even offer one price passes allowing several stops in various locations for a single fare. For example, Bahamas Air lets vacationers explore three Bahamian Islands within 21 days for $250 from Nassau (800-222-4262). Liat Airlines, offers an "island hopper" fare allowing three stopovers from among 15 Carribean destinations within 21 days for approximately $170 to $200. For about $350 travelers may choose from 26 islands, plus Venezuela and Guyana, within 30 days. (800-253-5011).

## AIRLINE TICKET CONSOLIDATORS

How would you like to fly from New York to Rome for hundreds of dollars less than full fare? Or jet to some other exciting destination for nearly half-price?

You can do just that if you purchase your ticket from a company specializing in discounted airline seats. These companies are known as flight consolidators, or "bucket shops" (so-called because they fill the buckets, or seats, on airplanes). There are about 100 consolidators operating in the United States supplying reduced airfares for "short notice" trips on both domestic and international flights. Here's how they do it.

**51**

# PASSPORT TO
# DISCOUNT TRAVEL

Consolidators buy seats at deep discounts on flights with plenty of empty seats, and then wholesale them to travel agents, or retail them directly to consumers at about 20% to 50% below regular coach rates.

Even with the retail mark-up, prices are typically much less than anything displayed on airline or travel agency computers, and sometimes come with fewer restrictions than normal advance-purchase excursion fares. First-class and business-class tickets often sell for 20% to 30% less than regulated fares, and full, non-discounted coach-class tickets for up to 50% less.

Although you can buy directly from some consolidators, you may receive better service and feel more comfortable using a travel agency. Although not all agencies sell for consolidators, many do. Check if they have any wholesale or consolidation fares available.

Because airlines prefer leaving you in the dark about where these discounts come from, they rarely ever mention "consolidation" fares. They would prefer to sell full-price tickets first, of course, but since some seats may remain unsold, they discreetly offer them through consolidators. Consolidators seldom advertise; travel agencies do the bulk of it. Scan through the ads in the Travel section of newspapers or in the classifieds in the back of travel magazines. You'll find listings for cut-rate fares, but hardly ever see an airline mentioned. These are usually consolidation prices.

Consolidators are a good source of discount fares on international flights. Most overseas fares are established during negotiations between individual governments and airlines, with the aid of the International Air Transportation Association (IATA). Inevitably, due to competition or other market factors, some carriers are left with unsold seats at these pre-determined prices which cannot fluctuate. To unload enough of the fixed-

# AIRLINES

price seats and still make a profit, foreign airlines turn a number of them over to consolidators at substantial discounts. Many consolidators are travel agencies or tour operators appointed by the airlines to sell surplus seats for them at less than the published, government-approved IATA rate.

Typically valid for one year from date of purchase, consolidation tickets are often relatively free of restrictions. Some, however, are non-changeable and non-refundable, and most cannot be used on another airline.

If you plan to purchase these tickets, try to avoid surprises. Read the fine print in any ads on wholesale fares, and ask to see, in writing, the seller's policies regarding consolidation tickets. After ordering your tickets, pick them up or have them mailed to you as soon as possible, so you can correct any itinerary or fare discrepancies. Paying by credit card whenever possible, enables you to request your card company to withhold payment if problems arise or if the airline ceases operations before you fly.

Consolidation tickets can help beat the high cost of business travel. One persistent frustration felt by business travelers is their inability to obtain low-cost excursion fares because of minimum stay restrictions, advance booking requirements or limited availability. Most discount fares are not designed for business travelers who need greater flexibility. Time is money, they say, and business flyers pay extra for the ability to make time changes. Consolidators offer both business and pleasure travelers another way to save on last-minute full-fare coach and first-class travel.

Some airline consolidators selling internationally to the general public are:

# PASSPORT TO
# DISCOUNT TRAVEL

In the United States . . .
>     Travac (800-872-8800)
>     UniTravel (800-325-2222)

In Europe . . .
>     Stohl-Air-Voyages, Geneva, Switzerland
>     Trailfinders, London, England
>     Airborne Travel, London, England
>     Bon Voyage, Southampton, England

## FLY AIR COURIER

If you want to save money and don't mind traveling light, you may be able to receive discounts up to 50%, or even fly free, by taking packages of freight for an air courier company. The packages count as part of your checked baggage, so for personal items, you may have to use carry-on luggage only. Consequently, this option is viable for those individuals who can comfortably travel overseas with what they carry with them.

Freelance air couriers rarely handle the packages, often containing documents, securities, or medicinal items. The packages are taken to the airport by a courier company employee, and picked up inside customs by another employee. The courier simply provides space for the items in his or her checked luggage.

Tickets are purchased directly from the air courier at a significant discount, in return, the courier company uses your free baggage allowance to ship its parcels. The courier company benefits by the timely arrival of its packages, and you benefit by flying for less. If shipped regular air freight, the company's packages may sit for hours or days on an international airline's freight loading dock before being expedited to their final destination. Packages checked with an air courier will arrive on the same flight.

Sometimes, prices for air courier tickets are a steal. Sample fares include $300 roundtrip to Europe, South America or Japan, or a $100 roundtrip to London or the Caribbean. If you can leave any time and go anywhere, you may even fly free! Unless you make arrangements well in advance, you may not be able to select your destination; you usually have to travel alone on short notice and be content to stay abroad for as long as the shipper says—typically, one to two weeks, though some trips allow stays for 30 days or more.

In the last few years, shippers such as DHL WORLDWIDE COURIER EXPRESS (718-656-8201), HALBART EXPRESS (718-656-8279), and SKYPACK (908-654-0600) have utilized independent air couriers. Recently, some of these companies have used their own employees to accompany their packages, rather than free-lancers. However, if you are lucky enough to contact them when they have an immediate need for couriers, you may be able to buy a ticket through them to England or Europe for as low as $200 to $250 roundtrip! Call large international shipping agencies for their latest policies.

If you'd like to learn more about becoming an air courier and traveling the world at cut-rate prices, read INSIDERS GUIDE TO AIR COURIER BARGAINS by Kelly Monaghan, which provides information about courier-booking services and package-expediting firms hiring independent couriers. It is available for $12.95 plus $2.00 for shipping from Inwood Training Publications, Box 438, New York, NY 10034. Another source of

# PASSPORT TO
# DISCOUNT TRAVEL

information is A SIMPLE GUIDE TO COURIER TRAVEL available for $12.95 plus $3 for postage and handling: P.O. Box 2394, Lake Oswego, OR 97035 (800-344-9375). THE TRAVEL UNLIMITED NEWSLETTER provides courier ideas and many other bargain suggestions. Subscription $25; write to Steve Lantos, PO Box 1058, Allston, MA 02134.

The following are some agencies representing courier services: (A fee may be charged for using them.)

• COURIER TRAVEL SERVICE, 560 Central Ave., Cedarhurst, NY 11516 (800-922-2359 or 516-374-2299), has offered bargains to Caracas, Venezuela for $250 and to Europe for $350. Some stays range from a week to two months.

• JUPITER AIR, 160-23 Rockaway Blvd., Jamaica, NY 11434 (718-341-2095), flies primarily to Hong Kong, offering stays of up to a month for approximately $600 roundtrip. A $35 fee and a refundable $100 deposit are required.

• NOW VOYAGER, Suite 307, 74 Varrick St., New York, NY 10013 (212-431-1616), has offered discount airfares to Amsterdam, Buenos Aires, London, Mexico City, and Tokyo. A $50 fee, good for one year, is assessed for their service.

• WORLD COURIER, 137-42 Guy Brewer Blvd., Jamaica, NY 11434 (718-978-9408), requires bookings several months in advance for week-long stays in London for as low as $200, and Milan for about $250.

# AIRLINES

## HITCH A RIDE TO EUROPE

One way to fly inexpensively to Europe is with AIRHITCH®, 2790 Broadway, Suite 100, New York, NY 10025 (212-864-2000). Airhitch was founded several years ago to help students afford overseas flights. Today, anyone can use them, not just students, but you must have a flexible schedule.

Airhitch arranges last minute "standby" flights on regularly scheduled commercial airlines to, or near, selected European cities. After choosing your preferred destination, you pay Airhitch about $200 to fly one way from Eastern cities such as New York, Philadelphia, Baltimore, Boston or Washington, DC; approximately $300 to depart from Western gateways such as Los Angeles, San Francisco or Seattle; and about $250 to fly from most other major American international airports. The price includes a $25 registration fee for listing with Airhitch.

The majority of flights used by Airhitch land at such cities as Amsterdam, Brussels, Frankfurt, London, Munich, Paris, and Zurich. Your payment guarantees a flight within a fixed number of days to either your preferred destination, or to a major city nearby. You must give Airhitch a range of at least five days during which you can depart on any flight close to your target city.

As your departure date approaches, Airhitch sends a travel voucher and a list of flights available. In most cases, you will get your first choice. However, if the plane is full, you may standby for any of the alternate flights. Airhitch gives you the option of paying for your return flight before leaving the United States, or while overseas at one of their seven European offices.

The main difference between Airhitch and regular travel agencies, ticket consolidators and last minute travel clubs is that

# PASSPORT TO DISCOUNT TRAVEL

these companies sell tickets for reserved seats to specific destinations on specific flights, whereas Airhitch sells standby tickets to any city close to your preferred destination on a variety of scheduled airlines.

## HOW TO FLY FREE

Simple. Get "bumped" off a plane. Not in the air, of course, but on the ground. Volunteer to give up your seat when your flight is overbooked. When the airline calls you to relinquish your seat voluntarily, or takes it from you involuntarily, you deserve to be compensated—your reward is normally a free roundtrip ticket.

When planes are full, airlines sometimes "bump" reserved passengers off flights by not boarding them. To minimize the number of empty seats at departure caused by no-shows (people who do not show up for their flights, and neglect to cancel their reservations), airlines overbook many of their flights. Overbooking and no-shows are the norm, and airlines, as a result, often accept more reservations than there are actual seats on the aircraft.

At departure time, when a flight remains overbooked, the airline requests volunteers to release their seats to accommodate other passengers. Volunteers yielding their seats normally proceed to their destination on the next available flight, deaprting the same day, or a day or two later. In return, most airlines reward volunteers with a free roundtrip ticket for a future flight to any city on their domestic route system. Not all airlines do this, but most will, if you ask them. At their ticket counters and boarding gates, many airlines post complete rules for the boarding priorities of reserved and standby passengers and denied-boarding compensation payable to voluntarily and involuntarily bumped passengers.

Here's how to give up your seat in the attempt to get a free ticket. Arrive at the boarding gate about 45 minutes to an hour before departure; tell the boarding agent you volunteer to relinquish your seat if the flight is full. Boarding agents compile lists of volunteers on a first-come first-served basis, so get your name in early. Arriving at the gate before the standard 30-minute check-in time will usually put you near the top of the list. If the flight is full and you get bumped, you double your money by receiving a free ticket for a future flight.

According to government regulations, a bumped passenger has the right to reject the airline's offer of a free flight for losing a reserved seat, and instead can choose to be reimbursed monetarily. If an airline cannot provide a bumped passenger with a domestic flight arriving within two hours of the originally scheduled time (or an international flight from the United States, within four hours of the original arrival time), the airline is obligated to compensate the passenger by paying double the one way fare, or $400, whichever is less.

If a bumped passenger gets to his destination within one to two hours of his original flight, he may receive the full one way fare up to $200. (The compensation amount is not based on half the roundtrip fare, but rather on the full one way coach fare, which is virtually always higher.) Most U.S. government-certified airlines abide by these industry standards.

To qualify for compensation, you must check in no later than the time recommended by the airline— usually 30 minutes for domestic flights, and one hour for international flights. If you are bumped off a shuttle, or other very short flight, or off a propeller-driven commuter plane, you will probably be offered

# PASSPORT TO
# DISCOUNT TRAVEL

denied-boarding compensation consisting of a free ticket for similar service only, not to anywhere the airline flies domestically.

In most cases, you are not entitled to receive compensation if: 1) you are bumped because your inbound connecting flight is late; 2) the flight is on a commuter plane with fewer than 60 seats; or 3) the flight originated outside the United States.

Normally, denied-boarding vouchers, also known as "flight credits," must be redeemed for an actual ticket within one year of the issue date, and may be used only by the bumped passenger. Occasionally, carriers will allow voucher-holders to transfer their flight credits to immediate family members. This should be clarified in advance, and approved in writing, by the airline representative at the time the voucher is given.

If you want to be clever about it, you could turn your one travel voucher into several free tickets. Book the reservation for your free trip on another flight which you think will become oversold. Then, if you volunteer to give up your seat, and the flight is full, you may get bumped again, thus earning another flight credit. You can turn that one in for another free roundtrip ticket on a future flight. Repeat the process as often as you like, but be prepared to take a long time to get to your destination if you play the bumping game—the next available flight may not take off for hours, or even days.

Bumping is prevalent on all airlines at certain times of the year. Some of the best opportunities to get bumped are: 1) during major holidays; 2) on weekends to popular resorts; or 3) over Spring Break from most college towns to anywhere that's hot and happening. Use your imagination to think of other times to fly when there is a chance of getting bumped. Also, remember to take carry-on luggage, so that if you are bumped, your belongings do not go on a trip without you.

# AIRLINES

## SPECIAL FARES

### Senior Citizen Discounts

Seniors get a break on most U.S. airlines through a variety of discount programs designed just for them. They enjoy substantial discounts on airfares, provided proof of age is shown at time of ticket purchase and departure.

Some airlines take a straight 10% off the price of the lowest applicable fare for passengers over 60; other carriers offer the same discount to those over 62, and also to a travel companion of any age.

Discounts for seniors are sometimes arranged by organizations such as the American Association of Retired Persons (AARP) and the American Automobile Association (AAA). Check with these and similar groups for information concerning travel specials for their eligible members.

An excellent program some airlines promote is the Senior Coupon Booklet. These booklets containing four or eight coupons enable a senior to fly anywhere in the continental U.S. for a set price per trip, averaging about $120 each way. The booklets cost approximately $480 for four flights, and $800 for eight flights. (Prices and offers may vary, so call the airlines for details.)

For example, flying from Miami to Los Angeles, make your reservation in advance according to the rules of the coupon. Go to the airport, exchange one of your coupons for a ticket, board the plane, and go! It's that simple. In other words, you fly clear across the country for about $120! Not bad compared to normal transcontinental fares.

# PASSPORT TO
# DISCOUNT TRAVEL

Coupons are typically valid for one year from date of purchase. Booklets may be purchased by anyone, but only used by the qualified senior in whose name it is issued. They make great gifts for golden-agers on the go.

Most senior coupon programs contain some restrictions. Airlines may limit the use of coupons to certain days, usually Tuesday, Wednesday, Thursday and Saturday, thereby avoiding the busier days of the week. Peak days near major holidays may be blacked out for travel as well. Senior coupons generally have no minimum or maximum length of stay requirements as long as the final coupon is redeemed within one year for a ticket. This ticket may be used for travel during the next year.

Senior coupon programs vary among airlines, so check with specific carriers for details. Some airlines require reservations at least two or more weeks in advance; others allow reservations to be made no earlier than five or six days prior to departure. Both approaches have advantages and disadvantages. If you have to attend an important engagement, making a reservation only five or six days in advance may not be enough time to guarantee seats on the flights you need. On the other hand, requiring reservations two weeks in advance prevents you from using a flight coupon on short notice or in an emergency. Some airlines waive advance reservation requirements if you have to use your coupons in a hurry, especially for situations such as a critical illness or the death of a loved one.

After making your reservation, take your booklet to the airline's ticket counter at the airport or city ticket office, and exchange your coupons for tickets. Since these tickets may be subject to a service charge for any changes, you should wait until the day of departure to pick them up. However, be sure to arrive at the airport at least 45 minutes before take-off, because you never know how busy the ticket counter will be. You may miss your flight if you cut it too close.

# AIRLINES

These senior coupon programs are great if you fly at least two roundtrips—or four one ways within two years, or if you fly far enough to turn a $120 ticket into a steal!

## Family Fares

On some airlines, families flying together can save substantially over regular coach fares. Airlines define families as husband, wife, and children ages two through 17. Infants under two years fly free. Step-children and step-parents may also qualify with proof of relationship. Grandparents traveling with grandchildren do not always qualify for a family fare, although some airlines will allow any adult and child traveling together to benefit from these discounts. Contact airlines for specifics.

To qualify for a family fare, a minimum of two family members must fly together on the same itinerary in one direction, but may travel separately in the other. Family groups normally have to be ticketed at the same time. Proof of children's ages may be required, and penalties may be imposed for changing or canceling tickets.

Family fares generally come in four forms: 1) a discount of about 10% or more off advance purchase supersavers for family members; 2) a 50% discount off supersaver fares for each child, age 2 through 17 traveling with an adult; 3) a straight 20% discount off full-coach; or 4) a drastic reduction for the spouse and children traveling with a full fare-paying parent. The best plan for your family depends on several factors. Be sure to shop around for the deal saving your family the most.

Here's how the fourth type of family plan works for short notice travel. For example, one adult family member pays a full coach fare of $250 one way. The spouse and children pay a

# PASSPORT TO
# DISCOUNT TRAVEL

fraction of that, approximately $80 to $120 per person, each way. Add that up, and the average price per ticket is hundreds of dollars less than the full fare for each person.

This type of plan makes it easy for a business traveler to bring the family along. (All prices quoted are illustrative only and not actual fares.) Suppose you are going to San Francisco from Denver on a business trip, but you do not qualify for a discount fare. A full coach fare is about $300, each way, however, under the family plan, you can bring your spouse and eligible children for about $100 each. Mathematically, the more family members going, the better. Because the more people traveling, the lower the average price per ticket ($300 plus $100 = $400; divided by 2 = $200 average price per ticket, each way for two people). With two kids and your spouse accompanying you, the average price comes down to $150 each. ($300 plus $100+$100+$100 = $600; divided by 4 = $150.) As you can see, this plan becomes a cost-cutter for families traveling together.

## Student Fares

Some airlines offer discounts to full-time students between the ages of 16 and 26, which may be a special price just for students, or a percentage off any fare.

Students may be required to show their high school, college or university I.D. as proof of full-time student status. Sometimes a driver's license with photo is accepted for high school students, 16-18.

Many students travel during their holiday breaks, making it difficult to obtain discounted fares. They should plan ahead and book travel reservations at the start of a new term. Each

# AIRLINES

semester, students should check the vacation dates on the school calendar, and ask their teachers when exams are given. Acting quickly is the best way to find bargains during peak travel periods.

## Military Fares

On many U.S. airlines, military personnel and their dependents receive discounts up to 50% off regular coach fares. Soldiers must present a valid, green "active duty" card. (A reservist's red card will not be accepted unless reporting for duty in a national emergency). Military dependents must present proof of dependency or show a tan "dependent" I.D. card. All spouses and any eligible children over the age of 10 should have one. In most cases, dependents do not have to travel with the active-duty military person.

Usually, military fares may be reserved or purchased at any time. Such tickets may be used one way or roundtrip, and are fully refundable. However, military fares are **not** always the best option for military personnel and their dependents.

In some cases, if certain booking, purchase, and travel restrictions are met, supersavers or max-savers may cost less than military fares. Military rates from San Diego to Cleveland may be $225 one way, reflecting a 50% savings off the full coach fare of $450. But the supersaver may be only $350 roundtrip! If returning to San Diego, the serviceperson would save $100 by buying the roundtrip supersaver, subject to the usual ticket rules and penalties for changes. This is not always a good option for military personnel whose orders can change abruptly. However, military fares remain a significant bargain compared to regular, short notice coach fares.

# PASSPORT TO
# DISCOUNT TRAVEL

## Compassion Fares

Some airlines offer discounts to seriously ill patients who must travel for medical treatment. Similar discounts are usually extended immediate family members escorting them to a treatment center. Agencies that assist terminally ill individuals, such as the Make a Wish Foundation, and the Children's Miracle Network, are usually eligible for these fares.

Typically, a minimum number of flights must be taken within a specified period of time to qualify. For example, four flights taken in six months, or eight trips within a year. These requirements may vary among airlines.

Documentation from a physician stating the nature of the illness, the need for treatment, and the physical ability of the patient to travel by air is usually required by the airline prior to arranging a compassion fare.

Lately, many airlines have begun offering discounts on last minute fares for medical emergencies. Every airline handles its medical fares differently, so be sure to shop around. Some carriers take 35% to 50% off their highest coach fare. Others offer their highest supersaver fare. Airlines may require the name and the relationship of the ill person, the name of the hospital or attending physician, and, in some cases, a medical statement indicating the urgency of the patient's condition.

## Organ Donor Fares

Some airlines provide savings of 33% to 50% off regular coach fares for organ transplant patients and their immediate families. The fare is valid for the initial surgery and any follow-up treatment. Usually a doctor's statement is required at time of purchase. Contact the airlines for more information.

## Funeral Fares

Several airlines offer "bereavement" or "funeral" fares to people suffering the loss of an immediate family member. These fares provide discounts of 35% to 50% off regular rates. As an act of kindness on behalf of those in mourning, the airlines often waive advance reservation, purchase, and minimum stay requirements. The death of a family member is painful enough without having to endure another shock...the shock of a high-priced airline ticket purchased on short notice to attend the funeral.

Only those individuals closely related to the deceased qualify for funeral fares. Brothers, sisters, sons, daughters, step-children, parents, step-parents, grandparents, grandchildren, and their spouses are usually eligible. Aunts, uncles, cousins, nieces and nephews often are not, nor are in-laws unless married to an eligible family member. Ask the airline for an exception to these rules if you need one. When reservations are made, the airline may ask for the name of the deceased, relationship, the name and phone numbers of the funeral home, hospital or attending physician.

Not all airlines handle bereavement fares in the same manner. Some simply waive all normal fare restrictions and charge a supersaver fare, though not necessarily the least expensive one. Others charge a full coach fare, possibly costing twice as much as a supersaver. Then, upon presentation of a death certificate, they will refund the difference between the full fare and the supersaver, or will issue a voucher as a credit on a later flight.

# PASSPORT TO
# DISCOUNT TRAVEL

To illustrate the savings involved, let's say you must fly from Dayton to El Paso to attend the funeral of a grandparent. Ordinarily, you'd have to pay about $350 for a one way coach ticket, $700 roundtrip. You would probably not qualify for a supersaver because of insufficient time to meet the advance booking requirement. However, with a funeral fare, you might receive a supersaver price of about $350 roundtrip, a 50% savings. On most carriers, your spouse and children would receive a similar discount.

As you can see, these funeral fares are a generous and humane gesture from airlines to their passengers in a time of grief.

## Clergy Fares

Some airlines offer discounts of 10% to 25% to members of the clergy, who may apply directly to participating carriers for a clergy card entitling them to their savings. Call to see which offer this program.

## SUMMARY: 20 WAYS TO SAVE MONEY

1) Plan your trip thoroughly in advance.

2) Read newspapers and travel magazines for news of airfare price wars.

3) Look for advertisements about bargains such as "introductory service" promotions, 2-for-1 deals, discount cou-

pons, and special fares for families, students, military personnel, and senior citizens.

4) Be flexible in your schedule.

5) Travel at odd times, off-peak, and off-season.

6) Avoid penalties by keeping your reservations after purchasing your ticket.

7) Utilize a travel agency equipped with a low fare-finder computer system.

8) Find a reputable, conscientious travel agent.

9) Volunteer to get bumped off a flight.

10) Fly to an alternate city or a "hidden" city.

11) Buy two roundtrip "specials" and split them.

12) Buy a roundtrip special and use it one way.

13) Know your discount fare options and restrictions.

14) Try a ticket broker or consolidator.

15) Enroll in frequent flyer programs.

16) Join "last minute" travel bargain clubs.

17) Check the classifieds for sales of unused tickets, bartered tickets and frequent flyer awards.

# PASSPORT TO
# DISCOUNT TRAVEL

**18)** Fly the low-cost airlines.

**19)** Fly as an independent air courier.

**20)** Do your research, and stay informed about the airline industry.

## AIRFARE COMPARISON CHART

Origination City_____

Alternate Origination City_____

Destination City_____

Alternate Destination City_____

Departure Dates: 1st choice_____

        2nd choice_____

Return Dates: 1st choice_____

        2nd choice_____

Number of Passengers _____

Ages of Children Passengers_____

Ages of Senior Citizen Passengers_____

| **Lowest Discount Fare:** | Airline A | Airline B | Airline C |
|---|---|---|---|
| Peak Price | _____ | _____ | _____ |
| Off-Peak Price | _____ | _____ | _____ |
| Peak Times | _____ | _____ | _____ |
| Off-Peak Times | _____ | _____ | _____ |
| Alternate City and Date Price | _____ | _____ | _____ |
| **Restrictions:** | | | |
| Booking Deadline | _____ | _____ | _____ |
| Purchase Deadline | _____ | _____ | _____ |
| Change or Cancel Fees | _____ | _____ | _____ |

# AIRLINES

**Lowest Walk-Up Fare:** _____ _____ _____
  Restrictions       _____ _____ _____
  Penalties       _____ _____ _____
  Alternate City and
    Date Fare       _____ _____ _____
**Special Fares:**
  Emergency Fare       _____ _____ _____
  Family Fare       _____ _____ _____
  Senior Fare       _____ _____ _____
  Military Fare       _____ _____ _____
  Promotional Fare       _____ _____ _____
**Service:**
  Outbound Departure
    and Arrival Times       _____ _____ _____
  Return Departure
    and Arrival Times       _____ _____ _____
  Non-stop or Direct
    Flights       _____ _____ _____
  Connecting City(s)       _____ _____ _____
**Miscellaneous Factors:**
  Frequent Flyer Mileage _____ _____
  On-Time Record       _____ _____
  Safety Record       _____ _____
  Financial Condition
    of Airline       _____ _____

# FREQUENT FLYER BONUS PROGRAMS

Nearly every major American airline has a frequent flyer program designed to encourage loyalty by rewarding passengers with discounts and free bonuses based on the number of miles traveled. The more miles flown, the bigger the bonus.

# PASSPORT TO
# DISCOUNT TRAVEL

Some airlines use a different approach in their frequent flyer programs. Rather than miles flown, they determine their awards according to the number of flights taken. They use a "trip-based" system with bonus points given for longer flights. For example, 10 short flights, or six long ones, might earn a free trip. Under this system, one might possibly receive equivalent awards faster with fewer flights than on a mileage accrual plan.

Membership in a frequent flyer program is free and open to anyone. Members receive an I.D. card and a numbered account that keeps track of their mileage balance or trip-points. Participating airlines partners, hotel chains, and car rental agencies reward frequent customers with additional mileage in their frequent flyer accounts.

Upon reaching certain mileage levels or award plateaus, some starting as low as 10,000 miles, the bonuses begin. Specific awards and award plateaus differ from one airline to the next. Some carriers are more generous than others, so shop around.

Usually the awards consist of discounted, upgraded or free airline tickets, hotel rooms, rental cars, cruises, or any combination thereof. High-mileage frequent flyers can earn free trips almost anywhere in the world staying at deluxe hotels and driving luxury cars at great discounts, and sometimes even free!

Contrary to what you might think, you do not have to fly very often to benefit from these programs which cost nothing to join. First of all, most programs give a "sign-up" or "first-usage" bonus of several thousand miles just for joining and taking a flight within a certain time. If you fly at least once a year, you should sign up.

Periodically, airlines send discount coupons to frequent flyer members. Even if you've never flown a mile with the airline, you can redeem these coupons for discounted tickets.

# AIRLINES

Don't forget, whenever you travel, you can earn extra mileage, sometimes as much as 1,000 miles or more, by staying at participating hotels, or renting from partner auto agencies.

Since there is usually no time limit, take as long as you need to reach your mileage goal. Every flight earns a minimum amount of miles, about 750 to 1,000 miles or actual mileage flown, whichever is greater. Fly first-class and get one and a half to two times more mileage per flight, depending on the specific airline's frequent flyer mileage formula.

You can earn mileage by flying on airlines other than your member carrier. If you fly on a partner airline, in conjunction with a flight on the member airline, you earn the mileage flown on both. For example, if you fly your member airline from Chicago to New York, and connect with a partner airline on a flight out of the country, you collect all the miles flown on both flights. International airline partners fly to the far corners of the world; by flying often enough, you can earn free international flights as well.

If you fly infrequently, stay away from programs which permit earned mileage to expire after a certain length of time. Some carriers allow mileage to remain in your account for only two or three years, so be sure to turn in those miles for a bonus award before they become worthless.

One method to increase your mileage quickly at no extra cost to you  is by taking connecting flights rather than flying non-stop to your destination.  For example, flying from Detroit to Tampa non-stop may earn 1,000 miles each way. Taking connecting flights involving two changes of plane, in Cincinnati and Atlanta, for instance, you would earn 3,000 miles each way (1,000 miles for each segment flown). A roundtrip between these two cities on non-stop flights would earn 2,000 miles, but your roundtrip flight with multiple connections garners 6,000 miles, —

4,000 miles more than you would have earned if you had flown straight through.

Another way to accrue mileage quickly and inexpensively is to take short flights featuring special low fares between nearby cities, such as Los Angeles and San Diego, or New York and Boston. Fly them on discount fares, and although the cities are only a few hundred miles apart, you still earn your minimum mileage allotment of 750 to 1,000 miles each way. Stay at a partner hotel, or rent from a participating car agency, and add another 30% to 50% to your total miles.

If you use credit cards, take advantage of the "affinity" VISA and Master Cards issued by most airlines which operate frequent flyer clubs. By using the credit cards for normal purchases (not just airline tickets), your frequent flyer account is usually credited one to two miles for each dollar charged, bringing you closer to an award level without flying. Details vary, so check with your credit card company or airline. Affinity cards can easily boost your mileage totals by 20% to 30%. The cards may offer other benefits such as "sign-up bonuses," automatic flight accident insurance, and free collision damage coverage when you rent a car from a participating agency. Although you may have to charge about $10,000 on your affinity card to get a discount on an airline ticket, that's still more than you would receive by not using an affiliated credit card.

To boost business in certain markets throughout the year, your member airline occasionally may offer double or triple mileage bonuses. Try to take advantage of these promotions because your mileage will skyrocket. For example, with a triple-mileage bonus, a simple roundtrip normally earning 2,000 miles suddenly earns 6,000. A multiple-connecting roundtrip flight, such as the Detroit-Tampa illustration earlier, could earn up to 18,000 miles for one roundtrip! (1,000 miles for each segment

# AIRLINES

flown, times three segments flown each way = 3,000 miles one way or 6,000 miles roundtrip, times three for the triple mileage bonus = 18,000 miles.)

Now the fun begins! Because many frequent flyer awards start at the 10,000 mile plateau. You could cash in your mileage and receive 25% to 50% off your next flight. At 20,000 miles you might fly free. At 30,000 to 40,000 miles, you and a companion might fly free, and receive generous discounts on hotels and rental cars. At 50,000 miles you might be able to fly free to Europe, Hawaii, or the Far East. At 75,000 miles, you and a companion could fly free overseas in first class.

Some airline programs offer gifts as an alternative to free flights. Rather than giving away flight passes, they provide a selection of gifts such as clothes, jewelry, computers, sporting goods, even cars. They figure that the last thing many frequent flyers want, having earned their awards by sitting for hours in airplanes, is another flight! Instead, they offer a choice of free travel or free gifts.

To request a frequent flyer award certificate which is redeemed for an airline ticket or merchandise, fill out the form on the back of your mileage statement and send it to the airline. They will deduct the appropriate mileage from your balance and issue your award certificate. If you desire to fly, make your reservations, exchange your certificate for a ticket, and you're off! Once you receive an airline award certificate, you usually have a limited time to exchange it. The ticket is typically valid for one full year from date of issue, unless otherwise stated. You must present the award certificate in person at the time the airline ticket is written. In most programs, award credit is not accrued retroactively in connection with any tickets previously issued or used before joining the frequent flyer program.

You will be asked to show identification when you claim

# PASSPORT TO
# DISCOUNT TRAVEL

your ticket and when you travel. Award certificates are issued **only** in the name of the frequent flyer member who earns the award, and may be exchanged for travel only by the person to whom it was issued, or by any individual or family member so designated by the program participant. Some airlines allow frequent flyers to transfer their award certificates only to immediate family members. Family relationship may have to be proved to the airline.

To transfer an award, the frequent flyer presents it in person to the governing airline, signs it, and designates the individual or family member who will use it. Almost all airlines allow non-family members to travel on a bonus award if accompanying the award recipient on an identical itinerary.

Be aware that only a limited number of seats are allotted for frequent flyer award travel on each flight. So book early, or you may not get your first choice. As usual, it's wise to plan ahead.

Join one or more frequent flyer programs and watch your mileage grow. It's like money in the bank, without taxes. You can discover clever ways to earn frequent flyer points, and learn how to get the most out of these programs by reading the following periodicals:

BUSINESS FLYER, P.O. Box 276, Newton Centre, MA 02159 (203-782-2155 or 800-359-3774)

BUSINESS TRAVELER INTERNATIONAL, Suite 1512, 41 East 42nd St., New York, NY 10017 (212-697-1700) Monthly. Lists comparison charts for various international fares. $36/yr. subscription rate.

# AIRLINES

FREQUENT, 4715-C Town Center Drive, Colorado Springs, CO 80916 (719-597-8889 or 800-333-5937) Subscription is $33/yr. for 12 issues. Lists information on flight bonuses, multiplying mileage, first class upgrades, participating partners and more.

FREQUENT FLYER, published by the Official Airline Guide (OAG) (800-323-3537) Monthly. Subscription: $24 annually.

FREQUENT FLYER MILEAGE PROGRAMS, Runzheimer International, Consulting Services Division, 555 Skokie Blvd, Suite 340, Northbrook, IL 60062 (708-291-9011). A review of frequent flyer programs and user options, $79.

Demand exists for unused frequent flyer award certificates. Although it's against the rules of practically every frequent traveler program for members to sell award certificates to an individual or to a coupon broker, several brokers deal in them. Some brokers pay about one to two cents per mile for the bonus award certificate. A 20,000 mile award will reap between $200 to $400 for the frequent traveler who sells it. The broker then tries to sell the award to someone else at a profit.

**Beware!** If the governing airline finds out a frequent flyer member has sold a bonus award, it might elect to eradicate that member's mileage account or expel the member from the program.

Although purchasing a frequent flyer award may not be illegal, it is unethical; most awards are transferable only to immediate family members, business associates, or other designated individuals.

# PASSPORT TO
# DISCOUNT TRAVEL

People buying unused award certificates can often save money on long-distance domestic and overseas flights. They use award certificates selling for about $300 on transcontinental flights, saving 10% to 50% over regular coach fares. Some business or first class frequent flyer certificates on international flights sell for approximately $500, hundreds less than regular rates for deluxe service.

Now the negatives: Some brokers may not refund your money if your ticket is confiscated, or if you decide not to travel as planned. If you elect to purchase a ticket through a broker, consider buying from a large agency. Smaller operators may have a limited selection and may not give refunds. Follow the dealer's instructions carefully to avoid foul-ups. The broker will either obtain the airline ticket for you, or will tell you how to pick one up yourself. Finally, always know your rights and obligations before purchasing a bonus coupon from a broker.

As mentioned previously, airlines have attempted to stop brokers from selling frequent flyer award certificates, even taking some of them to court. However, several coupon brokers are still in operation. Some of them are:

AMERICAN COUPON EXCHANGE, 800-222-9599

COUPON BANK, 800-331-1076

TRAVELER'S CHOICE, 800-458-6278

# AIRLINES

## TIPS FOR COMFORT

If you have specific dietary needs, or simply prefer a special meal, make your request at least one day before departure. Some of the meal-types most airlines can provide are vegetarian, low calorie, low cholesterol, low fat, low sodium, kosher, bland, seafood, fruit plate, and meals specifically for children, infants and diabetics. It never hurts to ask about the choices you may select as alternatives to regular airline food.

Most airlines allow passengers to bring sandwiches, snacks, and baby food on board, however opened cans and bottles are prohibited. Usually complimentary soft drinks, tea and coffee are served, and alcoholic beverages are available for purchase.

When sitting, rest your feet on your tote bag or over-nighter. This keeps the edge of the seat from cutting off the circulation in your legs—a major cause of swollen feet and ankles. A pillow placed behind the small of your back will also improve your comfort. U-shaped pillows which add comfort on long flights are sold in stores and mail-order catalogs. They provide excellent support to both head and neck, allowing you to sleep without strain.

Bring a sweater in your carry-on bag in case you feel chilly. Ask the flight attendant for a blanket and pillow as soon as you are seated; they may all be taken if you wait. Take a pair of slipper-socks in your tote to wear on the plane—not all airlines give them out. Slipper-socks will keep your feet warmer than your shoes, and they are more comfortable on a long flight because feet tend to swell a little.

The air is very dry in most jet aricraft. Tuck a small bottle or tube of moisturizer in your carry-on, or try this trick which

# PASSPORT TO
# DISCOUNT TRAVEL

models use on long flights—spray your face occasionally with water from an atomizer bottle.

The FAA requires domestic airlines to accommodate all but the most severely handicapped passengers. Requests for wheelchairs and on-board oxygen equipment must be made in advance. Other needs, such as stretchers in the cabin, may be met by some airlines, but not others. Check first before making reservations. Handicapped passengers or children may sit anywhere on the plane except the exit rows. Boarding gate agents are required to seat people in exit rows only if they are willing and able to assist fellow passengers in the event of an emergency.

Experienced travelers know that tedious hours in planes can be painful to the body. Stiff necks and shoulders, cramped arms and legs, reduced blood circulation, and lower back pain are just some of the maladies facing long-distance flyers. Recognizing these problems, several international airlines have prepared a series of stress-relieving exercises which can be performed in one's seat.

Japan Air Lines offers a free 5-page pamphlet, JAL HANDY, illustrating numerous on-board exercises. For a free copy, write to: JAL, Literature Distribution Center, P.O. Box 7712, Woodside, NY 11377.

Germany's Lufthansa Airlines supplies a free 24-page booklet with 19 exercises entitled FITNESS IN A CHAIR. For a free copy, write to: Lufthansa, 750 Lexington Ave., New York, NY 10022-1208.

Here are some exercises to do while seated on a plane:

1. Stretch your legs straight out with your toes up, and contract your thigh muscles.
2. With your legs straight, alternate pointing your toes up

and down to flex calf muscles and promote circulation in your lower legs.

3. With knees bent and toes on the ground, raise and lower your heels from the floor.
4. Sit back and breathe deeply, exhaling completely between breaths to help relieve tension.
5. Tighten and relax stomach muscles to aid digestion.
6. Lift and lower your shoulders, and roll your head around to loosen a stiff neck.
7. Move your arms up and forward while opening and closing your hands to reduce swelling.

## KNOW YOUR RIGHTS

Know your rights as a consumer, your duties as a passenger, and the rights and duties of transportation companies.

An airline ticket, for instance, is more than just a ticket; it is a contract between you and the airline. Basically, the airline promises to: 1) fly you to your destination, 2) arrive reasonably on-time, and 3) perform these functions at a specified price. You promise to: 1) check-in on time, 2) take the ticketed flights, and 3) meet the fare rules and restrictions.

Before changing your airline ticket, look at the flight coupon portion (showing your flight number, dates and times), find the fare basis code indicating restrictions applying to your ticket, including any penalties incurred. The fare basis code is usually found near the top-center of cardboard, computer-generated tickets. Handwritten paper tickets display the fare basis code on the flight coupons at the end of the lines showing your flights, dates, and times. Both types of tickets also display the fare basis code in an area called the fare ladder, which shows, step by step, the price of each flight and the fare rules governing them. If you have any questions about where these items are located or about the consequences of changing your ticket, call your travel agent or the airline's reservations department

Understand your options. Never be afraid to ask if you are uncertain about monetary penalties, or if you have any questions about tickets, fares and reservations. If you still have a problem, speak to a supervisor. Reasonable requests are usually accommodated by the airline's customer service representatives.

For more information regarding refunds, lost tickets, inadequate service, or other difficulties, send for a copy of FACTS AND ADVICE FOR AIRLINE PASSENGERS, from Aviation Consumer Action Project, P O Box 19029, Washington, DC 20036, $2. (See Appendix H for DOT "flying rights" fact sheets.)

## CHECK-IN AND DEPARTURE REQUIREMENTS

You must purchase your ticket at least 30 minutes (60 minutes, international flights) before your scheduled departure, unless an earlier ticketing time limit is specified, as is the case with most advance purchase discount fares.

When you first pick up your tickets, make sure they show correct flights, dates and times. Read the information on the ticket jacket, as well, noting regulations regarding overbooking of flights, check-in and departure requirements, baggage liability limitations, personal liability exclusions, and passenger accept-

# AIRLINES

ability.

Get your seat assignments and boarding passes from your travel agent or from the airline well in advance. This gives you a better chance of selecting the type of seat you prefer, window or aisle, smoking or non-smoking. If advanced seating is unavailable on your flight it could mean that the plane is quite full or even overbooked. For your comfort, select a less crowded flight, if possible. Try to arrive at the airport about 45 minutes to one hour before departure. Report to the boarding gate at least 30 minutes early so the gate agent knows you've arrived and doesn't give your seat away.

If you have not already obtained seat assignments or boarding passes, they must be assigned, as a rule, no later than 20 minutes (30 to 60 minutes, international) before scheduled departure. Present yourself at the designated boarding gate **no later** than 10 to 15 minutes (30 minutes, international) prior to take-off, or you forfeit your rights to compensation if you're bumped off the flight.

In the event you do not comply with these departure requirements, your reservations and seat assignments, including those for seats on continuing and return flights, may be cancelled, and your seat given to someone else. If that happens, you could be stuck for a while.

Even with a valid ticket, you could be denied boarding if you fail to meet the airline's departure requirements. You could also be denied access to the plane if you behave in a manner considered threatening to the security of the flight, or by acting in a way which may jeopardize the safety and comfort of fellow passengers. This includes joking about highjackings, bombs, weapons, or terrorists. You may be kept off a flight for public intoxication or improper attire (shoes and shirts are required).

Finally, never wait until the last minute to catch a flight;

# PASSPORT TO
# DISCOUNT TRAVEL

don't think you can breeze onto the plane as the flight attendant closes the door. This may look good in the movies, but it usually doesn't work that way in real life—you could be left standing at the terminal watching the plane take off. Think smart and plan ahead.

## LATE FLIGHT IN HAWAII

When I was younger, traveling in Hawaii, I cut it so close catching my return flight to the mainland, I could actually reach out and touch the plane as it rolled away from the gate. I could literally count the rivets on the nose of the fuselage as the plane backed away.

On that fateful day, I was planning to fly home from Honolulu. I left my hotel in plenty of time to arrive at the airport one hour before departure. Unfortunately, an auto accident stopped traffic on Highway H-1, the freeway from Waikiki to Honolulu International Airport. By the time I reached the exit ramp to the airport, I was almost too late.

I didn't give up though. I rapidly returned my rental car, and sprinted toward my departure gate past startled tourists. As I arrived, the gate agent quickly glanced at my ticket, took my boarding pass and told me to hurry—he should have saved his breath.

There I was, thundering down the jetway with my suitcases flapping at my side like two broken wings. At the end of the tunnel I saw the open aircraft door. Before reaching it, I heard the ramp agent say "goodbye" to the flight attendant as she slammed the door shut.

# AIRLINES

The ramp agent grabbed my arm, yelling that I was too late to board. (The jumbo jet's engines were screaming to life now, making it almost impossible hear.) "The door is secure," he hollered. "The pilot wants to leave; we're already 20 minutes behind schedule!" Did I care? I just wanted to get on that plane. I had to be at work the next day!

The massive Boeing 747 began rolling away from the gate. I yelled at it to stop—it didn't. I pleaded for it to stop—it still didn't.

On the jetway ledge, I was eye-level with the captain. I waved frantically at him to come back for me. He quizzically looked at me, shrugged his shoulders as if to say there was nothing he could do, saluted me smartly, flashed the thumbs-up sign, and kept on backing up.

There I was, sweating like a boxer, watching my plane pull away in front of my eyes. My heart was pounding; my mind racing—what to do? I thought of jumping onto the nose of the plane and affixing myself like a hood ornament! An amusing thought, but no good.

Now what? Well, what does any good, red-blooded American do when faced with a crisis? He prays. And guess what? It worked! About 20 seconds later, the plane started returning to the gate! The pilot, a good guy after all, I thought, was coming back to get me!

The sobering truth turned out to be quite different. In their haste to depart, the attendants failed to close the cabin door properly. The pilot noticed "door open" indicator light flashing on his instrument panel. He had no choice but to return and let the boarding agent reseal the door correctly. My prayers were answered!

When the door opened, I flew in like a rocket. The passengers assuming the pilot returned for me, must have thought I

# PASSPORT TO DISCOUNT TRAVEL

was a VIP. Not to shatter their illusions, I strutted down the aisle to my seat like a big shot. However, as soon as I sat down, I let out such a sigh of relief I removed all doubt as to my celebrity status. I was grateful just to be on board. From this near miss in Honolulu, I learned a valuable lesson about getting to the airport on time.

## WEATHER AND MECHANICAL DELAYS

When inclement weather disrupts flights, don't expect the airlines to recompense for your inconvenience. If you miss your flight or if it is canceled because of bad weather, you will probably not be reimbursed for your trouble. The same applies if prevailing conditions force you to stay overnight in a hotel. because your flight is postponed to another day. Neither will you be compensated if your suitcases in the confusion, have been sent somewhere else leaving you without a change of clothes.

Air carriers cannot control the weather. Mother Nature, after all, is not an airline employee, which explains why most carriers refuse to repay hotel or meal expenses incurred as a result of her nastier side. On occasion, some airlines may pick up part of the tab for hotel, meals, incidentals, and possibly even a change of clothes if a flight is canceled due to weather. If you honestly believe that the cause of your delay could have reasonably been circumvented by the airline, go ahead and ask for reimbursement of your expenses.

If you are delayed more than four hours, ask for a voucher to cover the cost of a meal. If delayed overnight while away from home, ask for a hotel voucher so you can spend the night comfortably (at the airline's expense) before taking a flight to your destination. Most airlines will give you these only if the cancellation is their fault, not due to weather, but it never hurts to ask.

## RESOLVING COMPLAINTS

If your travel is disrupted by something the airline can control, such as mechanical breakdowns or insufficient crew to fly the plane, you have every right to expect compensation for costs incurred while waiting. Some expenses that should, at least in part, be covered by the airline responsible for your inconvenience are: meals, hotel, and, if bags are missing, clothes and toiletries. You may not get all of it, but why not ask. When you do seek compensation, present your case calmly but firmly, with receipts to back you up.

Try to resolve the issue at the airport or ticket office, if possible, because speaking to someone face to face may speed up the process. If that fails, get the names of the airline employees with whom you dealt and write a letter to the carrier's office of consumer affairs, the company president, or even the chairman of the board.

Clearly explain the details leading up to your complaint: what happened, where, when, and with whom you have already spoken. Be specific, and state your case concisely. Explain the incident, the loss or damage suffered, and the compensation you seek. Be reasonable and realistic. Don't expect the world, but you might get a cash refund or a travel voucher for future flights.

If you receive no response after several weeks, follow-up your initial letter with a phone call to the consumer affairs department. Most complaint bureaus investigate incidents thoroughly before reaching compensation decisons. This may take up to a month or more. Be patient, but don't be afraid to prod the process along every once in a while with a phone call. As always, get the name of any customer service representatives you speak to.

If the airline is unable or unwilling to rectify the situation, and if you are serious enough, contact your lawyer for assistance and send a copy of your airline complaint letter, with a cover letter, to the Department of Transportation, Office of Consumer Affairs, 400 7th St. SW, Washington, DC 20590.

## REBOOKING

When flights are canceled by weather or by mechanical breakdown, most airlines do all they reasonably can to accommodate passengers on later flights, or on another carrier. Even if you are traveling on a restricted, non-changeable ticket, you should be rescheduled to fly on another airline if the original one cannot get you to your destination due to weather or mechanical disruption without causing you undue hardship.

First, find out if another airline arrives sooner than the next available flight on your carrier. Explain to the agent why you must reach your destination as soon as possible. If there is another flight on a different carrier which will get you there sooner, ask to have your ticket written for that airline.

If the request is reasonable, your ticket may be rewritten under "Rule 240," a loophole used by airlines permitting them to accept competitors' tickets in an emergency. If you can

# AIRLINES

convince them of the urgency of your trip, such as attending a wedding, a funeral or a vital business meeting, you may be placed on a Flight Interruption Manifest (FIM), allowing you to fly on another airline without additional charge.

If you are at the airport when the cancellation is announced, you will undoubtedly encounter a crush of anxious, stranded travelers at the ticket counter or at the assistance desk. Passengers from your flight, and possibly from other canceled flights, will be clamoring for help.

Inevitably, you will stand in long, slow lines, waiting to be rebooked. It may take hours to find alternative flights operating, especially in bad weather. When one airline starts canceling or delaying flights due to dangerous flying conditions, normally other airlines do the same. Nasty weather doesn't play favorites, so finding viable flight options into or out of affected airports can be difficult.

Handle this problem the right way. If the line at the airport is moving slowly, leave it and reschedule yourself, by phone.

Call the airline on which you are ticketed. Explain to the reservation agent what has happened, and ask to be reassigned. The reservationist will explore your options, and at no extra charge will attempt to book you on a later flight, or another airline. Calling an airline's reservation center will be much faster than standing in snail-paced lines at overcrowded customer assistance areas. After making your new reservation, take your ticket to the original airline's ticket counter for reissue where they will change it, and get you on your way.

If you are nervous about flying when dangerous weather conditions such as snow, ice storms, severe winds, or heavy rains exist in the vicinity of your origin or destination cities, or are forecast to hit those regions soon, ask to be rescheduled on a

# PASSPORT TO
# DISCOUNT TRAVEL

later or earlier flight. If you plan to drive yourself to the airport, or have a friend or acquaintance take you there, but would prefer not to motor in such messy road conditions, ask the airline to rebook you for a different time. When it becomes evident your flight will depart so late you will miss your connections, arrange to fly when conditions improve. After all, the last thing you want to do is become stranded at some intermediate airport waiting out a storm.

Normally, when holding non-changeable discount tickets, you would have to pay a penalty to alter your flights. Unless a departure is definitely canceled, most airlines insist that you take the flight for which you are booked, or pay an extra charge. However, if poor or deteriorating weather is clearly going to cause you to miss a flight, or undergo extreme inconvenience getting to or from the airport, exercise common sense, stand up for your rights, and ask to change your reservation. Be firm, and calmly express your concerns in a straight-forward manner. If you make a strong case for yourself, you will often get what you want. Frequently airlines are willing to shift passengers to other flights. If you encounter resistance to your request, speak to a supervisor. Don't be afraid to explain your situation, and your genuine concerns. Present your case logically and resolutely. You paid good money for your ticket; you have the right to request reasonable accommodation in order to assure your comfort and safety.

In addition to mechanical or weather delays, a flight can be late for other reasons. Check to see if it is on time before going to the airport. Phoning ahead may save you hours of needless waiting at the terminal.

Do your part to avoid delays by using the following strategies:

# AIRLINES

• **Book flights having a history of being on time**. The recent on-time performance record of every flight is available from airlines and travel agents. If possible, stay away from flights operating during peak morning and evening rush hours, when ticket counters, boarding gates, and runways are most congested.

• **Know the originating city of your flight.** The origin city and the number of stops enroute can affect a flight's on-time performance. For example, the last leg of a transcontinental or an international flight can be expected to run late because of multiple stops, or possible weather or air traffic delays. Try not to book such flights.

• **Avoid selecting the last flights** out of a city since they are often delayed. Later flights have a tendency to run behind schedule because of problems encountered earlier in the day. Keep this in mind if you are planning an itinerary involving a late-night connection so you don't get stranded along the way.

• **Fly to a less crowded airport** where you may encounter fewer bottlenecks. For example, fly into Dulles International instead of National Airport in Washington, DC; Newark International or Stewart Field instead of LaGuardia or JFK in the New York City area; Midway instead of O'Hare in Chicago; Oakland or San Jose Airports instead of San Francisco International, and Burbank or Orange County Airports instead of Los Angeles International.

For more information about other strategies and tactics, read THE AIRLINE PASSENGER'S GUERRILLA HANDBOOK by George Albert Brown, Blakes Publishing Group, Washington, DC.

# PASSPORT TO
# DISCOUNT TRAVEL

## BAGGAGE

Domestic airlines limit the number, size and weight of bags allowed per passenger. In most cases, each passenger may transport, free of charge, a total of four pieces of luggage— either two checked bags and two carry-ons, or three checked bags and one carry-on.

Carry-on bags must be small enough to fit in overhead bins or under the seat in front of you. Garment bags with hooks can be hung in the airplane's closet. However, by the time you board, the closet may be full; you cannot always count on space being there and may have to squeeze the garment bag into an overhead compartment, or send it on as checked baggage.

The average storage space on most U.S. aircraft should be able to accommodate carry-on articles within the following dimensions: Overhead compartments—10" high x 16" wide x 24" long; underseat—8" high x 16" wide x 21" long; closet—4" high x 23" wide x 45" long. Dimensions vary per aircraft, with some planes having larger or smaller on-board stowage areas.

Usually, personal items such as handbags, overcoats, umbrellas, cameras, binoculars, baby food for use during flight, and reasonable amounts of reading material may be carried on board without charge and are not considered part of the free baggage allowance. Canes, crutches, and metal walkers, are also permitted. Personal wheelchairs may be accepted as baggage and can be checked in with the luggage. Most airlines provide wheelchairs for use in the terminal. Reserve a wheelchair for all points enroute by calling the airline prior to departure. Motorized carts used to transport passengers in some airports cannot be guaranteed in advance, but may be requested.

# AIRLINES

On some airlines, sporting equipment such as golf clubs, skis, scuba gear, surfboards, and bicycles are accepted as part of a passenger's free baggage allowance; on other carriers these items may be subject to a modest transportation charge of approximately $25 to $75. Since policies vary and could change at any time, call the airlines for details before traveling.

Bows and arrows, scuba diver's knives, and unloaded hunting rifles, shotguns, and pistols may be accepted in checked baggage if packed in locked, hard-sided cases. Dangerous or hazardous material, such as propane tanks, compressed air containers, flammable liquids, toxic chemicals, and corrosives are normally restricted or prohibited on flights.

For your information, even some seemingly harmless items packed in suitcases such as matches, aerosol sprays, gas-filled cigarette lighters, and nail-polish remover can ignite or explode as the result of vibration, sudden motion, or changes in atmospheric pressure. Instead of packing potentially dangerous items, you should buy what you need after arriving at your destination. Cigarette lighters containing liquid petroleum gas or butane are permitted in the cabin of the plane, but are not allowed to be used in flight. (Most domestic flights under four hours prohibit smoking anyway.)

Delicate items, artwork, pottery, and fragile electronic equipment such as computers, radios, video cameras, VCR's, and TV's may be taken as baggage, but be careful. Airlines often waive any responsibility for such items. Unless you purchase extra-valuation insurance at check-in, you may not receive reimbursement from the airlines if such items are lost or damaged. Extra-valuation insurance is inexpensive (approximately $1 for every $100 of value) and well-worth every penny, because it covers the cost of replacing valuable, breakable items. Play it safe, and purchase the extra protection.

# PASSPORT TO
# DISCOUNT TRAVEL

If you are taking more than four pieces of luggage, or if you are taking items that are particularly large or heavy, you may have to pay excess baggage charges. These charges usually range from $30 to $50 per item. Exceedingly large or heavy bags may have to be shipped separately as airfreight. After all, passenger planes are not in the furniture moving business, and cannot be expected to transport enormous amounts of personal items for the price of an airline ticket. Check with the carriers for specifics about size and weight restrictions, excess baggage charges, and air freight fees. Baggage and weight allowances on inter-national flights are normally more stringent than on domestic flights. Call international airlines for details.

## LOST AND DAMAGED LUGGAGE

If your luggage is damaged enroute, immediately show it to an airline baggage service representative. If at fault, the airline will usually repair it for you free of charge. Similarly, if your belongings are lost or stolen, promptly file a claim with baggage service. Keep your original baggage claim tags or a photocopy of them; they are your only proof that your bags were ever checked. Whenever you file a claim, always get the names of the service agents with whom you speak in case you have to follow up. Make notes of your conversations for later reference.

If your bags have been missing for hours, with no precise arrival time yet known, you may need to replace some vital necessities such as medication. Ask the baggage service agent for cash to reimburse your essential purchases. Expect no more than about $50 from the airlines to cover the cost of the replacement items. If you must buy new clothes because your business suits or dresses are in a lost suitcase, talk to the airline's baggage service representative. Explain why replacement clothes are needed, and ask for reimbursement. If your request is denied, speak to a supervisor—if still denied, buy what you need anyway and keep your receipts. Then, file a formal complaint with the airline's consumer affairs department, explaining the legitimate necessity for your purchases, and seek justifiable compensation for the inconvenience and the cost incurred as a result of the airline misplacing your bag.

Some airlines insure the contents of each suitcase for a maximum of between $1,000 and $1,250; other airlines cover your total losses up to $1,250 regardless of the number of suitcases checked. If the value of your packed items exceeds this amount you should consider purchasing excess valuation insurance (approximately $1.00 for every $100 declared value). You may forgo purchasing extra valuation insurance if you already have secondary insurance, such as a personal property rider on your homeowner's policy, which makes up the difference between the value of your belongings and the airline's standard compensation limits.

Always take your valuables (jewelry, money, cameras, etc.), important documents (passports, etc.), and necessities (medications, toiletries, or other items) on the plane. Never place them in your checked luggage.

Most carriers compensate fairly for articles lost in their care. Avoid the hassle in the first place by taking only carry-on bags, if possible. Pack light and put all your things into one or two overnighters, such as a garment bag hung in the airplane's closet, or a soft-sided carry-on case or duffel bag stuffed into the overhead bin or under the seat in front of you. Since they are with you the whole way, carry-on bags cannot get mauled on the ramp by baggage handlers, crushed by other suitcases in the baggage compartment, or become lost along the way.

Some credit card companies such as American Express provide additional safeguards for your luggage. Charging your ticket with them automatically insures (in excess of the carrier's liability and other coverage), against loss or damage to your belongings. You may also purchase the same protection for about $5 a trip without having to use the cards to pay for your airline tickets. Contact credit card issuers for details. Under some policies checked items are covered up to $500; carry-ons to $1,250. You may also receive up to $200 for replacing items you need if bags are delayed six hours or more. Coverage for valuables such as cameras, jewelry and electronic equipment, may be limited to approximately $250.

If you must check bags, do so at least 30 minutes before flight time. Never wait until the last minute. Plan to arrive at the airport about 45 minutes to one hour before departure. Although not a guarantee, arriving early generally minimizes the chances of your luggage being misplaced or misrouted in the rush to get it to the plane.

If you do arrive later than you should, you may be asked to sign a "late check-in" baggage tag, which waives the airline's responsibility to pay for delivery of your luggage to you if it's delayed. Conversely, don't check your bags too early either. Most airlines will not accept bags more than four hours before departure, because any earlier is too risky. In fact, dropping off your bags more than 90 minutes early could result in having them shoved in a corner of the luggage area, where they may remain overlooked until after the flight has left.

If your itinerary involves a connection, try to book on the same airline all the way through, thus helping eliminate baggage-handling mistakes. If two or more airlines are involved, the

# AIRLINES

last carrier on which you fly is responsible for finding your bags, regardless of which one messed up.

Always place luggage tags with your name, and home or business phone numbers on both the outside and the inside of your bags. It is not wise to advertise your home address on the luggage tags. Ideally, attach another tag with the name, and phone number of your destination on the outside. Most luggage tags are not large enough to have all the recommended identification information written on them, so use more than one. You can pick up free luggage ID tags at airline ticket counters.

Why put a luggage tag inside? If you ever lose your luggage, and your ID tag has disappeared, you will wish you had information inside your suitcase—providing it has not been locked—so the airline baggage agent can positively identify it as yours and send it to you. Without knowing whose bag it is, where it is going, or where it came from, the agent can only put it in storage until you identify it in person. If you're lucky, you may be able to convince him over the phone that the suitcase is yours by describing its outward appearance or its contents. If the agent believes you, he will send it via a delivery service for which the airline may, or may not pay, depending on the situation

One last piece of advice. When you check your bags at the airport, look closely at the destination tags affixed to each suitcase to make sure the correct airport code is on them. If you don't know the airport code of your destination city, ask the ticket counter agent or a porter to tell you, and see that the correct ones are used on your tags and claim checks.

One sad couple spent much of their entire honeymoon in Hawaii wearing the same set of clothes because all their luggage went to the wrong place. Instead of sending their bags to Honolulu (code: HNL), the airline check-in agent using the wrong tag sent them to Houston (code: HOU). Had this unfortunate couple looked at their claim checks before relinquishing their luggage, they could have steered clear of this needless annoyance. Of course you would think that the check-in agent, a professional, should have known better, but airline personnel make mistakes, too. It's up to you to keep your eyes open.

## FLYING WITH YOUR PET

Based on flight time, my wife's dog, Teddy, an absolutely irresistible Maltese Terrier, was a seasoned veteran. Teddy had silky snow-white fur, intelligent black eyes, an engaging personality (he was liked by everyone who knew him, even the postman), and the patience of a saint (as a child, my wife would dress him up as a doll and leave him in a baby carriage for hours).

Beyond all this, he had the soul of an adventurer … and no wonder. His master, my wife's father, was a Navy jet pilot, and his dog took to the skies like a bird.

He took his first transcontinental flight when my wife was just a youngster. Teddy would be toted in a cabin kennel on board, where flight attendants and passengers alike proceeded to shower him with VIP treatment. He was even taken into the cockpit on occasion and visited with the pilots. What a ham!

By the time he was 16, he had flown coast to coast numerous times, (flight attendants knew him by name) and had participated in several cross-country car trips as well. Over the years, Teddy passed along his canine comments and criticisms on pet travel to my future wife, and she, in turn, passed them on

# AIRLINES

to me. From the most senior canine travel expert that I know, (he traveled in nearly 40 states, through several foreign countries, and spent countless hours in the air), I now pass along Teddy's savvy tidbits to you.

Before flying, check with your veterinarian to see if your pet is fit to travel. The doctor may suggest sedating your animal for the journey with pet tranquilizers. **Never** attempt tranquilizing your pet yourself without first discussing it with your veterinarian.

It's a good idea not to feed your pet for several hours before the flight. Your veterinarian can give you instructions on this pertaining to your particular pet.

Always make sure your pet wears an identification tag with your name, and phone number on it.

Some transportation companies restrict travel with pets. While, Amtrak, for instance, prohibits pets of any kind on its trains with the exception of dogs accompanying blind, deaf or otherwise handicapped persons, most airlines will accommodate house pets including hamsters, ferrets, rabbits and snakes. Some airlines limit pets to dogs, cats, and birds. If you have an exotic or unusual animal, check with the airline for any restrictions before bringing it to the airport.

Traveling with pets in the United States is common, but traveling with an animal overseas is not, primarily because the quarantine period during which a country keeps your pet isolated can sometimes last up to six weeks or more, making it impractical for most people to take their pets on a foreign jaunt. For more information obtain the free fact sheet, TRANSPORTING LIVE ANIMALS, from Consumer Affairs Office, I-25, United States Department of Transportation, 400 Seventh St. S.W., Washington, DC 20590.

The American Society for the Prevention of Cruelty to

# PASSPORT TO
# DISCOUNT TRAVEL

Animals (ASPCA) publishes TRAVELING WITH YOUR PET, listing foreign and state regulations, plus general safety and health tips. For a copy, send $5 to ASPCA, Education Department, 441 E. 92nd St., New York, NY 10128.

When flying with a house pet in the United States, the animal must be transported in an airline-approved kennel, regardless of whether the animal is accompanying the passenger in the cabin of the plane or placed in the aircraft's baggage compartment. The kennel must be hardsided, well-ventilated, and large enough for the pet to stand, sit, and lie down. You must also provide food and water in non-spillable containers if traveling more than four hours.

Cabin kennels must be small enough to fit under the aircraft's seats. Most airlines only permit one kennel each in first class and in coach, so reservations must be made in advance. Kennels of all sizes may be purchased at pet stores or directly from the airlines. They are not supplied free of charge by the airlines, nor can they be rented. After all, who would want to receive a kennel that another animal has traveled in for a number of hours?

Most airlines will accept practically any animal considered to be a pet by its owner, as long as it is comfortable inside the kennel, appears in good health, and is not offensive in any way. In case of some question about the animal's health, bring your veterinarian's letter of approval and a copy of your pet's vaccination records.

Pet transportation charges on most airlines cost about $30 to $60 per kennel, one way, on each airline flown, if accompanying a fare-paying passenger. If more than one airline is used, each charges its own pet transportation fee. With the exception of very little animals like small birds, puppies and kittens, the rule of thumb is, one animal per kennel, and one

# AIRLINES

charge per kennel, per carrier. When shipping an unaccompanied animal, it must go air freight.

If your itinerary involves connecting flights on the same airline, that airline will automatically transfer your pet for you from one plane to the other. If there is a long layover between connecting flights, you may be allowed to walk or water your pet before the next take-off. Ask the airline first for permission to do so. If your itinerary involves connecting flights on different carriers, you will have to retrieve the kennel yourself at the baggage service department of the first airline, and bring it to the second carrier in time to check-in and pay their pet charge.

In general, it is a good idea to wait until you arrive at the ticket counter with your animal on the day of departure to pay your pet transportation charge. Most airlines do not refund unused pet fees, so if you pay the charge in advance and Fido decides at the last minute he doesn't want to fly, you lose your money. Never pay your pet fees in advance. You won't save time that way, because you still have to go to the check-in counter at the airport on the day of departure to allow the agent to examine the pet and the kennel for acceptability.

If there is any question about a pet's health, the ticket counter agent may require a note from a veterinary doctor approving the animal for travel. In the interest of the animal's safety and well-being, when the weather is either very cold or hot, airlines may refuse to take it. Call them for specific temperature restrictions and pet regulations, and obtain a free copy of AIR TRAVEL FOR YOUR DOG OR CAT, which lists airline policies regarding pet transportation. Send a stamped, self-addressed envelope to the Air Transportation Association of America, 1709 New York Ave. N.W., Washington, DC 20006-5206.

Another excellent manual is TAKE YOUR PET USA listing hotels which accept animals. It offers tips on kennel selection,

# PASSPORT TO
# DISCOUNT TRAVEL

veterinarian advice, and transportation restrictions. Available at local bookstores and pet shops, or send a check for $11.95 to Artco Offset, 12 Channel St., Boston, MA 02210.

# Chapter 4

# HOTELS

**"The great advantage of a hotel is
that it's a refuge from home life."**
George Bernard Shaw

Hotel managers hate vacancies, because unoccupied rooms represent lost opportunities to generate revenue. Since their goal is to put heads in beds, hotel managers attempt to increase occupancy when bookings are down. They offer discounts and reduced rates to fill both unexpected and anticipated vacancies.

During the past decade, the number of hotel rooms world-wide have grown dramatically. This abundance of space creates intense competition and widespread discounting. Experts estimate that the average room is occupied at 25% below the normal "rack" rate (the rates posted in the hotel room ). By knowing what to do, you can get a discounted room.

The first step to saving money on lodging is plan your trip carefully. Set your budget, then study the areas you intend to visit. Choose where you would like to stay—in the heart of town, by the airport, along a river or coastline, or near museums, theaters, shops or other attractions. Decide whether you prefer to stay at a hotel, motel, guesthouse, or condominium. Find lodging alternatives to fit your pocketbook and your goals.

# PASSPORT TO DISCOUNT TRAVEL

When planning your trip, call hotels and motels directly; you may get a better quote from the local staff than from a central reservations agent. If hotels participate in toll-free booking services, call their 800 number first, and seek the best rates. (See the Appendix for a list of toll-free phone numbers of major hotel chains).

Get the local phone number from the information operator for the hotels. Call them directly and ask for their lowest prices. Don't be surprised if the hotels' reservationists quote better rates than those of a central reservations operator.

Occasionally, the national reservation centers of large hotel chains are unable to keep track of the constantly changing availability of rooms in their vast inventory. Representing tens of thousands of rooms worldwide, it's practically impossible for them to know the exact number of actual vacancies everywhere at once.

On the other hand, reservations personnel at each hotel know their actual number of bookings and are in the best position to offer good rates if rooms are plentiful. So, when shopping prices, calling hotels directly could open the door to big savings.

When visiting a city for the first time, you may discover good values by making advance reservations for a few days at a well-known, or chain-affiliated hotel. Then, once you have a feel for the area, move to other accommodations you may find,more appealing in terms of location, ambience, or price. Naturally, do not cancel your reservation at the first hotel until you find an acceptable alternative.

These days, it's a buyer's market for discount rooms. In the U. S., savings up to 50% are found regularly in Honolulu, Phoenix, Austin, and West Palm Beach, to name a few. In foreign countries lodging bargains exist too, depending primarily on the strength of the dollar versus local currency. When the

# HOTELS

exchange rate is good, dollars go farther and bargains seem abundant; when the dollar is lower, prices appear higher and bargains more scarce. Regardless of the exchange rate, discounts can be found practically anywhere, if you know how to look for them. As a rule, some of the best values are obtained in Greece, Portugal, Mexico, Jamaica and parts of South America.

Remember...never settle for the first price quoted— always ask for a discount.

## TYPES OF DISCOUNTS

The variety of hotel discounts offered today reflects the sophisticated marketing of a highly competitive industry. Hotels use the same system to fill rooms as airlines do to fill seats— "yield management"—the pricing of rooms based on demand, not on size or amenities.

Hotels reduce prices on rooms during slow times as an incentive to boost occupancy. For example, a hotel may set aside a certain number of rooms on weekends at 50% off weekday rates. Because of low occupancy then, hotel managers try to lure customers with attractive prices. Generally, discounts are not combinable with other specials. For instance, you wouldn't receive a 10% "corporate discount" on top of an already discounted weekend rate.

Some hotels reduce every room during the off-season. In Toronto, remarkable savings can be found during the winter at top-notch hotels such as the Four Seasons, the Hilton, the Sheraton, and the Inter-Continental. (Call directly or contact the Toronto Visitors Bureau at 800-363-1990.) Caribbean lodging prices often drop by 50% or more beginning in mid-April, which

# PASSPORT TO
# DISCOUNT TRAVEL

makes it a good time to go. FIELDING'S CARIBBEAN by Margaret Zellers, an excellent guides to islands, reviews some low-cost accommodations.

Some types of hotel bargains about which to inquire are:

- Corporate discounts
- Weekend discounts
- Off-season discounts
- Advance purchase discounts
- Frequent flyer tie-ins
- Frequent guest programs
- Less desirable rooms
- Kids-stay-free promotions
- Senior citizens specials
- Half-price cards and coupons
- Student, faculty, clergy and
  military discounts
- AAA and other travel club-member deductions

When calling hotels for prices, discuss the bargains mentioned above. Because there are so many types of discounts, you may have to specifically ask for them.

When calling a hotel and are quoted a standard room rate, don't accept it right away, unless you're desperate. Ask for a "corporate rate," saving about 10% to 20%. (You do not have to travel on business or work for a corporation to get this discount.)

Even if corporate rates are available, check if there are less expensive rooms on lower floors, or in less desirable locations—perhaps without a scenic view. Weekend rates may be even lower, or perhaps there's a "special" which lets kids stay free.

# HOTELS

Members of a participating airline's frequent flyer program receive bargain rates. By being persistent and asking the right questions when shopping for the best prices, you could very easily get that room for about half-price.

Inquire about advertised specials. Some major chains, facing excess capacity and diminishing occupancy, offer discounts up to 50% for reservations paid in advance. Some feature other inducements as well, such as gift certificates, room upgrades, or even savings bonds. Don't give up if a chain's toll-free operator says an advertised rate is sold out. Contact the hotel directly; they may be offering some rooms at special unadvertised discounts. Perseverance pays, but if pressed for time, call a travel agent who will try to find bargains by shopping at several hotels.

Central reservation services in certain areas coordinate room reservations for several hotels. Because of volume sales, these services usually offer discounts. New York, Los Angeles, San Francisco and vacation locales such as Las Vegas, Hawaii, and Florida , as well as ski and island resorts all use central reservation services.

In pricey San Francisco, for example, you might be able to save up to 50% at nearly 90 different properties by calling the city's booking service at (800-677-1550 or 800-333-8996).

CAPITOL RESERVATIONS (800-847-4832) in Washington, DC, performs a similar service for hotels in the District of Columbia and surrounding Maryland and Virginia.

EXPRESS HOTEL RESERVATIONS (800-356-1123) regularly offers rooms at 20% to 30% off at a variety of hotels in both New York City and Los Angeles.

There's no charge to use these reservation services. You may find others in the TRAVEL PLANNER, or by contacting city and state tourist boards.

# PASSPORT TO
# DISCOUNT TRAVEL

THE NATIONAL DIRECTORY OF BUDGET MOTELS, published annually, lists addresses and phone numbers of more than 2,000 low-cost chain motels across the United States and Canada. To order a copy, send $4.95 by check or money order to Pilot Books, 103 Cooper St., Babylon, NY 11701.

A good place to discover lodging bargains is in newspaper travel sections which contain many hotel advertisements and descriptive articles. Also, most travel guidebooks rate and price hotels and motels in many cities and countries. Travel clubs and automobile associations produce handy reference guides to lodging selections nationwide, including those offering discounts to members.

Excellent values are often found at smaller hotels off the beaten path. Many of these locally owned and operated establishments provide a personal touch sometimes missing at larger, high-volume hotels.

If you are the spontaneous type, you may be able to find good bargains by searching for lodging on the day of arrival. Several of the local hotels may offer very affordable rates. This approach to finding discounts is somewhat risky, however, and could backfire if you are unable to locate anything suitable. Consider it only if you have the time, patience, and energy to look for a room upon reaching your destination.

## ADDITIONAL DISCOUNTS

Some more ways to save money on lodging are:

• **Preferred Rates**. Many companies, large and small, negotiate "preferred" rates for employees traveling on business.

# HOTELS

Depending on volume and use, these rates chop as much as 40% off the normal price of a room. (These are not the same as "corporate" rates.) When preferred rate rooms are vacant, some hotels and travel agencies will offer them to non-business travelers.

• **Frequent Flyer Tie-ins.** Members of frequent flyer programs may be offered discounts at participating hotels. Some reduced rates apply whether or not the member actually flew on that airline to get to the hotel. Discounted or free rooms are also given as part of the bonus awards earned by frequent flyers.

• **Frequent Guest Plans.** Like the airlines, hotels offer membership programs to encourage repeat business and reward hotel chain loyalty. They offer their members special prices on rooms, airfares, and rental cars. If you travel a lot, look into joining several of these programs which could result in savings of 30% to 50%.

• **Less Desirable Rooms.** Smaller or less-appealing rooms can lead to lower prices. If a scenic view is not a priority, ask for a room on a lower floor or in the back of the hotel. These rooms, particularly, in older properties, are frequently discounted. In Europe or the Caribbean, where many full-service American-style hotels tend to be pricey, you may find affordable lodging if willing to forgo some of the glitz. Staying at a smaller hotel, or doing without room service or an in-room shower, may be all it takes to save up to $100 or so a night. Big savings on hotel bills can be achieved by simply scaling down your desires.

• **Senior Citizen Discounts.** Several hotel chains offer seniors 10% to 50% off regular rates. Marriott's Leisure Life

# PASSPORT TO DISCOUNT TRAVEL

program, for example, features half-price rooms for travelers over 62. Ramada's Best Years program gives 25% discounts to guests over 60. Some properties even provide greater reductions for senior members of hotel frequent-guest clubs. The American Association of Retired Persons (AARP), retired military personnel, postal workers, and other groups are usually eligible for discounts at hotels.

• **Automobile Club Discounts.** The American Automobile Association (AAA) and other auto clubs, offer their members discounts of 10% to 20% at hotel chains such as Marriott, Sheraton, Days Inn, Stouffer, Ramada, Quality, Rodeway, LaQuinta Inns, and others. Members obtain savings by showing their club card at check in. These auto clubs publish guidebooks, pricing and rating hotels, restaurants, and tourist attractions in many cities, noting which establishments give member discounts. You and your family can join AAA and other automobile clubs (Sears, Montgomery Ward, and Amoco, for example) for a reasonable annual fee. Check the white pages of your phone book for your local office.

• **Advance Purchase Discounts.** Some hotels offer 30% to 50% off published room rates to travelers who confirm reservations with a major credit card 30 days in advance. Marriott, Holiday Inn and Trustehouse Forte are several chains periodically promoting these savings.

• **Student, Faculty, Clergy and Military Rates.** If booked in advance, hotels offer discounts of 10% to 25% for eligible travelers. Ask specifically about these rates, and compare them with other discount options to get the best deal.

# HOTELS

Finally, be bold enough to bargain on the spot when you check into a hotel. It never hurts to ask the desk clerk if lower-priced rooms are available, or whether you can obtain a better or larger room for the same price. If the hotel is not too crowded, the clerk may gladly discount or upgrade your room.

## HELPFUL HINTS

When making a reservation for a hotel in an unfamiliar city, request map of the area with the hotel's location clearly marked. If planning to use public transportation, pick up a map of the bus, subway, and municipal rail systems. When overseas, have an English-speaking hotel clerk explain the local transportation system.

Before venturing out to see the sights, ask the concierge or hotel clerk about tipping, proper fares for taxis and public transportation, or surcharges for night-time or holiday trips. It's important to know in advance which cabs, buses, and water taxis are legitimate, and which are not. In some countries, the words "public transportation" refers to just about any conveyance which runs or floats.

Since licensing is not strictly enforced in many foreign countries, watch out for "gypsy" cabs and transportation services which may "take you for a ride" financially. In some places, so-called "private sightseeing" bus and boat operators have been known to charge three to four times the authorized rate. Find out which are authentic transportation companies and what appropriate fares should be.

If you do not speak or write the native language, carry the name and address of your hotel written in local script. This is crucial in areas where the alphabet is completely different from English, such as in Russia, the Middle East, and the Orient. Life is much simpler when you can show a legible address to a taxi driver or someone from whom you are seeking directions. Why get lost because you cannot spell or pronounce the name or address of your desired destination?

When it's time to pay your restaurant or hotel bills, check if a service charge has been assessed. Service charges cover tips for the waiter, busboy, or housekeeper, averaging between 10% to 20%. In many European restaurants, especially in Italy, a "table fee" is automatically added to your bill. If the service charge or table fee appears on your check, you may still wish to leave a little more money. If it has not been included, the rule of thumb is tip the same as in any American city—15% to 20%.

## HOW TO STAY AT UP TO 50% OFF

Hotels in many locations offer low weekend rates to help fill rooms vacated by business travelers heading home on Friday. Weekend specials save up to 50%, and often include such amenities as complimentary meals, show tickets, greens fees, or tennis court time.

Try to stay in cities on weekends when you are likely to find lower rates or promotions, such as discount coupons, "two nights for the price of one," or "special occasion rates" for anniversaries, graduations or family reunions. Call the hotel's central reservations toll-free operator or the hotel directly for specifics.

When making a reservation, always write down the name of the reservation agent and your room confirmation number. Having this information on hand when you check in provides leverage in case there is no record of your reservation and no room at the inn. Without it you may be left out in the cold. If unable to present your confirmation number and the booking agent's name you're out of luck! With proof of confirmation, most clerks will attempt to find a room at their hotel or another one, provided, of course, you arrive before the room cancellation deadline. If you show up too late, your room may have already been assigned to someone else. Avoid that worry by guaranteeing your reservation with a credit card which keeps your room waiting, no matter when you arrive. Unless guaranteed, your room could be given away.

On the other hand, if you decide not to use a room you've guaranteed with a credit card, be sure to cancel the reservation by the hotel's deadline (usually 4 p.m. to 6 p.m. on the day of arrival, or at some resorts, several days before). Failure to do so may result in your being charged for at least the first night, and in rare cases, for the entire length of the reservation whether or not you actually stay there. Check the hotel's cancellation policy at the time you make your reservation.

When canceling, remember to get a cancellation number and the reservationist's name. Such data is essential should you need to correct your credit card account when charged for a hotel room you never occupied.

# PASSPORT TO
# DISCOUNT TRAVEL

## HOTEL WHOLESALERS

As a national average, hotels fill only about 65% of their rooms each day, so naturally, hoteliers eager to increase occupancy, would rather discount rooms, as much as half price, than have vacancies. Sometimes they even offer rooms to whole-sale marketers to sell at reduced rates. Many well-known hotels and hotel chains throughout the world participate in wholesale programs.

For a modest annual fee, ranging from $30 to $100, wholesale companies sell coupon books for discounted rooms to travelers on a space-available basis. The wholesaler distributes lists of participating hotels, resorts, and condominiums, with details on special conditions and blackout periods during which they cannot be used.

Wholesalers generally give discounts on the more expen-sive rates, not weekend specials, which are about the same as a wholesale club's half-price offerings. Since less expensive rooms tend to sell out first, usually those at mid-to-high-prices are the only ones discounted. Consequently, weekday business travelers benefit more from wholesale marketing programs than do weekend vacationers or tourists, who tend to book rooms far in advance.

Reservations for rooms at wholesale rates are usually made with the hotel directly, not through the chain's toll-free central reservations number. In some cases, reservations are accepted up to a month or more prior to arrival.

Some of the following wholesale clubs offer free rooms when joining, provide rental car upgrades, money back guaran-tees, or directories of affiliated resorts worldwide. Membership fees up to $100 may be charged.

# HOTELS

• QUEST INTERNATIONAL, Schinook Tower, Box 4041, Yakima, WA 98901 (800-325-2400)

• ENTERTAINMENT/TRAVEL AMERICA AT HALF PRICE, 2125 Butterfield Rd., Troy, MI 48084 (800-521-9640)

• CONCIERGE, 1050 Yuma St., Denver, CO 80294 (800-346-1022)

• THE PRIVILEGE CARD, 3473 Satellite Blvd., Suite 200, Duluth, GA 30136 (800-359-0066)


## FOREIGN BARGAINS

### How to Save Money on Foreign Vacations

• Stay at generally less-expensive family-run hotels, guesthouses, or country inns.
• Shop for economical travel packages which include airfare, lodging and ground transportation.
• Design or select sightseeing excursions yourself, and use public transportation whenever possible.
• Take advantage of city "tourist cards" offering discounts on museums, attractions and municipal transportation.
• Eat at least some of your meals in small cafes, or buy picnic foods.
• Visit bargain countries, such as Spain, Portugal, Greece, Yugoslavia, Czechoslovakia, Poland, India, Thailand, and parts of Central and South America.

• Stay in smaller towns, which are normally more economical than larger cities.
• Use some of the housing options discussed below.

## Home Exchanges

How can you save on a lengthy trip abroad? Staying at a hotel, renting a villa, or a private apartment is fine for a few weeks, but what if you want to stay a month or more? One solution is swap houses with a foreign family who will reside in your home, while you stay in theirs.

How can you arrange an exchange if you don't personally know any families with whom to swap? Easy. Contact a "home exchange" company to show you a selection of houses, locations and prices, and handle the details of the transaction.

Before paying the fee (approximately $50), check on the reputation and history of the company. Contact the Better Business Bureau and your local consumer protection agency for any complaint history. Find out how long it has been in business; ask for references from people who have used its services; or see if your travel agent is familiar with the company.

Through its catalog, a good home exchange company should offer a wide variety of homes in several countries. Find out how many properties are represented, how often the catalog is published, where services are marketed, and how many times your home will be advertised. The tourist boards of most countries should be able to provide you with the names of home exchange agencies operating within their borders, and their history.

Before approving an exchange, take some common sense precautions to assure yourself about the family with whom you will be swapping. Your goal is to screen the people and determine their honesty and integrity. Correspond with the family frequently enough to feel confident about their background and reputation. This usually includes exchanging pertinent information such as place of employment, work and home phone numbers, and personal and professional references. In addition to exchanging photos of the houses, you could also exchange photos of each other. If you still don't feel comfortable about swapping with them, follow your instincts and don't do it. Home exchanges in the U.S. may also be arranged.

Two American-based companies specializing in home exchange vacations are:

• VACATION EXCHANGE CLUB, P. O. Box 820, Haleiwa, HI 96712 (800-638-3841). In business since 1960, this club prints two exchange books per year highlighting homes, condos and apartments worldwide. Fees: $50 to list your home in one of the books, (you receive both), and $55 to be an unlisted subscriber of both books. Half of the homes listed are overseas; the rest are in the continental U.S. and Hawaii.

• BETTER HOMES & TRAVEL, 185 Park Row, P.O. Box 268, Suite 14D, New York, NY 10038 (212-349-5340), charges $50 to list your home. No fee for rental info. Closing fees for finding an exchange partner range from $150 to $600 depending on the type of home and length of exchange.

• HOME BASE HOLIDAYS, Annlin Publications, Box 1562, Santa Clarita, CA 91386 (805-251-1238). $50 annual fee lists your home in their brochures. Write for a free sample copy.

# PASSPORT TO
# DISCOUNT TRAVEL

For a comprehensive list of agencies which arrange home exchanges, or to obtain information about vacation swapping with your children and pets, read TRADING PLACES: THE WONDERFUL WORLD OF VACATION HOME EXCHANGING, Rutledge Hill Press, $9.95.

## The Condo Connection

Staying at a condominium can save money and provide added space and comfort. Many condos accommodate four to six people for less than the cost of a suite or two hotel rooms. Most vacation condos are located in prime tourist areas, and provide kitchen facilities not found in standard hotel rooms.

Several organizations and agencies specialize in renting condos to travelers. One such company, CONDOLINK, based in Omaha, NE (800-733-4445) rents condos at over 2000 resort properties in Europe, the Caribbean, Mexico, and the United States. For example, some of their two-bedroom apartments in Puerto Rico rent for less than $100 per night; condos on other islands start at about $1,000 per week, even less in Europe and Mexico.

The RESORT PROPERTY OWNERS ASSOCIATION, Suite 304, 950 Skokie Blvd., Northbrook, IL 60062 (708-291-0710), publishes a comprehensive directory of over 1,000 vacation condos, rates the properties, lists current prices, and mentions discounts on selected rentals. The association also provides names of travel agencies and reservation services handling condo vacations. Initial membership, $75; annual renewals, $20.

# HOTELS

VILLA AND CONDOMINIUM VACATIONS, a helpful free guide to condo rentals, is available from Travel Resources, P.O. Box 935, Coconut Grove, FL 33133 (800-327-5039).

For information about Bed and Breakfast lodgings in the United States and Canada, including rustic farmhouses, ocean-front cottages, quaint guest homes, and city brownstones, send a stamped, self-addressed envelope to BED AND BREAKFAST, THE NATIONAL NETWORK, P.O. Box 4616, Springfield, MA 01101, or call 212-594-5687.

Tourist boards in most cities and states can also provide updated information on bed and breakfast lodging in their areas.

## EUROPEAN BARGAINS

Before going to Europe, research the various lodging options available. A handy booklet, PLANNING YOUR TRIP TO EUROPE, prepared by the European Travel Commission, provides important details about accommodations, attractions, passports, restaurants, rail passes, shopping, special events, travel packages, transportation discounts, tours, and weather. For your free copy, write to EUROPEAN TRAVEL, P.O. Box 9012, East Setauket, NY 11733.

TRAVEL EUROPE, a monthly newsletter, has news about advisories, tours, bargain airfares, promotions and specials. For a free sample, send a stamped self-addressed envelope to Box 9918, Virginia Beach, VA 23450. One year subscription is $20.

For a more off-beat approach try Rick Steves' EUROPE THROUGH THE BACK DOOR videos and guidebooks which present a laid-back look at traveling on the Continent (206-771-8303).

# PASSPORT TO
# DISCOUNT TRAVEL

## Finding Hotel Discounts

Even during peak season, you can save up to 60% on European hotels, when many chains, tourist boards, airlines, and travel agencies promote discounts to ensure good occupancy. These promotions cover a range of prices and accommodations, from guest houses to 5-star resorts.

For example, Hilton Hotels International (800-223-1146) and Inter-Continental Hotels (800-327-0200) slash their room rates by 20% to 50% in July and August, when most of their vacationing business clients leave behind empty rooms. Similar-ly, the 4-star Pullman Hotels and the 3-star Altea Hotels reduce prices across the board, charging a flat rate for all rooms of about $75 to $100 a night. In London, the Park Lane, a classic grand hotel, whose art-deco lobby and ballroom have been featured in several motion pictures and television programs, offers summer prices of less than $100 a night. For more information about this and other specials, contact Concord Hotel Reservations (800-888-4747), which represents over 50 hotels in more than 15 countries.

During the summer, some hotels in the luxurious CIGA chain offer a 40% savings for a minimum 7-day stay. Other hotel chains, such as Trustehouse Forte (800-225 5843), and Leading Hotels of the World (800-223-6800) also feature dramatic off-season specials in Europe and worldwide. Good sources for moderately-priced hotels in Europe and elsewhere include Best Western (800-528-1234) and Utell International (800-448-8355) Contact tourist boards for lists of hotels in your price range.

Many international airlines such as Air France, British Air, Swissair, and KLM Royal Dutch Airlines arrange discounts with participating hotels providing excellent rates due to volume sales. Their prepaid room vouchers guarantee the hotel bill will not fluctuate with the exchange rate. Some airlines even offer added incentives such as free rental cars or tours.

At certain times of the year, Alitalia Airlines slashes prices on its "Italy Loves You" air and land packages starting at around $100 per person, double occupancy for a 5-night stay in first-class hotels in Rome, Florence, Venice, Sorrento, Palermo, and Taorimina. Some extras include daily continental breakfast, hotel tips, and a "Best of Italy" card for discounts at many restaurants, boutiques and attractions. Call ITALY TOUR for details (800-237-0517).

Government tourist boards frequently promote hotel bargains. The German Tourist Office, 747 Third Ave., New York, NY 10017 (212-308-3300), oversees the 90-plus WUNDERHOTELS, which offer hundreds of rooms at guaranteed rates. It also distributes free NEW GERMANY GUIDES, highlighting some of the exciting tourist attractions formerly concealed behind the iron curtain. Ask about seasonal discounts on KD RIVER CRUISES on the Rhine and Elbe rivers.

The French Tourist Board (212-757-1125) publishes FRANCE DISCOVERY GUIDE, listing many hotel specials throughout the country, including $89 room rates in Paris and on the Riviera, and discounted weekly rental car rates. The government also promotes tourism to the storybook villages of eastern France by offering free guidebooks and advice with one phone call, 900-990-0040 (50 cents a minute).

In addition to promoting hotels, the British Tourist Authority (BTA) sponsors alternatives including apartments and bed-and-breakfast lodging. The booklet, ACCOMMODATIONS FOR BUDGET TRAVELERS, lists moderate-priced hotels, guest houses a and apartments in London and its suburbs. For a free guide offering tips on saving money on everything from lodging and

# PASSPORT TO
# DISCOUNT TRAVEL

transportation to tourist attractions, shopping and dining ask for AMAZING LONDON, from the BTA, 40 W. 57th St., New York, N.Y. 10019 (212-581-4700). Also, inquire about the Countdown Card which helps you save 10% to 50% while visiting London.

The BTA also sells guidebooks on guest houses and country inns in England, Scotland, and Wales. Send a note listing the material in which you are interested, and a self-addressed business envelope with $1.00 postage to: British Tourist Authority, Literature Distribution Center, 25-15 50th St., Woodside, NY 11377.

For more information about bed and breakfasts throughout Great Britain, send for the brochures, BRITAIN: BED AND BREAKFAST and STAY WITH A BRITISH FAMILY from the regional office of the BTA, Suite 470, 2580 Cumberland Parkway, Atlanta, GA 30339-3909 (404-432-9635). The BTA also promotes budget lodging in Scotland, starting as low as $30 a night. Ask about the Scottish grading and classification program describing accommodations in detail, so you know what to expect.

Some U.S.-based agencies handling London apartment rentals for travelers are:

AARP TRAVEL SERVICE (800-227-7737)
BRITISH TRAVEL ASSOCIATION (800-327-6097)
LONDON APARTMENTS (800-366-8748)

Some French apartment specialists are:

JET VACATIONS (800-538-0999)
EUROPA-LET, INC. (800-462-4486)

# HOTELS

## Rental Homes

If you need extra room and more privacy during your stay on the Continent, consider renting a home. Explore the excellent values of short-term leasing available in several countries. In France you can rent a 3-star "gite"—a private home supervised by the French government tourist office (GTO), starting as low as $200 a week. These comfortable homes feature two bedrooms, living room, kitchen, bathroom, and sometimes even a garden. Other countries offer similar lease programs. Contact their GTO's for details.

Want a truly exotic experience? Why not stay in an authentic European castle or château? B & D DE VOGUE INTERNATIONAL represents nearly 150 exclusive, privately-owned residences in France, Germany, Belgium, Italy, and Portugal. You can luxuriate in a number of magnificent properties including Renaissance castles, stately mansions, centuries-old manor homes, charming châteaux, and hunting lodges.

Now don't let the words "hunting lodge" fool you. These lodges aren't shacks in the woods. A gentleman's hunting lodge in Europe is something else entirely. Take Linderhof, for example, the famous mountain retreat built in the late 1800's for Bavaria's youthful "Mad" King Ludwig. Far from being a rustic cabin, it is simply one of the most magnificent estates in the world.

Tucked away in a peaceful river valley in the Alps of southern Germany, this elegant mansion, features stunning architecture and priceless art. Looking inside, you suspect this bachelor king was hunting something other than deer! Why else would he design his exotic Persian Lounge with its sensuous colors, peacock-feathered walls and gilded Middle Eastern artifacts? Why would he adorn his huge master bedroom's walls

123

# PASSPORT TO
# DISCOUNT TRAVEL

with lovely murals depicting idyllic romantic scenes? Why would he cover his ceiling with statues of naked cherubs literally floating out of the vaulted roof blowing golden trumpets and firing Cupid's arrows? Why build a waterfall to cascade soothingly outside his bedroom's 30-foot-high picture window? Why place a musician stand for a string quartet discreetly in a corner? Why erect a mammoth, four-poster, satin-sheeted bed in the middle of the room which can only be reached by climbing up several steps to its platform? Ludwig even went so far as to create his own underground grotto, complete with a subterranean lake and swan-shaped boat made of solid gold. What game was he really hunting?

Of course, whenever Ludwig wearied of the "rugged" life of the hunt, he could always return to one of his two other castles: Neuschwanstein, the magnificent real-life inspiration for Walt Disney's Cinderella Castle; and Chiemsee, a duplicate of the famous French Palace of Versailles, built on an island in the center of a beautiful alpine lake.

How fitting that he modeled this graceful lake retreat after the splendid residence of King Louis XIV. Among Ludwig's more exotic eccentricities (often alluded to as proof of his insanity by some of his subjects, who eventually murdered the disturbed, young king), was his delight in conversing during meals with the great deceased rulers of history—monarchs, Caesars and czars. His favorite guest of all, was the Sun King, Louis XIV of France, who had been buried for more than a century before Ludwig began hosting him at dinner!

Although your European residences may not be as grand as Ludwig's famous castles, you will still feel like royalty when the resident family welcomes you to gracious château living. Reservations usually require a minimum two-night stay, with prices starting at about $70 a night and climbing to many

# HOTELS

hundreds of dollars. Details and copies of the latest, richly illustrated Chateau Catalog are available at travel agencies, or from B & D DE VOGUE INTERNATIONAL, P.O. Box 1998, Visalia, CA 93279 (800-727-4748 or 209-733-7119).

Visitors to the United Kingdom may obtain a copy of COUNTRY HOLIDAYS, a free catalog of rental homes and cottages in England, Scotland, and Wales. Homes in picturesque hamlets, Victorian townhouses, and even castles are among the hundreds of selections presented in this vacation rental guide available from BRITISH TRAVEL ASSOCIATES, P.O. Box 299, Elkton, VA 22827 (800-327-6097).

Other agencies specializing in foreign home rentals include:

• HOMETOURS INTERNATIONAL (800-367-4668)

• VACATION HOME RENTALS WORLDWIDE (800-633-3284)

• VILLAS INTERNATIONAL (800-221-2260)

## HOSTELS

Imagine going to America's most popular tourist city, San Francisco—City by the Bay—with its Golden Gate Bridge, world-class restaurants, historic sites, breathtaking views, and magnificent Pacific coastline.

# PASSPORT TO DISCOUNT TRAVEL

An expensive place to stay, right?

Wrong!

You can reside in one of San Francisco's most ideal settings, overlooking the bay on a picturesque wooded hillside, just minutes away from famous Fishermen's Wharf, for about $20...repeat...$20...a night!

How? Not by sleeping in a car at Fort Mason Bayfront Park, but by staying at the San Francisco Youth Hostel located there.

If you are no longer a youth—don't worry. Hostels in the United States have no age restrictions. Anyone can stay in them if they are a member of American Youth Hostels (AYH).

AYH is the U. S. affiliate of the International Youth Hostel Federation, representing more than 5,300 hostels in 29 countries. Like the AYH, most international hostels allow members of all ages to visit. Exceptions to this rule are the hostels in Bavaria, Germany, which only permits guests up to 26 years old.

Annual membership dues are approximately $10 for youths under 18; $25 for members over 18, and $35 for families. (Membership fees are subject to change.) For more information contact: AMERICAN YOUTH HOSTELS, Dept. 863, P.O. Box 37613, Washington, DC 20013 (202-783-6161). They will send literature explaining membership benefits, and advising about the nearest AYH Council. Upon joining AYH, you receive a guide to hostels in the U. S., a twice-yearly magazine, discount travel information, and a membership card for entry to hostels worldwide.

Unlike a hotel, a hostel's dormitory-style surroundings are not designed for those who desire privacy and luxury. However, if you are on a tight budget, gregarious, and willing to share your living space, you will find a friendly welcome and

# HOTELS

meet fascinating travelers from around the world.

Accommodations in most hostels consist of shared, separate men's and women's bunkrooms, although some hostels have individual rooms for families and married couples. Many hostels close between 9:30 a.m. and 4:30 p.m., to encourage visitors to explore the surroundings.

As a courtesy, all guests are required to refrain from drinking alcohol and smoking on the premises. They are also asked to do a brief daily chore, such as sweeping a room, mopping a floor, or helping out at the front desk. This assures the hostel will be clean and functioning for the next visitors. It's a sort of "sing for your supper" arrangement, but the prices are so incredibly low, most budget-minded travelers don't mind a few minutes of community duty.

Groups are welcome. Hostels will make special arrangements for them if their facilities can handle it. Capitalizing on their unique locations and reasonable rates, many hostels host daytime and overnight functions for schools, churches, scout troops, ecology clubs, and creative workshops.

The locations of some hostels are truly spectacular. One, actually a restored lighthouse, is nestled on a rocky ledge along California's coast. The Montara Lighthouse hostel, snuggled on scenic shoreline 25 miles south of San Francisco, is just one example of the many wonderful hostel sites. Others are centrally-located in major cities, such as New York, Washington, New Orleans, London, Amsterdam, and Paris.

# PASSPORT TO
# DISCOUNT TRAVEL

## COLLEGES AND UNIVERSITIES

Cut lodging expenses by going to college! Not as a student, but as a visitor. During the summer, many colleges and universities open their residence halls to the general public at bargain rates. Most dormitory rooms only have single beds and lack private bathrooms. (The shared washroom facilities are usually located down the hall) However, some schools provide suites with kitchens, baths and extra beds or cots for children.

If you decide to stay at a college, check the campus rules first. Some schools may permit you to use their tennis courts, swimming pool, gymnasium, and other recreation facilities; other schools may not. At most colleges, pets, alcohol, and smoking are prohibited in campus housing.

Be sure to reserve your room well in advance since many dorms in prime locations fill up early. Some are wonderfully situated in Hawaii, New England, California, and New York City

In Hawaii, for example, Honolulu's CHAMINADE UNIVERSITY offers rooms only a mile and a half from Waikiki Beach for about $20-$30 a night (808-735-4760). In rustic New England, NEW HAMPSHIRE UNIVERSITY'S STRATFORD PLACE is close to the ocean and near dozens of lakes. It offers singles and doubles with kitchenettes for about $30-$40 a night, and two bedroom apartments for around $80 (603-868-2192). The University's hotel-style New England Center also hosts weekend "learning experiences" from March to July for retirees and senior citizens. Instructed by faculty members, classes delve into a range of subjects, such as architecture, music, politics, and foreign cultures. The weekend costs about $200 per person, including two nights' lodging, meals, and special events (603-862-1900).

# HOTELS

While the average prices of hotel rooms in New York City are the highest in the country, you can stay nearby for only $30-$50 a night at the STEVENS INSTITUTE, a 55-acre campus across the East River in Hoboken, NJ. For larger rooms with air conditioning and a private bath, expect to pay about $50, single, and $60, double. Budget meals are available in the college cafeteria, and recreation facilities may be used by guests. For more information, contact CAMPUS HOLIDAYS USA, 242 Bellevue Ave., Upper Montclair, NJ 07043 (201-744-8724).

Across the country on the West Coast, the UNIVERSITY OF CALIFORNIA IN SANTA BARBARA offers double rooms overlooking the Pacific Ocean for around $50 a night.

For information on these and over 600 other schools in the United States, Canada and overseas offering summer lodging, send for U.S. & WORLDWIDE TRAVEL ACCOMMODATIONS GUIDE from the Campus Travel Service, P.O. Box 8355, Newport Beach, CA 92660 ($13.00 plus $1.50 for postage).

# HOW TO STAY FREE

If you have a favorite sport, hobby, or special interest and there is a game, convention, or expo related to that interest, bring a group of 10 or more fellow enthusiasts along with you, and stay at the same hotel. A group of visitors occupying at least five to 10 rooms typically receives a complimentary room, or, at least, a deep discount from the hotel. You, as the group's organizer, may even be able to stay free.

# PASSPORT TO
# DISCOUNT TRAVEL

When calling the hotel, explain to the person in charge of reservations that you are organizing a group interested in staying there, if the rates are acceptable. Then, negotiate the best deal. Don't be shy—you are bringing in a nice amount of business to the hotel and should be rewarded with a free room or substantial discount. If your group is large enough, you may also be able to arrange discounts on tours and event tickets purchased through the hotel. Since offers vary, shop around.

# Chapter 5

# RENTAL CARS

**"Strong and content I travel the open road."**
Walt Whitman

Renting cars today is faster and easier than ever before. Innovations such as pre-written contracts and instant drop-off machines speed up the automobile pick-up-and-return process. Frequent renters whose lease agreements are prepared prior to arrival breeze through pick-up procedures. Frantic renters running late return their cars in a flash using instant drop-off machines. Bills are charged to credit cards, and receipts arrive by mail.

While the speed of the rental process has accelerated, searching for best prices has bogged down. Because rates fluctuate so widely from place to place, shopping for the best deal can become complicated and time-consuming. It is difficult to determine which car company has the best rate, until you estimate any extra charges you may have to pay. These extras are not always fully explained when calling for a quote and can significantly inflate your final cost.

To select a good value, you must understand the choices given. Unless you know the specifics of the rental agreement regarding mileage and drop-off charges, refueling costs, airport fees, surcharges and taxes, you may be driving up an expensive dead end. Comprehending the contract and its various options will help you avoid the shock of higher-than-expected rental bills.

## HOW TO RENT CARS AT UP TO 50% OFF

In most cases, rates depend on demand, location, competition, days of the week, time of year, and length of rental period. To get the best rates you must shop around.

Popular tourist spots such as Orlando, with its myriad attractions—Disney World, Sea World, MGM Studios, Universal Studios, Epcot Center, Kennedy Space Center, Cypress Gardens, and much more—usually feature lower mid-week and weekly rates than a business center such as Boston, because of abundant rental cars, competition and visitors.

There are a variety of ways you can save up to 50% on your next car rental bill; you don't have to be a tourist to get a good rate. When in a big city, rent a car on a weekend, if possible; in tourist areas, rent it during the week, or for at least a week.

Rental agencies in metropolitan areas such as Chicago, Dallas, and Philadelphia frequently offer weekend specials of up to 50% off normal weekday rates, since demand for cars there is greater on weekdays than on weekends. Inquire about weekend savings when renting in a large city, even if you don't plan to spend the entire weekend there. Some rental companies liberally define weekend to mean any two consecutive days between Thursday and Monday.

Leisure markets such as Florida, Southern California, and Hawaii tend to offer lower prices on mid-week and weekly rent-

# RENTAL CARS

als, and slightly higher prices on weekends. Renting a car at weekly rates (five days or more) normally saves 25% to 40% over standard daily rates.

You receive additional benefits when you patronize agencies participating in your frequent flyer program. In most cases, by renting from a "partner" agency, you can earn extra bonus miles in your frequent flyer account and may become eligible to receive discounted rates or car upgrades.

Many rental companies offer their best rates to those who book in advance. Some agencies hold reservations for up to a year, guaranteeing the rate, regardless of how much the price may increase from the time you make the reservation to the time you actually pick up the car. Some guarantee these rates only with a credit card deposit. Make sure which policy applies when reserving.

Sometimes, you can save by renting from smaller agencies or local companies rather than from large national or international chains. In many cities, smaller rental companies attempt to steer customers away from the big boys by offering attractive rates.

You can find these low-price agencies in local yellow pages. Since these agencies generally operate in just one, or possibly a few cities or states, they seldom advertise nationally. You may have to do some research to find them. Contact the area's Chamber of Commerce for information about local car rental agencies or ask an acquaintance in the city you will be visiting, to check the yellow pages. Refer to the TRAVEL PLANNER at your travel agency to see if any regional car companies are listed at your destination.

Upon arriving, check the prices at local car rental companies, whether or not you have a reservation with another agency—you may find a lower rate. In some locations, car availability is no problem even at smaller agencies, unless you are renting during a peak season, or when a special event is taking place.

To find a local car rental agency, ask for a recommendation at the airport information booth or check the yellow pages and baggage claim/ground transportation area of the airport for local ads. When calling these agencies you may be pleasantly surprised by the excellent prices available, even at the last minute.

Good deals may be found at the big companies too, not to mention the convenience of their in-airport locations, and speedy service. Larger agencies have solid reputations, huge fleets of newer cars, and more locations to serve you. Ask rental clerks the average age and mileage of cars in stock.

Economists define cost as price over value, meaning consumers invariably receive good value for their dollars by spending more for a superior product than by paying less for an inferior one. In other words, you get what you pay for. The same applies with rental cars. Don't base your decisions solely on price—consider the company's reliability, as well as the quality of their automobiles.

When driving in relatively isolated areas, even if it's more expensive, consider renting from a company with a national network of cars and mechanics to assist you in case of an accident or malfunction. You may think you have found the best deal at some local "Rent-A-Bomb" agency, but if the car breaks down, your so-called bargain could blow up in your face.

With all the variables involved, knowing which agency offers the best deal can be complicated. Call at least three companies to compare prices. Ask for bargain rates (weekday, weekend, or weekly), special promotions, or frequent flyer tie-ins. Also inquire about extra charges such as drop-off, refueling, insurance, and transfer fees which some off-airport agencies assess for shuttling customers to and from terminals. These levies could add anywhere from 50 cents to as much as 10% of the basic rental charge to your bill.

## UNDERSTANDING THE RENTAL AGREEMENT

No matter where you rent a car, be sure you understand the contract thoroughly before signing. Items to check on your rental agreement are:

• **Rental rates**. What are the daily, weekend, and weekly rates? What is the charge for extra hours if the car is kept beyond the specified return time?

• **Mileage charges**. What is the charge for each mile driven? How does it compare with an unlimited mileage rate, or a fixed mileage rate with fees for extra miles?

• **Deposit Requirements**. Is a deposit required? If so, how much and can it be paid by cash or credit card?

• **Age Restrictions**. Are there restrictions for drivers between the ages of 18 and 25, or over 75?

• **Insurance Coverages and Collision Damage Waivers.** Does the rental policy include insurance and collision damage coverage in the basic price, or is it extra? Are these coverages mandatory or optional?

# PASSPORT TO
# DISCOUNT TRAVEL

&bull; **Personal Liability**. What are the limits of the coverage—does it guard against property damage, bodily injury, and medical expenses?

&bull; **Drop-off Charge.** Can you return the car at any designated location free of charge, or do you have to pay an extra fee if dropped-off at a location other than where rented?

&bull; **Fuel charges**. Should you return the car full, empty, or the with the same amount of gas which was in the tank when picked up? How much does the company charge for gas to fill the tank to the proper level?

## MILEAGE CHARGES

Rental fees vary according to the type and size of the car, length of the rental period, and the geographic location. The best bargains are usually found in high-volume, year-round tourist areas, such as Hawaii, California, and Florida. The highest rates are often found in cities such as New York and Chicago.

There are five types of rates: 1) daily, with mileage charges; 2) daily, with mileage charges if driven beyond a limited number of free miles; 3) daily, including unlimited free miles; 4) weekend discounts; and 5) weekly specials. Weekend and weekly prices often include free unlimited mileage, or a limited amount of free mileage, beyond which, every additional mile is charged.

When planning to drive, do **not** rent a car with mileage charges, which can soar faster than zero to sixty. For example,

# RENTAL CARS

if the charge is 50¢ per mile, and you drive 100 miles, $50 plus tax is added to your daily rental cost. If you drive 200 miles, $100 is tacked on to your bill. Be careful, and choose a rental agreement to suit your needs.

Inquire about "unlimited mileage" rates. If available, this option may carry higher daily fees, but no mileage charges. On a long drive your dollars go a lot farther. Let's say the daily rates for a compact car are either $25 a day, plus 30¢ per mile, or $40 a day with unlimited mileage. Which rate should you take? It depends on how long you keep the car and how far you plan to drive.

Suppose you intend to rent the car for 3 days and plan to drive about 100 miles a day. Select the unlimited mileage rate and save about $45. How? The 3-day total for the flat rate is $120 (3 days x $40 = $120). The 3-day total for the daily rate plus mileage is $165 (3 days x $25 = $75 + a $90 mileage charge [30¢ x 300 miles] = $165). By doing these basic calculations and comparing rates you can save money even before hitting the road.

## FUEL CHARGES

Many agencies rent cars with a full tank of gas. They usually advise you to return it full, otherwise they will charge you about **twice** the normal price of gas to top it off.

Some firms rent cars with whatever gas is left in the tank by the previous user. Unless otherwise advised by the clerk, return the car with an equivalent amount, or be prepared to pay a higher price for fuel when the agency refills it to the same level.

---

Some companies offer a different option. Each car is filled with half a tank of gas charged to your contract at nearly double the average price. Renters are advised to return the car with the tank as close to empty as possible.

From the renter's point of view, this approach has three disadvantages: 1) The renter pays more for the gas than purchased at a service station; 2) No refund is received for any gas left in the tank; and 3) in attempting to return the car empty, the renter may run out of gas before getting back. Although the rates of these agencies seem competitive, renters initially pay more for fuel.

## INSURANCE OPTIONS

### Collision Damage Waiver

The Collision Damage Waiver (CDW), sometimes referred to as the Loss and Damage Waiver (LDW) on rental car contracts, is **not** insurance. It is a "risk-transfer" agreement eliminating the possibility of being sued by the rental company for damages caused by an accident or vandalism while the car is in your possession. Unless purchasing CDW, it is the renter's responsibility to pay for any loss or damage up to the full value of the vehicle, plus related expenses. Acceptance of the CDW releases you of the responsibility for loss or damage to the car unless resulting from violation of the rental agreement.

The price of the CDW, about $10 to $15 a day, is little enough to pay for peace of mind. On the other hand, it may be a lot to pay for protection you may not need. If your personal

# RENTAL CARS

auto insurance already covers rental cars, purchasing the CDW may be unnecessary. Don't assume anything—read your policy or ask your insurance agent to review your coverages **before** renting.

If unprotected, uncertain about your coverage, or planning to rent in a foreign country, by all means take the CDW. The few extra dollars are worth it, because it waives liability for any damages, or the loss of revenue to the rental company while the car is in the shop. Without this protection, you could be totally responsible for anything that happens to the car. The CDW does **not**, however, eliminate liability for any damages or injuries you may inflict upon the person or property of others.

The next time you see ads proclaiming super-low rental rates, scan the fine print to see if CDW is included. Some companies mandate it; others offer it as an option.

People whose personal auto insurance covers them in rental cars sometimes take the CDW anyway. They figure why make their own insurance company pay for damages, which could increase their risk of being charged higher premiums, being assigned points against their policies, or even being dropped altogether by the insurance company.

These individuals realize that without CDW, they must pay to repair even minor damage. The cost of replacing a cracked windshield or a blown tire, for instance, probably falls below most personal auto policies' deductible. Clearly, repairing the glass or rubber costs much more than the expense of the CDW in the first place. Why take a chance? Let CDW pay for it.

Before renting, ask your credit card issuer if it provides any CDW insurance protection. Some major credit card companies will automatically insure your rental car, if you use their card to pay for it. They supply secondary, or back-up coverage, meaning they pay any repair or replacement expenses for a rental car **not** covered under your primary auto insurance.

These cards do **not** usually cover most recreational vehicles, trucks, and exotic cars such as Porches, Ferraris, and Mercedes. Verify your credit card company's rental policy in advance—it could save you a lot of money.

Some rental agencies offer a choice of CDW options:

1) Full protection for about $5-$15 a day, regardless of car size. Choose this if your credit card, or your personal or business auto insurance policy does **not** provide rental protection.

2) Sets a limit on the amount of damage coverage, usually about $3,000. This option is for business travelers who want to cover their personal liability when renting a car on company business. The cost is normally about $6 to $10 a day.

3) The renter's deductible on his personal auto policy is covered for a few dollars a day. Alamo and General Rent-a-Car are two companies offering these, or similar insurance options.

Car rental agents usually earn a commission from selling the Collision Damage Waiver, so it's no wonder some of them push it so hard during the sales pitch. Don't be pressured into thinking you must pay for the total cost of all damages immediately upon repair, even if you have insurance which covers it. As long as you have adequate protection against damages and loss in a rental car, either from your own personal auto insurance, or your credit card's complimentary coverage, you should consider refusing CDW.

If properly insured, do not be intimidated by gimmicks used by a few unethical rental agents to force purchasing CDW.

# RENTAL CARS

One is "the credit card block." If you refuse the CDW option, some agents insist on putting a hold of up to several thousand dollars on your credit card until the car is returned. Problems could arise from this if the hold maxes-out the available credit on your charge card, preventing you from using it, even in an emergency. If a car rental agent demands a credit block, rent from another company!

Another gimmick used is to demanding a copy of a customer's auto policy to show coverage. Some agents say you must either produce proof of insurance on the spot, or pay for CDW. Once again, don't be pushed. The insurance identification card you carry in your wallet is all you need to show the agent.

It is probably wise to play it safe and take CDW, reducing hassles and worry, and increasing peace of mind. It may be worth it to pay a little extra to avoid trouble if something goes wrong.

An acquaintance of mine learned the hard way. She rented a car in Florida and decided not to purchase CDW, because she was going to use the car for only one day. After going only few miles, one of the tires blew out. She hadn't hit a pothole or anything else to cause the rupture, so she naturally assumed that the tire was faulty. Nonetheless, when she returned the car, she was informed by the agent that since she had not purchased CDW she would have to pay for a new tire. According to a clause buried deep in the small print on the back of the contract, she was responsible for any "road hazard" damage to the tires

Three points to remember: Always read the fine print on the rental agreement; expect the unexpected on the road; and take CDW if you don't want to pay for any unpleasant surprises.

# PASSPORT TO
# DISCOUNT TRAVEL

## Liability Insurance

The basic rental charge from many agencies automatically includes primary limited liability insurance which protects the renter and additional authorized drivers against responsibility for injuries to third parties due to an accident with the car. Rental clerks of companies not providing complimentary liability protection will tell you that this standard coverage is not included, and may try to persuade you to purchase their optional insurance. If your personal auto policy provides liability protection in a rental car, you may refuse to buy the agency's primary coverage. However, if you are uncertain about your coverage, or want to increase it, you may elect to purchase the Liability Insurance Add-On (LIA) or the Liability Insurance Supplement (LIS). These options, costing about $5 to $10 a day, increase the standard liability protection against damage claims up to one million dollars.

## Medical Protection

Personal Accident Insurance (PAI), another option offered on most car rental contracts, pays benefits in the event of accidental death during the rental period. In some policies, these benefits apply whether or not you are actually in the rental car at the time of death. Passengers in the vehicle are covered for injuries resulting from accidents. Personal Effects Coverage (PEC), usually included free as part of the PAI option, provides for loss or damage to personal effects during the rental period. The cost for PAI, with or without PEC, runs about $2 to $4 per day.

# RENTAL CARS

Some PAI policies help pay for medical expenses if you or any passengers are injured in an accident involving the rental car. This secondary protection works in conjunction with personal medical insurance policies, and pays up to a specified limit after your primary medical coverage runs out. If your auto or medical insurance provides adequate protection, you may not need to purchase the PAI. If you have any questions, consult your insurance company.

## INSPECT THE RENTAL CAR

Why pay for damages caused by someone else? Before driving a rental car, examine it thoroughly. If you notice a dent, or anything broken or scratched, show it to the rental agent immediately and have the damages indicated in writing on your contract or a rider stating they existed **before** you took the car. Be smart—don't learn the hard way.

When returning a car, a friend of mine was told he would have to pay for a dent he hadn't even noticed on the passenger door. In disbelief, he looked at the damage which was more like a "ding" than a dent— no scratches, no missing paint. He hadn't purchased CDW because he was keeping the car for only a day.

When his credit card bill arrived, an extra $350 appeared under the rental charge. Naturally, he protested to the agency, but to no avail. The rental representative explained to him that $250 covered the cost of actually repairing the dent, $50 reimbursed the agency for two day's of lost revenue while the car was in the shop, and $50 was assessed for "administrative fees."

Even though his personal auto insurance covered him, he

still had to pay all but $50 of the bill himself, because the deductible was $300.

If ever in a similar predicament, you may not have to pay all those charges. Have the agency give you a written explanation of the damages and copies of receipts showing exact repair expenses. Check with other auto body shops to see whether the repair costs are in line with the amount of the damage. If not, **don't pay**!

Avoid paying the "loss of use or loss of revenue" charge. Unless the agency can show they had no other cars in stock to rent while your car was being fixed, they may **not** be able to claim loss of revenue. They are required to prove their entire automobile inventory was in use at the time, and that they actually lost money by not being able to rent your car. You should dispute these bills if the rental company charges them on your credit card.

The important point here is: **always** examine the rental car carefully, and point out even minor damage immediately to the rental agent **before** driving it off the lot. Make sure the damage is noted on your contract. **Inspect the car thoroughly:**

• Check the entire outer body of the vehicle. Look for dings, dents, and scratches on all fenders, doors and lower body panels. Check for broken lights, lenses or cracks in the windows and windshield.

• Make sure all lights work properly, including the high beams, directional signals and brake lights.

• Examine the tires for proper inflation, sufficient tread and good condition. Count all four hubcaps.

# RENTAL CARS

• Check the spare tire for inflation and wear, and see that the jack works.

• Try the controls: windshield wipers, horn, heater, defroster, air conditioner, radio, and car phone.

I'm sure after reading this checklist a few of you are wondering, "Is he kidding? Who has time to do all that?" Well, here's how I learned first-hand the importance of making sure everything on a rental car is operational.

One winter day, high in the Wasatch Mountain Range of western Utah, I was driving from a ski resort to Salt Lake City. It was the end of a terrific ski trip and I was planning to fly home that day. I left for the airport early in order to take a leisurely drive through the mountains. Coming around a curve on the narrow road, I noticed that the right front tire was flat.

No problem, I thought. I'll just change the tire and put on the spare. I remembered glancing at the spare tire when renting the car, and it looked fine. But on that freezing morning when hauling out the tire and plopping it on the ground, it was totally out of air.

Stuck in the mountains on a secluded, snow-covered road, with more snow threatening to fall, I started to wonder if I would make it to the airport at all. Knowing I had to do something, I thought I'd put on the spare tire anyway. Although it was flat, it was still in better shape than the blow-out. I'd try to nurse the car down the road until reaching a telephone to call for help. But when I looked in the trunk, the jack was missing! When examining the car at the rental agency, I recalled seeing the spare tire, but not the jack. No wonder. It wasn't there! Now I was really stuck!

Finally, a kind soul happened by and drove to a pay

phone to called for a tow truck. Eventually, I made it out of the mountains, arriving at the airport in time to catch a later flight home.

Because of stories like this, I emphasize the point: Always check the condition of the spare tire and the jack in your rental car. The few extra seconds is all it takes to avoid hours of aggravation.

A final safety tip: If ever stranded on the road, never get into a stranger's car. Instead, ask a good Samaritan to call the police, or a towing company for assistance.

## RENTAL CAR FROM HELL

In some parts of the world, the good reputation of a rental company has little in common with the quality of the car you may receive. A case in point.

Many years ago, a friend and I rented a car from one of the "big three" American renta! companies in Cozumel, Mexico, a small island off the Yucatan Peninsula in the Caribbean. Since the island has only a few car agencies, we chose to play it safe by reserving a car from a major rental company before leaving the United States.

Upon arriving at the rental counter in the Cozumel Airport, we saw the two male clerks on duty conversing languidly. One was sitting on the counter, the other had his feet propped on the desk. One took my pre-paid reservation voucher, looked at it and handed it back to me. He shrugged and said no cars were available right now, but one would be returning soon. He suggested we wait.

# RENTAL CARS

We did. Almost an hour and several complaints later, we gave up and decided to take a taxi to our hotel. Just as we were getting into the cab, a beat-up, smoke-belching Volkswagen Beetle with a rental sticker pulled up. One of the clerks rushed out of the terminal to inform us that our car had arrived.

Approaching the vehicle suspiciously, we immediately did a double-take. Believe it or not, the back seat was missing! I thought, if the back seat is gone, what else is wrong?

It didn't take long to find out. Attempting to open the passenger door, it stuck. We then noticed a gaping hole in the dashboard where the radio used to be. All that remained were strands of disconnected wires sticking out. By the way, did I mention the windshield was cracked, too?

Reaching over to check the air conditioner, guess what? The control knob was jammed in the off position and I couldn't budge it. (The air conditioner probably didn't work anyway.) When I rolled down my window, it fell off its track and slid down into the doorwell, permanently!

By now, I was really steamed! I jumped out of the car and slammed the door. You guessed it—the door handle came off in my hand! That did it! I marched back to the office in the terminal, with rental contract and door handle in hand, and slammed them down on the counter. "Gentleman," I said, "I **don't** think I'll be renting that car. It had a breakdown just **sitting** outside, and this door handle is all that's left of it!"

Fortunately, the two men had a sense of humor and an earnest desire to correct the problem. Minutes later, a much better car arrived. After examining it thoroughly with satisfactory results, we were finally on our way.

The bottom line is, regardless of what company you rent from, **always inspect** the car **carefully** before driving.

# PASSPORT TO DISCOUNT TRAVEL

## SAFE DRIVING TIPS

Anyone who has ever had their car break down on a highway far from home knows the story: exorbitant towing charges, rip-off repair rates, Draconian auto mechanics, and irretrievable time lost on a vacation or business trip. Even when driving a relatively new car, try to prevent such possible pitfalls by planning ahead and being prepared.

Before beginning an auto journey, have a qualified mech-anic check the car for any hidden problems, or at least check the following items yourself before starting out:

## PRE-TRIP CHECKLIST

• **Lights**. Make sure they are all working properly, including the turn signals.

• **Wiper blades**. Keep them in good condition and in working order.

• **Fluid levels**. Top-off the oil, gas, radiator, window washer fluid, brake, transmission, and power steering fluids.

• **Hoses and belts**. Feel the belts to see that they are snug and in good shape, not cracked, split or worn. Hoses should give a little to the touch—not too hard, not too soft.

# RENTAL CARS

• **Tires and jack**. Check for proper inflation and adequate tread. See that all parts of the jack are operable, and that the spare tire is in good shape and is properly inflated.

• **Air conditioner/heater-defroster**. Make sure it cools adequately in hot weather, and heats sufficiently in the cold.

• **Undercarriage**. Look for any signs of troublesome leaks and excessive rust, especially on the mufflers and exhaust pipes. While driving, note the car's steering and handling, the brakes, the shock absorbers, and the wheel alignment. Listen for any tell-tale rattles or squeaks.

• **Miscellaneous.** Depending on length of trip, pack a flashlight with fresh batteries, a can of aerosol tire inflator, a blanket, drinkable water, first aid kit, extra coolant/antifreeze, some snacks and beverages.

Even after completing the pre-trip checklist, something could still go wrong. Inevitably, cars break down at the most inopportune time.

One winter afternoon in Philadelphia several years ago, an acquaintance picked up a car from an "auto driveaway" company to take to Nashville for a transferred military family who wanted it delivered to their new home. He inspected the car himself and was assured by the agent that it was mechanically sound. Everything seemed fine, so off he went.

Before entering the Pennsylvania Turnpike, he decided to grab a sandwich. Walking back from the sub shop he noticed a puddle under the car. At first he thought someone had dropped a bottle of soda, but there was no broken glass. When he knelt down and touched the liquid he realized it was gasoline! While he was inside, a seam in the gas tank had ruptured spewing fuel onto the ground.

Fortunately, my friend listened to his stomach that day, because stopping for food gave him the chance to spot the leak. Otherwise, he might not have noticed it until he had completely run out of gas on the turnpike. Still later, the heater conked out, leaving him to freeze his buns, feet, and hands for the rest of the trip. He had to make another stop to buy three blankets, which he wrapped around himself to complete the mission.

## YOUR CONFIRMATION NUMBER

As with airlines, hotels and tours, any time you make a reservation, get a confirmation number and the name of the booking agent. Nothing is more frustrating than arriving at the rental counter to find no car ready, and no record of your reservation. Or if a car is available, the rate is much higher than the one you were quoted. Avoid this aggravation by showing the rental clerk your confirmation number and the name of the reservations agent. With such evidence, most agencies will attempt to accommodate you. As always, be firm and stand up for your rights.

# RENTAL CARS

## RENTAL LIMITATIONS

### Age Restrictions

Some major agencies refuse to rent to anyone under 25, and most require renters to be a minimum age of 21. A few charge up to $10 a day extra when renting to young people. An exception is made for business travelers over 18 whose employer has a corporate account with the rental agency. Similarly, some restrictions may apply to drivers over 75.

### The Second Driver

Many agencies charge extra for anyone sharing the driving with the renter, including spouses. Some agencies assess a fee for each extra driver, while others charge a flat fee for any number of them. A few rental companies make exceptions for spouses, and most firms waive all extra fees if the invoice is charged to a business account and the second driver is a co-worker. Policies vary, and should be taken into consideration when looking for the best deal.

### Forbidden Areas

Some companies prohibit their cars from being driven in certain areas where the terrain is particularly rugged or dangerous. If you drive a rental car into a forbidden zone and the car breaks down, you may be stuck in more ways than one. In addition to being stranded in an isolated place, you will be assessed all towing and repair bills, which could be enormous.

One such prohibited area encompasses the "saddle road" running across the central spine of the big island, Hawaii. This serpentine road bisects the island's landmass, connecting its two main cities: Hilo and Kona-Kailua.

This taboo road winds through two of the world's tallest mountains, the Mauna Loa and Mauna Kea volcanoes. Thousands of years ago, eruptions from these twin peaks created this exquisite Pacific paradise. Mauna Kea is the world's tallest mountain, measured from its base on the ocean floor to its summit above sea level, over 40,000 feet. Across an enormous valley stands the equally impressive Mauna Loa.

The area around this road is periodically used by the Army for military maneuvers and live artillery practice. Often heard amidst this breathtaking scenery is the earth-shaking thunder of exploding shells. One can easily imagine why every traveler obeys, without question, the signs posted along the road, "Warning! Live Ammunition. Remain In Your Car."

If your car breaks down on this forbidden volcanic road, watch out—being blown-up by a wayward shell may be the least of your worries. The staggering tow charge may be even worse. If the explosives don't get you, the cold will—in the winter months, you could possibly freeze to death. Close to the equator, most of Hawaii is tropical and mild, but in the higher elevations near 15,000 feet, the temperature plummets and snow falls. Without the foresight to bring warm clothes, you could be in danger of frostbite, or worse.

Before you take your rental car into unfamiliar territory, find out where you may and may not go. For example, when renting a car in Western Europe, you are usually not insured for loss or damage if driving in former Iron Curtain countries.

# RENTAL CARS

## RENTAL CAR PRICING CHART

### Rental Car Pricing Chart

Rental Dates: From_____to _____ (____days)
Present insurance applicable to rental car:

    Personal accident (auto):_____

    Collision/comprehensive
    (auto or credit card benefit): _____

    Personal effects/property
    (homeowner's insurance):_____

|  | Company 1 | Company 2 | Company 3 |
|---|---|---|---|
| **Make/Model:** | _____ | _____ | _____ |
| **Size:** | _____ | _____ | _____ |
| **Mileage Limit:** | _____ | _____ | _____ |
| **Pick-up location:** | _____ | _____ | _____ |
| **Drop-off location:** | _____ | _____ | _____ |
| **Base rate:** | _____ | _____ | _____ |
| Daily: | _____ | _____ | _____ |
| Weekly: | _____ | _____ | _____ |
| Weekend: | _____ | _____ | _____ |
| **Additional fees** | | | |
| Mileage: | _____ | _____ | _____ |
| Dropoff fee: | _____ | _____ | _____ |
| Additional drivers: | _____ | _____ | _____ |
| Underage driver: | _____ | _____ | _____ |
| Airport Surcharge: | _____ | _____ | _____ |
| Special Equip. Fee: | _____ | _____ | _____ |

# PASSPORT TO
# DISCOUNT TRAVEL

**Insurance Fees**
Personal
  Accident Ins.:   _____      _____      _____
Personal
  Effects Ins.:   _____      _____      _____
Additional
  Liability Ins.:   _____      _____      _____
  CDW:   _____      _____      _____
**Fuel costs**
  Per gal.   _____      _____      _____
  Flat rate:   _____      _____      _____
**Other**
**Discounts:**   _____      _____      _____
**TOTAL:**   _____      _____      _____
**Refundable**
**deposit:**   _____      _____      _____
**Late Charges:**   _____      _____      _____

# RENTING CARS OVERSEAS

When renting overseas, be sure to understand the rental contract completely before signing on the dotted line. Know what is included in the price, and what is extra. In many countries, rental agreements, including those of major international agencies, are often written in the local language, not English. Unless you read and speak the language fluently, renting in a foreign country may be troublesome. Deciphering rental agreements is taxing enough in English, let alone an unfamiliar language. Although many foreign rental agents speak English, make sure you understand each other clearly—whatever language is spoken.

# RENTAL CARS

For discounts overseas, you must usually make your reservation at least two to seven days in advance. You generally receive better rates by doing so before leaving the United States. When planning a trip to Puerto Vallarta, Mexico, a few years ago, I was quoted a rate of $210 per week for a Class C (mid-size) vehicle. I found out later that if I had rented without making prior reservations in the United States, I would have paid twice that amount. The official published rate in Mexico for a similar car was nearly $400. Returning to the U.S., I called the rental agency to ask about the difference in price and was told that the higher rate quoted in Mexico was correct; my lower rate was valid only because I had reserved in advance in the States.

Reservations made in the U.S. for a rental car overseas normally work without a hitch and are as routine as picking up a car in North America. There are exceptions, however. You may be quoted one price over the phone here, but be charged an unexpectedly higher rate at your destination.

Whenever problems arise about reservations or rental cars not satisfactorily resolved, speak to a supervisor. If the supervisor cannot help, take it up with the rental car company when returning home. Get the names of the people you speak with, and make notes of what they say.

One time in Italy, I was expecting to save 20% (about $75) off a weekly rental rate based on membership in a participating auto club. Not so, said the agent in Milan. Despite my insistence (I even showed a copy of the club's membership benefits, which listed the overseas rental discount), the agent and his supervisor refused to honor it, saying they reserved the right to adjust their local prices and policies at any time, and were not obliged to comply with every discount mentioned in the United States.

# PASSPORT TO
# DISCOUNT TRAVEL

Breakdowns in communication between a rental company's stateside reservationists and their international representatives happen just as easily as they can between a renter and a clerk face to face. Be prepared to make the best of it. Upon returning, bring the matter up with both the auto club and the customer service office of the rental agency.

Once, in the beautiful Central American country of Costa Rica, I rented a car from a major international agency. At the counter, I asked for and received assurances that unlimited mileage was included in my daily rate. This was important since I planned to drive extensively throughout the country for a few days.

Starting before daybreak, I drove up a steep, winding pass to the peak of Poas Volcano, over 10,000 feet elevation. I hoped to see the sun rise over the Atlantic Ocean and set in the Pacific. Guided by the dawn's early light, I eventually reached the top of the mountain, and drove around its immense crater—the only place in the world where you can see both the Atlantic and Pacific Oceans from one spot.

After exploring the active, steamy volcano, I left the gaping caldera to examine the weather-resistant cacti, stunted pine trees, and tiny birds hardy enough to survive the harsh conditions along the fiery rim.

I descended into the forests of the central highlands, and headed toward the unspoiled beaches of Manuel Antonio Jungle National Park on the lovely Pacific coast. I drove to this lush area where rain forests, rich with monkeys, parrots, birds, and butterflies of all descriptions, meet the shore. I arrived at this Eden just as the sun slid slowly into the sea.

What a great day! Everything was perfect—until I returned the car. The original agent was not at the counter. The one now on duty informed me I would have to pay over $100 in

# RENTAL CARS

extra charges, because I had not kept the car for the minimum three days required for the unlimited mileage rate. I responded that when picking up the car, I was not told about the minimum period required to qualify. Too bad, the man said, those were the rules.

Since I was already at the airport ready to catch my flight home, I didn't have time to argue, so I paid the money. Considering the wonderful journey I had, I figured it was worth it.

This illustrates another point: always verify the specifics of agent's promises and the rental agreement, in writing before driving off. Double check the fine print in the contract concerning mileage charges, taxes, insurance, and other requirements.

In Europe try some of the new services offered to rental customers. For example, Avis offers a "message service" to its renters on the Continent and in Great Britain, which allows them to leave and retrieve international messages from family, friends, and business associates at any time, night and day. To send or receive messages, customers call a special number directly in the United Kingdom, or toll-free from France, Holland, Belgium, West Germany, Italy, or Switzerland. When renting a car phone, the message center will, at your request, pass on that number to callers who wish to reach you in your car.

For more information, see your travel agent, or phone AVIS INTERNATIONAL RESERVATIONS (800-331-1084) at least 48 hours before leaving North America. Other international rental agencies have recently introduced similar services.

# PASSPORT TO
# DISCOUNT TRAVEL

## LEASING FOREIGN CARS

One way to save money on automobile transportation overseas is to lease a new car rather than rent a used one. The "lease" is really a sale-and-buy-back arrangement on paper. Essentially, you buy a car for at least three weeks and then sell it back to the dealer.

The main advantage of leasing versus renting is not having to pay approximately 25% in taxes on rental cars. Another benefit of short-term leasing is that, as a non-resident, you do not have to pay any sales or "value-added" taxes.

France, with one of the highest tax rates in Europe, is a leader in lease agreements. Visitors can obtain a Peugeot with unlimited mileage for 23 days at about $30 a day from KEMWEL AUTO VACANCES, 106 Calvert St., Harrison, NY 10528 (800-234-1426). Longer leases, of up to half a year, have even lower rates. After the cars are bought back by the dealer, they are sold to appreciative residents and rental agencies who pay lower prices and taxes for used cars rather than higher prices and taxes for new ones.

Even though the auto "purchase" period must be for a minimum of 23 days, drivers returning their cars early may still save money. If planning to use a car in Europe for at least two-weeks, look into leasing. To get the best deals, try to arrange your buy-and-sell package about four to five weeks before departure.

An English-speaking representative from Peugeot will meet you when you arrive in Paris, and bring you back to the airport for departure. Cars leased in France may usually be driven beyond the border and dropped off, for an extra fee, in London, Frankfurt, Rome, Milan, or Madrid.

# RENTAL CARS

EUROPE BY CAR, One Rockefeller Plaza, New York, NY 10020 (212-581-3040, or in California, 213-272-0424) leases a variety of cars, which may be picked up and returned in most French cities. The economical Citroen CV6, a four-door with manual transmission, goes for about $500 for 23 days (prices subject to change). They also handle lease arrangments in Brussels for Volkswagen and Audi, and will answer any questions you have about leasing, renting, or buying a new car.

The Renault Automobile Company offers attractive leasing programs in France and Spain, featuring rates up to 25% less than conventional rental agencies. Cars may be returned in many European cities for a drop-off charge. RENAULT is located at 650 First Ave., New York, NY 10016 (800-221-1052).

Contact the tourist boards of other countries which you will be visiting to see if they are aware of any automobile companies participating in similar lease/buy back programs

## INTERNATIONAL DRIVING TIPS

When planning to drive in foreign countries, determine whether you need an International Driver's License. Many nations allow U.S. citizens to drive within their borders as long as they have a valid license; some, however, require an international one. Ask your travel agent, auto clubs, or the consulates of the countries in which you'll be driving. You can usually obtain an International Driver's License from your local Department of Motor Vehicles and from most branches of the American Automobile Association. Allow a month for processing.

Car rental companies abroad normally have restrictions

for drivers under 25 years and over 70; such as higher deposit requirements. Contact agencies for details.

Before you go, review road maps of the areas you'll be visiting. Plot two routes for any car trip so you will have an alternate plan—one scenic, one direct—in case you need to make adjustments based on prevailing road, weather, or traffic conditions.

Rand McNally and AAA are good sources of maps for the U.S. and foreign countries. Tourist boards and consulates can supply maps of their areas. European road guides from Michelin, the tire company, are extremely informative. They denote scenic and historic routes, and rate them according to interest, beauty and time. Michelin guides are sold at book stores and travel specialty shops in the U.S., and at many newsstands, and gas stations in Europe. Prentice Hall Press (800-733-3000) publishes DRIVING TOURS, (approximately $18 each), a series of guides describing desirable auto itineraries, scenic routes, and historical sites in Britain, Canada, France, Italy, Mexico and the U.S.

Memorize the meanings of international road signs which use pictorial symbols instead of words, and are generally self-explanatory. You'll see them in Europe, Canada, the Caribbean, Mexico, South America, and the Orient. Knowing them in advance allows you to make quick decisions, and you don't have to guess what signs mean while driving on congested roads. Maps and auto guide books usually display and translate the most common signs. Some of the universal international road signs and transportation symbols are illustrated on the following page.

# RENTAL CARS

## International Road Signs and Travel Symbols

### Prohibition Signs

NO ENTRY

ROAD CLOSED

CLOSED TO
MOTOR VEHICLES

CLOSED TO
MOTORCYCLES

CLOSED TO
PEDESTRIANS

NO LEFT (OR RIGHT)
TURNS

NO U TURNS

OVERTAKING
PROHIBITED

SPEED LIMIT

END OF
SPEED LIMIT

### Mandatory Signs

DIRECTION
TO FOLLOW

TRAFFIC
CIRCLE

PARKING

HOSPITAL

MECHANICAL
HELP

TELEPHONE

FILLING
STATION

CAMPING SITE

CARAVAN SITE

YOUTH HOSTEL

### Danger Signs

CURVE

INTERSECTION

OPENING BRIDGE

ROAD WORKS

TUNNEL

PEDESTRIAN CROSSING

WATCH OUT FOR CHILDREN

ANIMALS CROSSING

ROAD NARROWS

SLIPPERY ROAD

DANGER

MAIN ROAD AHEAD

STOP AT INTERSECTION

161

# PASSPORT TO
# DISCOUNT TRAVEL

Remember, most foreign countries measure distance in kilometers, not miles. One kilometer is about two-thirds of a mile (0.62 miles per kilometer; 100 kilometers equals 62 miles). So, while driving on the German autobahn at 100 kph, you're actually moving at about 60 mph, practically a snail's pace on that superhighway which has no speed limit—except how fast your car, and your nerves, can go.

Budget for higher gasoline prices overseas. In most countries, gas is three to four times more expensive than in the U.S. Fuel is normally sold in liters or imperial gallons. (An imperial gallon is slightly more than our gallon. A liter is a little less than a quart; one gallon equals about 3.75 liters.)

Some foreign gas stations keep at least one self-service pump open 24 hours a day. You can fill up anytime, paying by depositing cash into the machine, or by automatically charging it to your credit card. For some reason this convenience is not widespread in the United States, although it seems like a good idea.

On a long road trip, try to pace yourself. Avoid driving too much in any one day. Traveling 100 miles on an American interstate highway or a European expressway is a lot quicker and less stressful than traveling 100 miles over narrow, serpentine country lanes. Speeding along a modern thruway at 80 or 90 mph shrinks distance and shortens time, but may also turn your journey into a blur. Plan to enjoy yourself without getting exhausted.

# RENTAL CARS

## HOW TO DRIVE FREE

It's simple: find someone who needs his car delivered somewhere, and drive it for them as an auto relocator.

How do you find someone who needs a car transported? Call "auto driveaway" companies listed in the yellow pages of most metropolitan phone directories. They find drivers to transfer cars belonging to individuals moving long distances due to a job or military reassignment. These people often fly, rather than drive, to their destinations and need their cars transported to places such as Miami, San Diego, Las Vegas and New Orleans.

Sometimes driveaway companies even pay drivers a small stipend based on mileage. In most cases, they require bonding, which is a process insuring against damages or losses while the car is being transported. During the bonding investigation, certain personal details are examined, such as credit and banking history, driving record, and criminal record, if any. Normally, a bonding fee is assessed; most driveaway companies will assist you with the paperwork. The entire procedure could take up to a month or more to complete, so allow the time for it.

When driving these cars, some companies will allow you to bring along family and friends, others may not. Specific arrangements with driveaway companies vary. Usually, the company does **not** pay for out-of-pocket expenses such as meals, hotels, gas, oil, tolls, and return transportation. If you can arrange to drive another car back to your home town, you can enjoy virtually free roundtrip travel.

Driveaway cars are not always available when and where you want them. Be patient and keep looking. If the timing is right, and a car needs to be delivered somewhere you're inter-

# PASSPORT TO
# DISCOUNT TRAVEL

ested in visiting, drive it there and save a bundle on transportation costs.

Another way to drive for very little is to ferry automobiles for rental agencies occasionally needing cars deployed to other locations around the country. Agencies often pay these drivers, or offer them free use of the cars while driving to these destinations.

I recall one memorable journey along California's Route 1, the famous Pacific Coast Highway. While reading a travel magazine. I noticed that a leading rent-a-car agency was looking for drivers to transport several vehicles from Los Angeles to San Francisco. I called up, applied, met their qualifications, and was given a car in L.A. to drop off in the City by the Bay within three days.

What a trip I had touring one of the world's most beautiful highways, with its spectacular ocean vistas, rugged shoreline, and thick forests. I drove around the towering Big Sur Mountain, visited William Randolph Hearst's immense, opulent San Simeon Castle, spent the night in picturesque Monterey, and lunched at charming Carmel-by-the-Sea, all without paying a dime for the car, except gas and tolls.

Truck leasing companies such as Ryder, U-Haul, Hertz-Penske and Budget, frequently need their vehicles transferred to other places too. Call to see what driveaway opportunities may be available. Have fun, buckle up, and always drive safely!

# RENTAL CARS

## HELPFUL DRIVING TIPS

### Traveling With Children

When traveling with children: 1) keep them safe; 2) keep them occupied; and 3) keep a flexible schedule to meet their eating, sleeping, and bathroom habits.

Make sure children use proper carriers, car seats or seatbelts whenever they are in the car. Everyone should use a seatbelt. No exceptions!

State laws require children under 40 pounds to use approved child safety restraints, available for infants and toddlers. Check with your local law enforcement authorities or automobile clubs for details about which seat you need for your children. *(Some approved samples are shown on the next page).*

Safety rules should be set and agreed upon by everyone before leaving. They should include: no distracting the driver, no playing with doors or door handles, no sticking heads, arms, or feet out the windows, and no thowing any objects inside or out of the car.

To keep children occupied, bring plenty of toys and games, as well as a pillow or two for naps or demarcation lines—not pillow fights! Young children may enjoy coloring or picture books, story tapes, or soft stuffed animals. Take a surprise toy or game along for when they really get bored or cranky. Older children may enjoy puzzles, magazines, books, audio cassettes, hand-held computer games, magnetic chess, checkers or other travel games.

Try involving the youngsters with the trip. Let older children help navigate using a road map, and looking for signs. Play

# PASSPORT TO DISCOUNT TRAVEL

## CAR SEATS

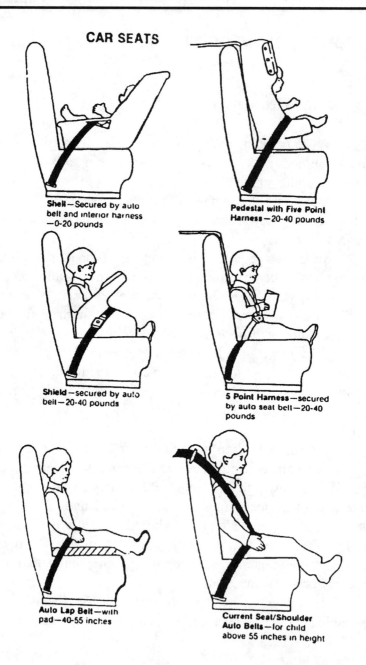

Shell—Secured by auto belt and interior harness —0-20 pounds

Pedestal with Five Point Harness—20-40 pounds

Shield—secured by auto belt—20-40 pounds

5 Point Harness—secured by auto seat belt—20-40 pounds

Auto Lap Belt—with pad—40-55 inches

Current Seat/Shoulder Auto Belts—for child above 55 inches in height games counting license plates from different states or make a game out of counting just about anything such as trucks, oil wells, billboards, types of cars, etc.

A wise parent will also include several plastic bags with wet and dry washcloths, motion sickness bags and medicine, cool water or juices, and a basic first aid kit. Stop and take plenty of breaks to let the kids exercise. Try picnic lunches in wayside parks and tourist stops.

Try making the trip an exciting learning adventure. Write to the Tourism Boards of the countries or states you'll be traveling through, or check your library, bookstore, or automobile club tour guides for material. While driving through a particular area, ask your children questions about the region. Talk about the capitol of the country or state, its languages or dialects, history, famous sites and people, popular attractions, major industries, or recreation.

Depending on the age of the child, provide a notebook and materials with which they can draw scenes of the trip or even keep a diary. This will keep the children occupied and entertained, and at the same time give them a project for "show and tell" at school when they return.

A guide to family travel by car, train and plane entitled, TRAVELING WITH CHILDREN AND ENJOYING IT, by A. K. Butler (Globe Pequot Press), dispenses advice on planning and coping with the kids on a lengthy trip.


## Traveling With Your Pet

Across the U.S. and around the world, many pet owners love to take their pets with them whenever they travel.

# PASSPORT TO
# DISCOUNT TRAVEL

Dogs are particularly upbeat about road trips. Hanging their heads out a window at 55 m.p.h. with jowls flapping, fur blowing, wind howling, eyes watering, and scenery racing by in a total blur is enough to make most dogs ecstatic.

A few pointers for taking your pet on a road trip are: make sure your pet has a collar with an identification tag giving your phone number and requesting a collect call if found (do not include name and address for security reasons); carry a leash and use it; bring pet food and a water bowl. Consult your veterinarian about what to give your pet in cases of car sickness; don't leave your pet in a car with windows closed, especially in warm weather. Bring flea spray or bath and flea dip—you don't want your pet scratching and uncomfortable, and you certainly don't want to share his fleas in the car.

When staying in a hotel, be sure to put a note on the door advising the maid your dog or cat is inside so that she is not startled, and is prepared to prevent it from running out the door. You may also consider confining the animal in the bathroom or its carrier while you are out of the room.

When driving with a small animal, place it in an airy, comfortable carrier, securing it with a seat belt or strap to prevent it from flying if you stop suddenly. For larger animals, there are seat belt extenders and/or harnesses available from PET AFFAIRS, (800-777-9192) or MASTER ANIMAL CARE (800-346-0749).

TAKE YOUR PET USA, by Arthur Frank, contains an alphabetical listing of U.S. hotels accepting pets, and their approximate room rates. It provides tips on security and loss prevention, and hotel etiquette for pets, and mentions the names of several veterinarians in many cities. Available at local bookstores and pet shops, or from Artco Offset, 12 Channel St., Boston, MA 02210. Enclose a check for $11.95.

# RENTAL CARS

For more information about pet-friendly hotels and motels consult regional tour books published by the American Automobile Association, or read the brochure TRAVELING WITH TOWSER, available for $1.50 from Quaker Professional Services, 585 Hawthorne Court, Galesburg IL 61401.

ON THE ROAD AGAIN WITH MAN'S BEST FRIEND lists lodging options for pets in various parts of the country. Published by Dawbert Press, Box 2758, Duxbury MA 02331, these directories cost approximately $12 each. Specify the regions in which you are interested.

AIR TRAVEL FOR YOUR DOG OR CAT is available from Air Transport Association (ATA), Dept. CF, 1709 New York Ave. N.W., Washington, DC 20006-2506. Send $1 with stamped, self-addressed envelope.

PETS-R-PERMITTED, by Annenberg Communications gives advice on boarding or taking pets when traveling. It names over 1,000 pet sitters and veterinarians nationwide, and more than 3,000 hotels and motels welcoming visitors with pets. Write: ACI, P. O. Box 66006, West Des Moines, IA 50265-9410 (515-224-4872).

# PASSPORT TO
# DISCOUNT TRAVEL

# Chapter 6

# CRUISES

"I must go down to the seas again,
To the lonely sea and the sky.
And all I ask is a tall ship,
And star to steer her by."
John Masefield, "Sea Fever"

## GREAT VACATION VALUE

According to many travel experts, cruises are today's top vacation value. Nearly everyone enjoys sailing on luxurious ships to sensuous ports-of-call, satisfying every whim while being pampered by an attentive, friendly crew. Passengers appreciate the "put-your-wallet-away" policy of all-inclusive pleasures, such as gourmet food, first-rate entertainment, casino gambling, moon-light dancing, sunny islands and round-the-clock service. Most people are amazed by the abundance of food served. In addition to the three basic meals, they may enjoy mid-morning, mid-afternoon, midnight buffets, and 24-hour room service. Voyagers also like the opportunity to burn up those extra calories with dance classes, aerobics, saunas, work-out rooms, rowing machines, swimming, snorkeling, volleyball, and shuffleboard. Other activities include: backgammon, bingo, bowling, talent shows, costume parties and first-run motion pictures. On a cruise you can enjoy a fantasy-like vacation where your signature alone obtains everything you want. But remember, reality replaces fantasy when the bill arrives.

## WATCH THOSE HIDDEN COSTS

Cruises cost an average of $150 to $300 a day per person, double occupancy, plus taxes, tips, port charges and departure fees. Port charges account for an extra $35 to $75 per person, depending on the itinerary and the number of stops. Tips run about $3 a day for your dining room waiter and cabin steward who makes the beds and handles room service; $2 a day for the busboy, and 15% of the bar bill for the barmaid or deck steward.

There are many temptations to spend additional money on a cruise. Some may not occur to you until you set sail. Skeet shooting, video games and driving golf balls off the deck all cost extra. Calling ship-to-shore can be expensive— a 10-minute call could cost up to $100. Ask what the charges will be before phoning.

According to the Cruise Lines International Association, most passengers spend about $25 a day on shipboard expenditures over and above the daily tips to service employees and the $10 per day average for land tours and excursions. At that rate, a couple on a 7-day cruise could wind up spending more than $500 above the advertised cost. Keep this in mind when budgeting your trip.

Normally these incidentals are not paid for in cash, but are charged to your credit card. Most ships allow you to leave an

# CRUISES

imprint of your charge card at the purser's office so you can sign for everything as you go. Amidst all the fun and excitement, you can easily lose track of how much you're spending. When the bill comes at the end of your voyage, you may receive quite a shock. Be smart, plan ahead for additional expenses, and enjoy your vacation without unpleasant surprises.

Extra cash usually goes towards souvenirs, massages, dry cleaning, shore excursions and alcoholic beverages. Wines range in price from $7 a bottle up to $150 for premier vintages. Cocktails cost $2.50 for house brands, up to $6 for name brands. Bottled beer runs about $2 domestic, $4 imported. Shore excursions and tours vary from $10 to $500 depending on location, length and level of luxury. Merchandise from the ship's trendy boutiques tend to be expensive, as are the services of hairdressers, barbers and beauticians.

Like most people, you will probably be lured into trying your luck at the gambling casinos, strategically located along busy walkways on the main decks. Be smart and set aside some cash as "gambling money." This should **not** come out of funds budgeted for other important cruise items, such as tours, souvenirs, etc., so that you can enjoy gambling, win or lose, without affecting the rest of your trip.

For all these extras, budget an additional $200–$300 because optional amenities make cruising even more fun.

# PASSPORT TO DISCOUNT TRAVEL

## SHOP FOR THE RIGHT CRUISE

Cruises normally last 3, 4, 7, or 14 days, although longer and shorter sailings are available. Prices vary according to the ship's reputation, duration and destinations of the cruise, and size and location of the cabin. Cruise ship quality and rates fluctuate; a higher price does not necessarily ensure a higher level of enjoyment. Some of the more expensive cruises are quite elegant, but may not provide the type of fun you seek, or are simply not within your budget.

Before weighing anchor, increase your chances for an enjoyable cruise by researching the wide variety of ships and itineraries available. Talk to people who have sailed on cruise lines in which you are interested. They've been on them, tasted the food, enjoyed the entertainment, and visited the ports-of-call. Their experience is helpful in selecting a cruise that's right for you.

Travel agency cruise specialists can help assess the multitude of options. These professionals sail on many ships, and will gladly discuss their favorites. Travel agents charge nothing for their services, so take advantage of their knowledge of quality bargains. Ask to look through their OAG CRUISE AND SHIPLINE GUIDE, which present itineraries, ship diagrams, sailing dates, special features, and entertainment attractions.

When four people share a cabin, the price per person is exceptionally low, about half the cost of double occupancy. With the exception of deluxe staterooms, cabins are typically rather small, ranging from approximately 86 square feet to 250 square feet, yet may cost about the same price. Usually, cabins are equipped with pull-down single bunk beds stacked close together in relatively tight quarters. Cruising four-to-a-cabin requires fairly close intimacy, but results in everyone saving money. Be sure to inquire about the exact size of a cabin, so you'll know what to expect.

Cabin size and location are important factors in selecting affordable cruises. If you must economize, select a smaller inside one. Don't worry if it doesn't have a window, because if it's a good cruise, you won't be spending much time looking out the porthole. More likely, you will be on deck enjoying panoramic views, or participating in some activities.

Cabins located on lower decks are usually less expensive than those on upper decks because they are closer to the sound and vibration of the engines. Select a cabin away from elevator shafts, kitchens, and crew quarters, because the ship's service generates sounds from these locations 24 hours a day. For those moments when you need your rest, you will appreciate being in a cabin far from these noisy areas.

## INSURE YOUR CRUISE

After spending your hard-earned money on a long-anti-cipated voyage, the last thing you need is a sudden emergency interrupting or canceling your trip. In addition to the disappoint-ment of not going, you could lose the money you paid for the cruise. Since emergencies may happen, you risk forfeiting your entire investment if you have not purchased trip cancellation/interruption insurance.

The chapter entitled, INSURE YOUR TRIP, explains travel insurance, how to determine coverage needed, and where to purchase it. In addition to trip cancellation or interruption, other insurance is available to cover theft, baggage loss, medical emergencies, natural disasters, terrorism, and the bankruptcy of the travel operator. Travel insurance should be considered before taking any trip.

## DRESSING FOR THE SUN

In the tropics, bring sunglasses, sunscreen and protective, lightweight clothing. Even half an hour of morning or late afternoon sun can result in a burn. Often, the very garments most travelers pack to keep cool— items light in color and wide in weave—are those least capable of blocking the sun and protecting the skin.

When packing, hold up the garment—if a great deal of light shines through, the weave is too loose allowing harmful ultra-violet rays to reach your skin. Use sunscreen underneath your clothes to counter the penetration of unhealthy rays. Thicker, opaque fabric, tightly woven cottons and linens protect more effectively than nylon or polyester knits. Bright colors, blue denim, dark whipcords, and similar cottons are a good bet.

Loose fitting clothes of natural fibers allow more air circulation to keep you cooler. Broad-brimmed hats and opaque parasols are good shields against sunlight reflected from water. A little caution and common sense will save you from nursing a sunburn instead of enjoying your cruise.

# CRUISES

## CRUISE COMPLAINTS

Unfortunately, not all cruises are the dream voyages portrayed in television commercials. Sometimes things go wrong. Suppose the food quality or service is consistently under par, or the air conditioner or plumbing in your stateroom doesn't work? What if the cruise isn't ship-shape and the crew unsympathetic to your requests? To whom do you complain and what sort of response should you expect?

Problems often arise from meal seatings. Complaints are made by non-smokers assigned to share tables with smokers. Many people ask for the later, second seating, but despite assurances from the cruise salesperson, do not get it. Travel agents may request the second seating, but **cannot** guarantee it. Most cruise lines make seating selections on a first-come-first-served basis. Get your selection confirmed in writing directly from the cruise line. Those who book at the last minute may not get their first preference.

Take your food or dining complaints to the ship's maître d´. Your service problems are handled by the purser's office, the equivalent of a hotel's front desk. When things go awry, pursue the matter immediately. If you fail to get satisfaction from the first person, see the supervisor, or the purser. Reasonable problems should be resolved quickly; if not, send a letter to the cruise line's coordinator for passenger affairs when you return. If justified, you may be compensated with a partial refund, or a discount on a future cruise

One unfortunate couple was stranded in a port city when their cruise-sponsored bus failed to pick them up after a day's outing. Keeping their wits and making the best of a bad situation, they made their way back to the ship, and retained their cab and boat launch receipts. When they finally got on board, they went straight to the ship's activity director, demanded an explanation, and obtained reimbursement for their expenses.

The cruise business is competitive. They want you to sail with them again and recommend them to others. Cruise companies strive to maintain a good reputation, and will usually satisfy valid complaints.

## HOW TO CRUISE AT UP TO 50% OFF

Start with some research. No captain of a ship commences a voyage without first studying his charts. Similarly, you should study cruise options before embarking on the quest for discounts. Read cruise advertisements in newspaper Travel sections. Call cruise lines and travel agencies for information about sailings. Most have toll-free numbers for request brochures and information. A list of toll-free numbers for major cruise lines is located in the Appendix.

Read descriptive material thoroughly, especially the fine print about refunds and cancellation deadlines. This knowledge will help you sail for less. Because of slow sales or last-minute cancellations, ships are sometimes left with vacant staterooms a few weeks before weighing anchor. Cruise operators desperately want to fill those empty cabins, and may offer them at up to 50% off the regular price.

Contact cruise lines or travel agencies for details on obtaining bargains on short notice. Sometimes cruise lines will advertise discounts directly to the general public. Other times they will offer wholesale prices on cabins to travel agencies or

# CRUISES

cruise discounters who attempt to fill the ship. Several cruise wholesalers are mentioned later in this chapter and in LAST-MINUTE BARGAINS.

A schedule flexible enough to act quickly and take advantage of these short-notice savings is important. It also helps to be able to sail at off-peak times when discounts are more plentiful. Avoid peak seasons, such as mid-winter, summertime or spring break.

## CRUISE BY FREIGHTER

Adventurous sailors travel inexpensively by hopping a freighter—not as a stow-away, but as a passenger. Two advantages freighters have over cruise lines are they take you where tourist ships don't, and cost about half as much per day—around $75 to $150 per person. Most freighter treks last much longer than vacation cruises (frequently two weeks to a month or more) and result in a higher total expenditure. A 30 day freighter cruise averaging about $100 per day would cost $3000. The price per day on a cargo ship may be less than on a cruise, but the overall expense may be more.

Some other advantages of cruising by freighter include smaller crowds, off-beat ports-of-call, and a sense of camaraderie among sailing companions. With less to do on a freighter than on a typical cruise, most of the entertainment depends on the people on board. By and large, your fellow voyagers will be well-rounded, seasoned travelers who know how to relax and have a good time. They appreciate meeting other cargo cruisers at the easy-going pace of a freighter.

# PASSPORT TO DISCOUNT TRAVEL

An example of a freighter itinerary is sailing from Charleston, South Carolina or some other eastern United States seaport, through the Panama Canal, all the way to New Zealand and Australia on an ACT/PACE cargo ship. For more details on this and other steamship voyages, contact ACT/PACE, Suite 8101, One World Trade Center, New York, NY 10048 (800-221-8164 or 212-775-1500).

Passengers on cargo ships is not a new idea. They have been sailing on them since ancient times. Freighters have changed a great deal over the centuries. Gone are dingy tramp steamers and leaky rust-buckets. In today's global economy dependent on international trade, many old transports have been replaced by sleek, containerized cargo vessels. Comfortable passenger compartments on many cargo ships offer modern amenities such as air conditioning, in-room showers, and toilets. On some freighters, nicer staterooms for passengers may be spare officers' quarters or even ship owners' suites.

While accommodations on some freighters may not be considered luxurious, they are quite liveable. Ask about cabin sizes so you'll know what to expect. While schedules and itineraries on steamers are not always strictly adhered to, if you have the spirit of adventure and a little extra time, you may find, as many others have, that traveling by cargo ship is a unique and economical way to see the world.

Usually, freighters feature lengthy voyages with numerous stops. Unlike many tourist sailings, freighter journeys often last 30 to 60 days, with extended periods on the open seas and long layovers in port for freight handling. Ships may dock for two or three full days, allowing passengers leisurely time to explore the port cities and surrounding areas.

Not all freighter voyages are long; some of the more popular shorter sailings lasting 10 to 14 days, are those between

# CRUISES

America and Europe. Below are four shipping lines taking passengers to and from the Continent at an average cost of $100-$150 a day:

- CAST SHIPPING features weekly trips between Montreal, Canada and Antwerp, Belgium; 12 days each way.

- LYKES LINE departs two to three times monthly from New Orleans, LA or Port Elizabeth, NJ to the Netherlands, Germany, England, and Italy; 12 to 14 days each way. Some ships also sail on to Egypt, Israel, and Turkey.

- MEDITERRANEAN SHIPPING LINES sails from Norfolk, VA; Baltimore, MD; New York City, NY; and Boston, MA to Antwerp, Belgium; Bremen and Hamburg, Germany; Felixstowe, England; and LeHavre, France; 11 to 13 days each way, weekly.

- POLISH OCEAN LINES departs weekly from Port Newark, NJ to LeHavre, France; 10 days each way.

One shipping line cruises the Norwegian fjords on mail boats holding 130 to 320 passengers, sailing along Norway's spectacular coastline, and stopping 35 times during the two-week-long round trip. Contact BERGEN LINE, 505 Fifth Ave., New York, NY 10017 (212-986-2711 or 800-323-7436).

Perhaps the world's most luxurious cargo liner is IVARAN LINES' *Americana*. This 600-foot ship holds nearly 100 passengers in style. Its elegant four-story complex on the aft deck features a swimming pool, bar, lounge, gym and beauty salon.

# PASSPORT TO
# DISCOUNT TRAVEL

Usually sailing between Miami and South America, it anchors Rio de Janeiro, Brazil; Montevideo, Uruguay, and other famous and not-so-famous ports in the southern hemisphere.

To find out more about these and other shipping companies, consult the STEAMSHIP GUIDE at a travel agency or library. It lists freighters accommodating passengers, and outlines approximate itineraries and departure dates.

The relatively few freighters accepting passengers are usually booked solid. Call a travel agent early for advice and reservations. Since freighters rarely accommodate more than a few passengers at a time, it hardly pays for them to advertise. You will have to do a little work to find out about them. Some other publications designed to help you in your search are:

• FREIGHTER SPACE ADVISORY, published twice a month by Freighter World News, 180 S. Lake Ave., Suite 335, Pasadena, CA 91101 (818-449-3106), reports availability and discounts on those cargo ships it represents as a booking agent. The subscription fee is reimbursed as a credit toward cruises purchased through them.

• TRAVLTIPS published by a travel agency in Flushing, NY, issued six times a year for members who pay a modest annual fee credited towards your first voyage. Each brochure contains articles about freighter travel, space availability, destinations, and schedules. For direct bookings, contact TravLtips, P.O. Box 188, Flushing, NY 11358 (800-872-8584 or 718-939-2400).

• FORD'S FREIGHTER GUIDE, published twice a year by Ford's Travel Guides, 19448 Londelius St., Northridge, CA 91324 (818-701-7414), lists itineraries, accommodations and rates, plus information on river and canal cruises, and the names of travel agencies specializing in freighter bookings. About $20 a year.

• FREIGHTER TRAVEL NEWS, published by Freighter Travel Club, 3524 Harts Lake Rd., Roy, WA 98580, carries first-hand accounts of recent freighter trips, along with updates on sailings. Annual subscription, approximately $20.

## CRUISE WHOLESALERS

Several wholesalers specialize in 3 to 14-day cruises reserved several weeks or more in advance, featuring specials such as two for the price of one, or deluxe cabins for less than the price of standard. When you find a good deal, act quickly because they may sell out. In most cases, shopping for short-notice discounts works best if you have a flexible schedule enabling you to take advantage of excellent values.

Normally, cabins sold by cruise discounters are filled on a run-of-the-ship basis, meaning the best cabin available at the time of confirmation. Cabins are reserved only after payment is received. The cabin selection process, therefore, is somewhat hit-or-miss, and certainly limits one's freedom of choice. Since most cruise lines sell out their lowest and moderate-priced cabins first, your chance of getting a prime cabin at a discount is good.

The companies, listed alphabetically below, discount cruises 5% to 50% and also provide information about destinations, group and theme cruises through their newsletters and toll-

# PASSPORT TO
# DISCOUNT TRAVEL

free hot-lines. Most do not charge membership dues.

• LAST MINUTE CRUISE CLUB, 870 Ninth St., San Pedro, CA 90731 (213-519-1717), specializes in 4 and 5-star rated ships offering cabins at savings up to 50%. Free listings sent by mail.

• SOUTH FLORIDA CRUISES, 3561 N.W. 53rd. Court, Fort Lauderdale, FL 33309 (800-327-7447), details sailings primarily from Florida.

• SPUR OF THE MOMENT TOURS AND CRUISES, 10780 Jefferson Blvd., Culver City, CA 90230 (213-839-2418; or for reservations only 800-343-1991 or 800-233-2129 in CA), specializes in last-minute cruises with savings up to 50%. Lists  sailings twice a month.

• WORLD WIDE CRUISES, 8059 W. McNab Rd., Fort Lauderdale, FL 33321 (800-882-9000 or 305-720-9000), features low rates and last-minute specials on major lines. Take 15 people along, and you cruise free.

Some other travel clubs also offering discount cruises are:

• ALL CRUISE TRAVEL in San Francisco (800-862-7447)

• CRUISE LINE INC. in Miami (800-777-0707)
• CRUISES OF DISTINCTION in Montclair, NJ. (800-634-3445)

# CRUISES

• CRUISE SHOPPER'S HOTLINE (900-740-3400) is a cruise information clearinghouse which charges $2 a minute featuring weekly updates on cruise bargains. Have a pencil ready, or tape record the data on your answering machine, because the details are recited rapidly. Callers receive a coupon for $25 off the price of any 7-day or longer cruise mentioned.

## CRUISING WITH THE KIDS

According to humorist Robert Benchley there are two classes of travel — first class, and with children. On today's ships, however, you can bring your kids and still enjoy yourself. Contemporary cruises are for everyone—not just for honeymooners, senior citizens, or swinging singles. Many feature special activities for youngsters of all ages.

CARNIVAL CRUISE LINES, for example, gears some events for children ages 4 to 12 such as  scavenger hunts, drawing contests, and ice cream and soda parties with the crew.

For teenagers, trivia games, ping-pong tournaments, disco parties, and "lip-sync" contests mimicking favorite pop singers help fill their days. Youngsters can enjoy video games in the arcade, swimming in the pool, and mixing with peers in their own teen clubhouse. They can fly a kite off the deck , see a movie, or play volleyball. Parents seeking a respite from their progeny can slip away on shore excursions while their offspring play on board.

NORWEGIAN CRUISE LINES' coordinators plan and supervise youth activities, including treasure hunts, cookouts and even a "circus at sea" where kids can clown around, juggle and do acrobatics—without getting into trouble.

REGENCY CRUISES has special packages for families, single parents, and grandparents at discounted rates. In addition to regular activities such as pool parties, talent shows and games, for youngsters, they host many family reunions. For special occasions they offer champagne bon voyage parties, souvenir photo albums, and "happy reunion" cakes.


## HOW TO CRUISE FREE


There was once a popular tune that went, "...you gotta have friends..." The same applies if you want to cruise for free.

Gather your friends, classmates, fraternity brothers, sorority sisters, church members, or co-workers and take them on a cruise with you. Usually, if your entourage fills ten cabins, you and your companion will probably sail free. Contact various cruise lines and see what you can arrange for your group. Remember, don't be afraid to negotiate! Since you're bringing in a fair amount of business to the cruise line, you deserve to be compensated, either with a deeply discounted cabin or a free one. Offers vary, so shop before you sail.

# CRUISES

## HOW TO CRUISE FREE AND MAKE MONEY

How would you like to earn $5,000 every time you take a cruise?

Impossible?

No. It's true, and you can do it! Not by winning big in the ship's casino, but by working as an independent "outside" sales consultant for a cruise line or travel agency.

You can make extra money, and sail to exotic places, by using spare time selling travel and cruises. Not directly employed by the travel company, you can set the hours you want to work from your home or the travel office.

One enterprising woman devised an appealing and profitable marketing strategy. She signed an agreement with a cruise line earning an average of $100 for every cruise passenger she booked.

To attract customers, she concentrates on selling theme cruises which she advertises in newspapers, club periodicals, church notes, posters, and fliers distributed throughout the community.

Her most successful is the "Murder Mystery", a version of the popular party game in which guests try to deduce who the murderer is among them. On a cruise, some clues are given out in advance with the boarding passes, and later, professional actors perform the crime dramas during or after meals. It's a lot of fun, the participants enjoy it, and it works well on the high seas.

Her advertisements announce the sailing dates, historical period of the crime, and her phone number. Interested "detectives" are invited to try their luck at solving the case. She

# PASSPORT TO
# DISCOUNT TRAVEL

sets her goal at 50 passengers, netting her $5000 and a free cruise! Not bad for someone working out of her home.

What cruise themes can you conceive? Be creative! Sports, cooking, drama, fashion? The premise behind a theme cruise is: if it's fun on land, it's fun at sea. Some themes used by cruise ships include theater at sea, learning a foreign language, natural history expeditions, meet-the-celebrity sailings, and comedy cruises.

Call cruise companies for their list of themes, and work the ones you prefer, or create your own!

If you'd like to work for a cruise company, but don't know where start, read Mary Fallon Miller's How to Get a Job With a Cruise Line, available at book stores or for $12.95, plus $2.50 postage from Ticket to Adventure, P. O. Box 41005, St. Petersburg, FL 33643 (800-800-8466).

# Chapter 7

# TOURS

**"A tourist is a fellow who
travels thousands of miles
so he can be photographed
standing in front of his car."**
Emile Ganest

Think of anywhere in the world you would like to visit, and chances are there's a tour going there. From an enchanted weekend on a Caribbean island to a once-in-a-lifetime journey around the world, tours provide a sensible way to travel. In addition to international tours offered through travel agencies, many organizations and universities offer a variety of interesting, educational tours.

Tours alleviate the hassle of visiting as many places as possible in a limited amount of time. They hit the highlights of an area efficiently and comfortably, saving time for seeing other interesting locations and taking pictures of more than just yourself standing in front of your bus. With some preparation on you part, you can tour for up to 50% off regular prices, and possibly even free!

# PASSPORT TO DISCOUNT TRAVEL

## TYPES OF TOURS

Generally, tour packages include airfare, hotels, airport transfers, sightseeing, and some meals. Prices vary according to accommodations and service, usually categorized as "standard," "superior" and "deluxe."

Tours come in all styles, lengths, and prices, ranging from inexpensive bus tours of a few hours to deluxe, extended tours of several weeks or more.

- **Escorted Tours**. Tour directors accompany a group throughout the tour, stay in the same hotels, and are available for advice and planning.

- **Hosted Tours**. Local agents or "hosts" are used at major destinations for a limited time to assist tourists with sightseeing and independent plans.

- **All Inclusive Tours**. A full-time tour director, a complete package of transportation, hotels, most meals, sightseeing, transfers, and gratuities as well as practically all travel needs are included, except personal expenses such as laundry, souvenirs, and extra beverages.

Below are several types of meal plans offered on tours:

- **European Plan (EP)** or **Bed and Breakfast (B&B)**. Continental breakfast is included in the price of your room.

# TOURS

- **American Plan (AP).** Three meals a day.

- **Modified American Plan (MAP).** Two meals a day (breakfast and dinner).

- **Table d'hôte.** A fixed-price menu with limited choices.

By American standards, a continental breakfast is quite light, consisting of coffee, rolls, bread and jam. American, English, or Dutch breakfasts are generally full meals with eggs, cereal, juice, meat, cheese, bread and jam, according to the customs of the country. Outside the United States, coffee and tea are rarely included with meals, other than breakfast, and must be paid for separately.

Tour hotels are typically designated as "deluxe," or "first class" (superior); "standard" (moderate); and "tourist class" (economy). These categories vary greatly among tour operators, places, and countries. For example, a hotel listed as deluxe in one brochure may be described as standard in another; a first class hotel in Moscow may be considered tourist class in Paris. Ask your tour operator for clarification. Reputable companies should be able to give you detailed evaluations of the properties they represent.

## UNDERSTAND THE BROCHURE

Understand all information about your tour before paying any money. Just as it's fun to browse trip itineraries and gaze

# PASSPORT TO DISCOUNT TRAVEL

at photographs in travel brochures, its also important to carefully read the details explaining exactly what you are getting. Data about the tour's inclusive and exclusive costs are usually found in the fine print. Peruse it thoroughly to know what's covered, for budgeting your trip accurately. For example, are airport transfers to and from hotels included in the price? Do you have to pay for meals? What about tips for luggage handlers, tour guides, and bus drivers?

It is customary to tip the tour director at the end of the trip, depending on the person's performance, about $2.50 per day. Let your instincts be your guide; if a tour director performs well, tip generously—if not, don't.

Understand the terminology in tour brochures. If uncertain, ask the tour representative. For example, an "air-cooled" sightseeing bus may mean you can open the windows and let the air flow through! "Average temperature 70 degrees" may mean it's 90 degrees during the day and 50 degrees at night. Phrases such as "you may want to cruise this glorious isle," or "you'll enjoy the exciting night-life..." may mean these are extras for which you'll have to pay.

Does the tour itinerary clearly state "visit," or is the wording ambiguous about whether the sightseeing is included in the price, or will cost extra? If the brochure lists particular tourist attractions as being "viewed," ask whether they are merely viewed from afar while passing by, or do you actually stop and visit. Also, know what is **not** included in your travel package. Most brochures spell this out clearly, usually on back pages under the headings "general conditions" or "terms of transportation."

If you are taking a pre-paid package tour, check the cancellation and refund policy, usually located on the last page of the brochure. Know exactly what happens if you change your mind. Cancellation penalties vary; you may get a refund, but then again, you may not.

Is the tour guide directly employed by the tour operator? An employee will have your best interests at heart, whereas guides not directly employed by the company may not be as attentive to your needs. Tour leaders contracted for a trip are also expected to provide quality service and stay with the group from start to finish. It's their job to see that everyone is taken care of and has a good time. Ask for references from people who have traveled with that guide. Talk to them so you'll know what to expect.

**Questions to Ask:**

• Has your tour operator been "checked out" in advance by the seller? Does the travel agent have first-hand knowledge of the operator's reputation, the tour director's performance and the suitability of any transportation being utilized? Contact other travelers who have used them.

• What can the company marketing the tour tell you about your hotel accommodations, services, and other features? A major airline may have sold you a tour, but has anyone from their tour department ever personally taken it? Ask them how it was. Get details.

• Has someone from the tour company or travel agency actually stayed at the hotel(s) recently? Hotels are frequently bought and sold; managements change and so does service. Get a recent recommendation.

# PASSPORT TO DISCOUNT TRAVEL

• What are the hotel locations and amenities? What restaurants, entertainment, and other attractions are nearby?

• Are taxes, service charges and gratuities included? Outside the U.S., by government decree, most hotels and restaurants must charge 10% to 15% for tips. Those employees such as valet, housekeeper, or concierge expect additional tips. Are these out-of-pocket expenses you have to pay, or does the tour price cover it?

Read How to Select a Package Tour from the United States Tour Operators Association (USTOA), 211 E. 51st St. Suite 12-B, New York, NY 10022 (212-944-5727). This booklet lists guidelines for selecting tours, explains what to look for in brochures, deciphers travel language, and defines common terms used in brochures and contracts.

## INSURE YOUR INVESTMENT

Can you risk losing the hard-earned money you paid for a tour if illness or an emergency forces you to interrupt or cancel it? Shouldn't you insure your vacation investment?

Travel insurance may be purchased for trip cancellation/interruption, theft, medical emergencies, bankruptcy of the tour operator, baggage loss or damage, and more. See the chapter, INSURE YOUR TRIP for complete details about types available, determining your needs and where to purchase.

Using an experienced travel agent or reputable tour operator does not necessarily guarantee a flawless trip. Something

# TOURS

still can go wrong. When that happens, your travel agent should go to bat for you in an attempt to work out a satisfactory settlement, perhaps obtaining a refund or credit vouchers for future travel. Since agents are not always successful—you should consider purchasing travel insurance.

Research the reputation of tour operators. Do they belong to travel industry affiliations? Do they participate in default programs sponsored by The American Society of Travel Agents (ASTA) or by the National Tour Association (NTA)?

Concerned merchants in the tour industry have taken steps to ensure the quality and consistency of tours by creating a multi-million dollar consumer protection program. Anyone purchasing a tour conducted by an active member of the United States Tour Operators Association (USTOA) is automatically covered by this plan which refunds tour payments or deposits if one of its member companies declares bankruptcy or becomes insolvent. It also reimburses the consumer if the USTOA active member fails to return deposits or payments within 120 days following the cancellation, or total non-performance, of the tour.

Details of this consumer protection plan, and a list of participating tour operators, are described in the free brochure THE STANDARD FOR CONFIDENT TRAVEL, available through USTOA, 211 E. 51st Street, Suite 12B, New York, NY 10022 (212-944-5727).

Unfortunately, not all tour operators participate in this program. Before booking with a company not belonging to USTOA, do a little investigating on your own. Find out how long the outfit has been in business and whether any complaints have been filed against it with the Better Business Bureau or with ASTA's consumer complaint department. Ask for contacts of former client's as references.

While there is no guarantee that everything on your

# PASSPORT TO
# DISCOUNT TRAVEL

journey will go smoothly at all times, you can do your part by purchasing appropriate travel insurance and being informed, prepared and unafraid to stand up for your rights. Be assertive in seeking reasonable solutions.

## HOW TO TOUR FOR UP TO 50% OFF

Which tours go where you want to visit? Refer to the Consolidated Air Tour Manual (CATM), a directory used by travel agencies listing reputable tour operators who work with commercial airlines. It details itineraries, prices and special features.

Before selecting a tour, gather as much information as possible. Read descriptive literature carefully, especially the fine print, paying particular attention to the "final payment" and "cancellation/refund" policies.

Look into air charter group packages which are often less expensive than individual tours using regularly-scheduled airlines. Charters may sometimes be less reliable or punctual than commercial carrier tours, hence the trade off.

One international charter operator is TOWER AIR (718-917-8500 or 800-221-2500), headquartered in New York. Another is AMERICAN TRANS AIR in Indianapolis which handles individual and group bookings to Orlando, Las Vegas, Cancun, Jamaica and the Virgin Islands (800-225-2995). Look in your yellow pages under "Airlines" for other charter companies serving your area, or contact your travel agent. Commercial airlines often provide equipment for charter operators; ask them if they know of any charter flights available. Trains and bus lines

# TOURS

also offer charters for economical group tours.

Unfortunately, for the tall, large, or claustrophobic traveler, space on charter flights is typically minimal. Individual space is scarce; these planes are often designed to carry as many people as possible.

Group tours are the key to extra savings, since as the departure date nears, any unsold space has to be filled quickly. Charter companies occasionally end up with empty seats, which you may be able to obtain at a bargain.

Call the tour operator or a travel agent close to the cancellation/refund deadline and inquire if there are any openings. If there aren't, put your name on a waiting list in case cancellations occur. When they do, you may receive a discount of up to 50%, because tour operators are eager to fill those vacancies. Don't be afraid to ask! Negotiate for the best possible deal—they'd rather give you a discount than depart partially filled.

## SINGLES TOURS

Singles tours are designed for college students, recent graduates, and young professionals between the ages of 18 and 35. These popular tours generally cost less and attract people of similar interests who wish to cover a lot of ground during the day, and live it up at night. To save money, young travelers are usually willing to forgo luxurious accommodations. Most hotels used on singles tours are small, clean, centrally located, tourist-class establishments. What they may lack in style and polish is made up in local charm and dollars saved.

# PASSPORT TO
# DISCOUNT TRAVEL

Such tours are ideal for travelers on tight budgets, offering the security of group travel, and a comfort level superior to hostels, hitchhiking, or sleeping in the park. Parents whose children are touring will be happy to know a guide is accompanying them the whole way.

Tour packages normally quote prices based on double occupancy (two persons per room or per ship's cabin). The extra money singles usually are asked to pay, the "single supplement," is intended to replace the hotel's or ship's perceived loss of revenue caused when only one person occupies a room For example, one person may be charged $100 a night as opposed to two people paying $120. One person eats and drinks less than two, and is likely to spend less in restaurants and shops.

Many singles prefer traveling with a group of peers rather than traveling alone or with people having little in common. Those on a singles tour usually do have to pay the 50% to 100% single supplement. These tours arrange to have two individuals of the same sex share a room at the less expensive double-occupancy rate, saving both of them money. For more information, read TRAVELING ON YOUR OWN: 250 GREAT IDEAS FOR SINGULAR VACATIONS, by Ellen Berman (Clarkson N. Potter, Inc.)

Several companies specializing in youth and singles tours are:

• AESU, Suite 248 West Quadrangle, Village of Cross Keys, Baltimore, MD 21210 (800-638-7640 or 301-323-4416)

• TRAFALGAR TOURS, 21 E. 26th St., New York, NY 10010 (800-352-4444 or 212-689-8977)

# TOURS

• INTERNATIONAL EDUCATION EXCHANGE, 205 E 42nd St., New York, NY 10017. (617-266-1926-Boston Office). IEE is not an agency, but it does provide helpful ideas for young people traveling abroad. It publishes "Student Travel Catalog" ($1) listing a variety of summer work, study, and volunteer programs for high school and college students desiring to spend their vacations overseas. Free copies are available at Council Travel offices nationwide.

• SINGLE GOURMET, 133 E. 58th St, New York, NY 10022 (212-980-8788) caters to those preferring to indulge their taste buds while traveling. Primarily a social dining club for singles, with chapters in various cities, it plans national and international trips with a focus on food.

• RAINBOW ADVENTURES, 1308 Sherman Ave., Evanston, IL 60201 (708-864-4570) offers international tours for women over 30.

• SINGLEWORLD, 401 Theodore Fremd Ave., Rye, NY 10580 (800-223-6460 or 914-967-3334) offers cruise programs to the Bahamas and the Caribbean.

For more energetic singles:

• TREKAMERICA, P. O. Box 1338, Gardena, CA 90249 (800-221-0596 or 213-323-5775) promotes adventurous camping trips in the United States and Canada.

• COLLEGE BICYCLE TOURS, 22760 Kenwyck, Southfield, MI 48034 (800-736-2453 or 313-357-1370) hosts multi-country European excursions for cyclists, ages 18 to 30.

# PASSPORT TO
# DISCOUNT TRAVEL

• OUTDOOR WOMAN, P.O. Box 834, Nyack, NY 10960 (914-358-1257) publishes a newsletter highlighting hiking, camping, and other outdoor activities designed for those who appreciate the environment. Send $3 for a sample newsletter. Annual subscriptions cost about $25.

To explore the suitability of group travel and itineraries which may appeal to you, send for the pamphlet: TRAVEL TOGETHER! from the National Tour Association, P.O. Box 3071, Lexington, KY 40596 (800-284-4682 or 800-755-8687). It provides travel tips and specific advice on selecting tours, listing more than 550 leading tour companies in North America.

Singles, not part of a group tour, preferring to travel independently, can still avoid paying the single supplement by sharing a room. While the lack of privacy may be unappealing, it eliminates the single surcharge, which adds substantially to the cost of a tour, hotel, or cruise package. For example, some European tour single supplements run as much as $400 or more.

To avoid the supplement, some resorts may help find single roommates of similar age, sex, and smoking preference. Hyatt Regency's Beaver Creek Resort near Vail, Colorado, locates compatible singles to split the cost of a ski trip. Phone numbers are exchanged, and arrangements made before arrival. If Hyatt fails to find a match, the lower "double rate" still applies. Check with Hyatt reservations (800-233-1234) for further details.

American Express Tours and Perillo Tours also offer a singles-sharing plan for their clients. Call them or your travel agent for suggestions on saving money when traveling alone. Book far enough in advance for the tour company to find a suitable roommate.

Singles traveling to popular resort areas should be able to

get a single rate without the supplement. This is generally true in parts of Hawaii, Florida, and Mexico. Every hotel has different pricing policies, so shop around.

Some companies specialize in finding tour partners for a fee. The agencies listed below will put you in touch with other interested travelers through ads, newsletters, direct mail, or phone.

• ODYSSEY NETWORK, 118 Cedar St, Wellesley, MA 02181 (617-237-2400). A $50 annual fee enters your name in their computer system for matching with travelers of similar interest. Newsletters list upcoming trips and travel bargains.

• PARTNERS IN TRAVEL, P.O. Box 491145, Los Angeles, CA 90049 (213-476-4869), $40/yr. membership; publishes "Smart Traveler," a guide to budget travel. Newsletters for those seeking travel companions, feature a Guest/Home Exchange program among members on the East and West Coasts.

• SINGLES VACATION NEWSLETTER, c/o Travel in Twos, 239 N. Broadway, Suite 3, North Tarrytown, NY 10591 (914-631-8409) charges $20/yr. for four issues listing a variety of international trips. For a $10 membership fee they'll match clients of the same sex and provide travel agency services, trip planning, and reservations.

• TRAVEL COMPANION EXCHANGE, P.O. Box 833, Amityville, NY 11701 (516-454-0880), a nationwide matching service for single travelers from 17-75. Memberships range from $36 to $66 for six months.

# PASSPORT TO
# DISCOUNT TRAVEL

## SENIOR TOURS

Many seniors have both the time and money to travel extensively.

Take Jean and Ray, my wife's aunt and uncle, for example. Having retired, travel is now their primary leisure occupation. Since Jean is Australian, the couple often skips winter in the States and goes Down Under just in time for summer. They also take escorted tours criss-crossing other countries they want to explore. For years we received their colorful postcards and lively letters describing scenes around the world, such as Hong Kong harbor, wintery Leningrad, the bazaars of Morocco, and the misty hills of Scotland. Their latest postcard detailed their adventures on a trip through newly-opened Eastern Europe.

Many organizations, alumni associations, senior citizen groups and retirement communities arrange tours. Whether you are going with a group, or on your own, there are plenty of resources available to help make your travels enjoyable and trouble-free.

One such resource is the free, informative booklet, GOING ABROAD: 101 TIPS FOR MATURE TRAVELERS, from Grand Circle Travel (800-535-8333 or 800-248-3737).

Another helpful publication is TRAVEL TIPS FOR OLDER AMERICANS, available for $1 from the Superintendent of Documents, U.S. Government Printing Office, Washington, DC 20402, listing important health, safety, and travel information for seniors.

Members of the American Association of Retired Persons (AARP) participate in a variety of tours and cruises developed by AMERICAN EXPRESS TRAVEL, 400 Pinnacle Way, Suite

450, Norcross, GA 30071 (800-927-0111). A couple may join AARP for $5. (One spouse must be at least 50 years of age.) Address: 601 E St., Washington, DC 20049 (202-434-2277).

THE MATURE TRAVELER is a fact-filled monthly newsletter suggesting economical trips in the U.S. and overseas; lists seniors-only bed-and-breakfast establishments, plus travel industry jobs. Annual subscription, $23.50. For a sample copy, send $2 to THE MATURE TRAVELER, P.O. Box 50820, Reno, NV 89513.

Another source of information about senior tours, discounts, vacations, study programs, and RV travel is THE 50+ TRAVELER'S GUIDE by Anita Williams and Merrimac Dillon (St. Martin's Press.)

A company specializing in tours for grandparents traveling with grandchildren, 12 to 17, is GRANDTRAVEL, 6900 Wisconsin Ave., Suite 706, Chevy Chase, MD 20815 (301-986-0790 or 800-247-7651).

THE EVERGREEN BED AND BREAKFAST CLUB for travelers over 50, saves money for its members by offering lodging at more than 500 homes for as low as $10 singles and $15 double per night. For information send a stamped self-addressed envelope to THE EVERGREEN CLUB, 1926 South Pacific Coast Highway, Redondo Beach, CA 90277. Annual dues: $40 singles, $50 for couples.

Other companies catering to the ever-growing mature traveler market are:

• A.J.S. TRAVEL CONSULTANTS, 117 Beach 116th St., Rockaway Park, NY 11694 (718-945-5900)

• FOLKWAYS INSTITUTE, 14600 Aldridge Rd., Portland, OR 97236 (800-225-4666)

# PASSPORT TO
# DISCOUNT TRAVEL

• GRAND CIRCLE TRAVEL, 347 Congress St., Boston, MA 02210 (800-248-3737)

• INTERHOSTEL, University of New Hampshire, 6 Garrison St., Durham, NH 03824 (800-733-9753)

• SAGA INTERNATIONAL HOLIDAYS, 120 Boylston St., Boston, MA 02116 (800-343-0273)

• SENIORS ABROAD, 12533 Pacato Circle North, San Diego, CA 92128 (619-485-1696)

For more physically-oriented travel, contact:

• CANOE COUNTRY ESCAPES, 194 S. Franklin St., Denver, CO 80209 (303-722-6482)

• INTERNATIONAL BICYCLE TOURS, P.O. Box 754, Essex, CT 06426 (203-767-7005)

For seniors traveling solo who would like to find a travel companion with whom to tour, contact:

• GOLDEN COMPANIONS, P.O. Box 754, Pullman, WA 99163-0754 (208-883-5052). Yearly membership is around $80. Newsletters list tours, hotels, discounts, get-togethers, and home exchanges.

• MATURE TRAVEL MATES, P.O. Box 26832, Tamarac, FL 33319 (407-338-4203)

# TOURS

• SHARED ADVENTURES - A WOMAN'S TRAVEL NETWORK, Fairview Plaza, 420 W. 75th St., Downers Grove, IL 60516 (708-852-4433)

Several travel associations have started marketing their services to travel planners, coordinating tours and cruises for senior clubs and retirement communities. They shop for good values in transportation, lodging and meals, handle all bookings, and take care of most details. If the planners sign up enough people, they get to go free, or at a discount. For details contact:

• GROUP LEADERS OF AMERICA, Box 129, Salem, OH 44460 (216-337-1027)

•THE NATIONAL ASSOCIATION OF SENIOR TRAVEL PLANNERS, 44 Cushing St., Hingham, MA 02043 (617-740-1185)

• SECOND WIND TRAVEL CLUB, P.O. Box 1142, Redondo Beach, CA 90278 (213-370-5094)


## WALKING TOURS

Walking tours are growing rapidly in popularity. Lewis Mumford once said, "Restore human legs as a means of travel. Pedestrians rely on food for fuel and need no special parking facilities." Since more and more people enjoy walking as their main form of exercise, dozens of companies now offer leisurely paced tours through beautiful areas of the United States and other countries.

# PASSPORT TO DISCOUNT TRAVEL

Walkers have the time and opportunity to get to know an area and experience its local pleasures. In addition to providing healthy exercise, these tours offer a pleasant contrast to the fast moving pace of motor-coach excursions. Typically one or two weeks in duration, they involve a small group of 10 to 20 people who wander through scenic and historic sites and cover 5 to 8 miles a day. The trekkers stay at fine manor homes and country inns, dine at specially selected restaurants, and unwind in the evenings with their group and guide.

Associations such as the AARP, the Smithsonian Institution, naturalist clubs, alumni groups, and state and local tourist boards package and promote walking tours. WALKING magazine also provides tips about resources, sites and special events. To subscribe write: WALKING, P. O. Box 56561, Boulder, CO 80322-6561, or call (800-678-0881).

Some companies specializing in walking tours for all ages are:

• ALL ADVENTURE TRAVEL, 4690 Pawnee Place, Boulder, CO 80303 (303-499-1981).

• Alternate Travel, 69-71 Bambury Rd., Oxford, England OX2 6PE (800-527-5997).

• BRITISH COASTAL TRAILS, 150 Carob Way, Coronado, CA 92118 (619-437-1211 or 800- 473-1210). Ask for their latest copy of "Walking Tours of England, Ireland, and Scotland."

• BUTTERFIELD AND ROBINSON, 70 Bond St., Toronto, Ontario, Canada M5B 1X3 (800-387-1147)

# TOURS

- JOURNEYS!, 1536 Northwest 23rd Ave., Portland, OR, 97219 (800-344-8890).

- SOBEK TOURS, P. O. Box 1089, Angels Camp, CA 95222 (800-777-7939 or 800-227-2384)

## HOW TO TOUR FREE

By organizing a group of at least 10 to 20 people, you should receive a free tour for yourself and possibly your companion. BRYAN WORLD TOURS of Topeka, KS (800-255-3507) promises a free trip for anyone signing up five people for one of their tours.

Get all the information you can about the tour you want to take and volunteer to lead your friends. Talk to your fraternity brothers, sorority sisters, teammates, co-workers, neighbors, union members, church-goers, or anyone else you know. Post sign-up sheets, and send out flyers to get people interested in your tour. Plan far enough ahead so people can arrange their vacation schedule around the trip. Three to four months in advance is not too early to start.

## VOLUNTEER VACATIONS

Some people pay less than full price for unusual vacations by volunteering. They give their time and energy to organ-

# PASSPORT TO
# DISCOUNT TRAVEL

izations needing small teams of caring, dedicated workers to assist in important projects worldwide. While sacrificing luxury and leisure is not for everyone, many feel rewarded by the adventure, stimulation and sense of accomplishment resulting from doing something good for others, or for the environment.

Some volunteers build houses for the homeless, both overseas and in the U.S., conduct whale censuses in Hawaii, dig for dinosaurs in Utah, survey sea life in the West Indies, study volcanic activity in Iceland, and hunt archeological artifacts in Mexico.

If interested in such pursuits, look into the history and reputation of the group you'll be helping. No governmental or travel industry watchdogs exist to monitor these travel programs. Be careful before committing any money to them. Check with the Better Business Bureau or consumer protection agencies for complaint reports. If uncertain, go with the more well-known organizations.

Have a good idea of what to expect on these ventures. Sometimes the work may be strenuous, dull or routine. You may have to outfit yourself and provide your own equipment, which is an added expense. Check if the leader has experience handling diverse groups of volunteers and choose a group that is not too large, about 10 to 20.

Make sure that insurance is included, or be prepared to purchase it separately. It should protect you in case of political unrest, terrorism, illness, or emergency medical evacuation. In some cases sponsoring organizations may require volunteers to sign waivers of liability, provide a doctor's statement of health, and obtain any required inoculations.

Although you work on this type of vacation, these journeys aren't free, ranging in cost from several hundred to several thousand dollars. They last from one week to a month or more,

# TOURS

and can encompass such diverse options as conducting plant research in rain forests, clearing mountain hiking trails, or whale-watching from a yacht in Alaska .

In most cases, fees cover lodging, meals and miscellaneous expenses, but not transportation to the site. Use skills learned in this book to find travel bargains to your destination. Some of costs may be tax deductible as a charitable contribution. Keep a log of expenses, hours worked, and duties performed. Consult a tax advisor for details.

Some organizations offering volunteer travel programs include:

• APPALACHIAN MOUNTAIN CLUB, Trails Conversation Corp, Box 298, Gorham, NH, 03581 (603-466-2771).

• CEDAM INTERNATIONAL, Dive Expeditions, One Fox Road, Croton-on-Hudson, NY 10520 (914-271-5365).

• EARTHWATCH EXPEDITIONS, 680 Mount Auburn St., Box 403TL, Watertown, MA 02272 (617-926-8200).

• FLORIDA STATE PARKS, 3900 Commonwealth Blvd., MS535, Tallahassee, FL 32399-3000. (904-488-8243).

• GLOBAL VOLUNTEERS, 375 East Little Canada Rd., St. Paul, MN 55117 (800-487-1074).

• HABITAT FOR HUMANITY, 121 Habitat Street, Americus, GA 31709-3498 (912-924-6935).

• INTERSEA RESEARCH, Box 1667, Friday Harbor, WA, 98250, (206-358-5980).

# PASSPORT TO DISCOUNT TRAVEL

- NEW YORK BOTANICAL GARDEN, Travel Program, Bronx, NY 10458 (212-220-8647).

- SIERRA CLUB, 730 Polk Street, San Francisco, CA 94109 (415-923-5630).

- SMITHSONIAN INSTITUTION, 490 L'Enfant Plaza SW, Room 4210, Washington, DC 20560 (202-287-3210).

- VOLUNTEERS FOR PEACE, Box 202, Tiffany Rd., Belmont, VT 05730 (802-259-2759).

For other sources: contact state, local and federal parks or other national or international organizations which may sponsor similar programs.

The publications below can provide additional information about volunteer travel (also check your library and bookstores):

- ENVIRONMENTAL VACATIONS, John Muir Publications (800-888-7504).

- HELPING OUT, American Hiking Society, Box 20160, Washington, DC 20041-2160.

- VOLUNTEER VACATIONS, Chicago Review Press (707-892-9364).

# Chapter 8

# TRAINS

**"To travel by train is to see nature and human beings, towns and churches and rivers, in fact, to see life."**
Agatha Christie

The "romance of the rails"—the mystique, intrigue, and adventure of passenger trains—has long been alluring to travelers the world over. Coursing through the countryside, these gently swaying communities-on-rails are considered by many to be the civilized way to go. For more than a century, these huge iron arrows aimed at endless horizons have symbolized man's far-reaching goals and capabilities.

An Amtrak commercial says, "There is something about a train." What makes them so special? Is it the atmosphere on board, the newly-made friends, or constantly changing scenery? Perhaps it's the passengers' comfortable sense of "belonging" on a train—a feeling rarely experienced flying in a jet at 35,000 feet.

Routes, destinations, accommodations, and amenities on American, Canadian, and European trains are presented on the following pages. Discussed are tour packages and trips for all budgets, and how to qualify for the many discount fares and passes available on trains worldwide.

All aboard!

# PASSPORT TO DISCOUNT TRAVEL

## AMTRAK

Amtrak, America's interstate passenger rail system, serving more than 500 cities and towns along 24,000 miles of track, crisscrosses the country through teeming metropolises and beautiful natural terrains.

Amtrak's modern fleet features lounge cars with televisions and VCRs, two-story glass dome observation cars, cafe, and full-service dining cars. The cafe sells sandwiches, snacks, drinks, and alcoholic beverages; hot breakfasts, lunches, and dinners are served in the dining car. On most trains, advance reservations are not required for these specialty cars.

For a small added charge per ticket, travelers on some Amtrak trains sit in "Custom Class," enjoying free orange juice, coffee, and newspapers. These cars, fitted with larger seats, feet and head rests, and telephones, operate on popular routes in the East, West, and Midwest.

Amtrak stations in New York, Chicago, Philadelphia and Washington, DC, provide lounges for up to 100 passengers holding tickets for "Custom Class," parlor cars, or sleepers. Lounges are equipped with telephones, fax machines, baggage areas, and restrooms. Free coffee and soft drinks, and in some locations, small conference rooms are also available. Lounge staff report on departure times and track locations, and can make or change train reservations. For Amtrak information, call 1-800-USA-RAIL.

Trains are usually more efficient than automobiles or airplanes, in terms of speed and expense, for trips up to 500 miles. Flying between Providence and Boston, for instance, costs about $100 and takes almost two hours (including time getting to and from airports)—taking the train, costs about $30 and roughly an hour's travel time.

# TRAINS

In the Midwest, trains offer the advantage of going to many small towns not served by airports, or served only by small aircraft. In bad weather, some people reluctant to fly propeller-driven planes known as "puddle-jumpers," find trains an excellent alternative.

Amtrak trains called Superliners, used in the West because Eastern tunnels are too low for them, feature double-decker cars with some seats and bedrooms upstairs for maximum views. Superliners require reservations for both coach and bedroom accommodations.

No reservations are required in the Superliners' glass-enclosed lounge cars. These scenic and social centers, where people may converse, play cards, or just gaze at the scenery through large, wrap-around windows, sometimes show feature-length films and cartoons.

On a long train ride consider reserving private sleeping quarters. Though quite small compared to hotel rooms, these well-designed living spaces are comfortably equipped with all the amenities: taped music and station-arrival announcements on room speakers, a large picture window, reading lights, climate controls, 120-volt electrical outlet, mirror, closet, sink, toilet, and even a newspaper delivered with your morning wake-up call. Some rooms have fold-down tables and enclosed showers; linens, towels and soap are supplied.

On Eastern trains sleeping accommodations, with the exception of economy class Slumbercoach, are considered "first class." An attendant is on duty full time, and meals are included in the price. Bedroom selections include: Roomette (for one person), Bedroom (for two adults or one adult and two small children), and Single or Double Slumbercoach (a smaller bedroom for one or two, without complimentary meals). Sliding partitions in double bedrooms can be opened to create a suite for larger parties.

# PASSPORT TO
# DISCOUNT TRAVEL

On the split-level Superliners, there are four types of bedrooms: Economy, Family, Deluxe, and Special. Economy Bedrooms, located on upper and lower levels of sleeper cars, are designed for one or two persons, and contain a couch which converts into a small bed, and an upper bed folding out from the wall.

Family Bedrooms have windows on both sides of the train, and occupy the entire end of the sleeping car . Each accommodates two adults and two children with a couch and two seats which turn into bunk beds; bathroom facilities are located nearby, not in the room.

Deluxe Bedrooms for two are situated in the upper level of sleeper cars. They have upper and lower berths, plus a private shower, sink, and toilet.

The Lower-Level Bedrooms on Superliners are reserved for senior citizens and anyone who may need space for a wheelchair. Most trains in Amtrak's fleet are designed with special bathroom and sleeping facilities for handicapped passengers.

Splurge on a bedroom or a roomette if you can. Coach is fun, but loud snorers, fussing babies, and all-night talkers can be annoying. Overnight travelers in coach are given a pillow, but no blanket—bring along a sweater or light blanket for warmth in winter when the heat provided may not be sufficient, or in summer when the air conditioning tends to be cranked up. In sleeper compartments, all necessary bedding is supplied, and room temperatures are controlled by individual thermostats.

Long-distance trains may encounter delays, so don't schedule a vital appointment too close to your anticipated arrival time. Since telephones are not available on every train, you may not be able to advise waiting parties of the delay.

If you are in a hurry to cover long distances, fly—but, if you have the time to relax, unwind, and enjoy the scenery, take the train.

# TRAINS

## Tours By Train

Amtrak's GREAT AMERICAN VACATIONS packages are designed as independent or escorted tours for individuals and groups. On escorted tours practically everything is taken care of, including hotels, sightseeing, baggage handling, transfers and tips. Amtrak provides travelers with information about train trips, in combination with hotel, tour and sightseeing packages.

The following are some Amtrak Tours:

• **Golden West Tour** whisks you to glamour spots such as Las Vegas, Los Angeles, and San Francisco.

• **New Orleans-Cajun-Gulf Coast Tour** traverses the deep South communities of New Orleans, Baton Rouge, Biloxi and Mobile.

• **National Parks Tours** take you to America's wonderful wilderness. A variety of customized excursions are available ranging from an overnight Yosemite Valley sojourn to the more adventurous "America the Beautiful" Tours through six national parks: Glacier, Yellowstone, Grand Teton, Zion, Bryce Canyon, and Grand Canyon.

One-day Sightseer tours or Rail/Air combination packages are available. A sample combinations tour would be: fly out West, explore the Pacific coast by train, then fly back home, saving considerable time. Another option may be to take the train cross country and fly home.

Rail/Sail and Circle Tours combine trains, buses and cruise ships in one package. These all-inclusive tours originating

# PASSPORT TO
# DISCOUNT TRAVEL

from many U.S. passenger ship ports feature hotel and sight-seeing in numerous cities. For more information about escorted, group, or independent tours, call Amtrak or your travel agent.

## Amtrak Route System

To give you an idea of areas served, here is a list of aptly named Amtrack routes:

**EASTERN TRAINS**: (Cities of origin and major stops are indicated; other cities may be served enroute. Routings may change at any time.)

**The Adirondack** – New York City to Albany and Montréal through the Hudson River Valley, the Catskill and the Adirondack Mountains, the Lake Placid region, and the St. Lawrence Seaway

**The Montréaler** – Washington, DC, to Montréal, through Baltimore; Philadelphia; New York; Hartford, and the White Mountains of New England

**The Northeast Corridor** – Boston to Washington, DC through Providence, or Springfield, MA; New Haven; New York; Philadelphia; and Baltimore

**The Colonial** – Boston to Virginia Beach, VA, with stops in Colonial Williamsburg and Norfolk

# TRAINS

**The Virginian** – New York to Richmond via Trenton, Philadelphia; Wilmington, Baltimore; and Washington, DC

**The Silver Service** – New York to Tampa and Miami with stops in New Jersey, Pennsylvania, Delaware, Maryland, Virginia, the Carolinas, Georgia, and Florida

**The Palmetto** – New York to Savannah, and Jacksonville, FL; with stops in every state enroute

**The Auto Train** – Washington, DC to Orlando, FL (actually, Lorton, VA, 15 miles south of Washington, to Sanford, FL, 30 miles north of Orlando). The auto trains takes you, your car and all the baggage you can pack into it, 700 miles non-stop.

**The Lake Shore Limited** – Boston and New York to Chicago and/or Detroit; through Albany, Syracuse, Rochester, Cleveland, Toledo, and South Bend. (Most Chicago trains offer Amtrak "thruway" bus service to Madison, WI)

**The Empire Corridor** – New York to Toronto through Niagara Falls and Buffalo

**The Broadway Limited** – New York to Chicago through Trenton, Philadelphia, Harrisburg, Pittsburgh, and Fort Wayne

**The Pennsylvanian** – New York to Pittsburgh through the Pocono and the Allegheny Mountains

# PASSPORT TO
# DISCOUNT TRAVEL

**The Capitol Limited** – Washington, DC, to Chicago through Harper's Ferry, the Blue Ridge Mountains, Pittsburgh, Canton, and Fort Wayne

**The Cardinal** – New York to Chicago through Philadelphia, Washington, DC, Charlottesville, the Shenandoah Valley; Charleston, the Ohio River Valley; Cincinnati and Indianapolis

**The Crescent** – New Orleans to New York through Birmingham, Atlanta; Charlotte, Charlottesville, and Washington, DC

**The Gulf Breeze** – Mobile, Montgomery, and Birmingham, to New York with dozens of stops along the way

## MIDWEST ROUTES

**The Chicago Hub** – Chicago to Milwaukee; Flint and Detroit, Champaign, Indianapolis, St. Louis, Kansas City, and nearly 30 other Midwest towns

**The City of New Orleans** – New Orleans to Chicago through Memphis, with connecting service to the River Cities, Kansas City, and St. Louis

# TRAINS

## WESTERN ROUTES

**The Texas Eagle** – Chicago to Austin, through Springfield, St. Louis, Little Rock, and Dallas with connections to Houston and Los Angeles

**The Sunset Limited** – New Orleans to Los Angeles, through Houston, El Paso (near Carlsbad Caverns National Park), Tucson and Phoenix

**The Southwest Chief** – Chicago to Los Angeles through Kansas City, Albuquerque, Flagstaff, past the Grand Canyon along the route of the historic Santa Fe trail

**The California Zephyr** – Chicago to Oakland and San Francisco via Omaha; Denver; the Rocky Mountains; Salt Lake City; Reno, the Sierra Madre Mountains, and Sacramento

**The Desert Wind** – Chicago to Los Angeles through Denver, Provo, Salt Lake City, and Las Vegas through Arches National Park, and the Mojave Desert

**The Pioneer** – Chicago to Seattle through Boise, Portland, and Tacoma, with connections to Vancouver, Canada

**The Empire Builder** – Seattle and Portland to Chicago through Spokane, Glacier National Park, Minneapolis, and Milwaukee

# PASSPORT TO DISCOUNT TRAVEL

**The Coast Starlight** – Los Angeles to Seattle, through Santa Barbara, San Jose, Oakland, and Eugene, with connections to San Diego and Vancouver

**The San Diegan** – San Diego to Santa Barbara with intrastate California service through San Juan Capistrano, Long Beach, Anaheim (home of Disneyland), and Los Angeles

**The San Joaquins** – Oakland to Bakersfield, through Fresno and other intrastate stops, with connecting bus service to Yosemite National Park and the Napa Valley Wine Region

## Amtrak Fares

Fares on Amtrak vary according to the length of trip, class of service and time of year. There are two types of charges: Rail Fares, covering transportation; and Accommodation Fees, assessed for options such as "Custom Class" on some intercity Metroliners, and sleeper car service on long-distance trains.

Roundtrip excursion fares are usually your best value. Offered in limited numbers on most routes and usually valid for 180 days, some are non-refundable and subject to certain restrictions and blackout periods during which they do not apply.

Amtrak's popular One-Way Plus $7 Return Fare, is an economical excursion rate offered on some direct routes involving no change of trains. For example, the one-way coach fare between New York City and Orlando is approximately $150; by adding $7 for the return, the roundtrip becomes a real bargain.

# TRAINS

The lowest fares are typically offered on off-peak travel days, so plan a second choice of dates and times in case your first choice is unavailable. To obtain one of the limited number of discount fares, make your reservations well in advance. Ask for any less expensive or promotional fares currently available. If your plans change, don't forget to cancel your train and tour reservations immediately to obtain the maximum refund.

For longer journeys, consider All Aboard America fares, which apply in or between the East, Midwest, and West regions of the country. For one fare, you can travel anywhere within one, between two, or through all three regions, with up to three stopovers along the way. You can travel to one city, stay a few days, then go to two other cities before returning.

You can cover a lot of ground with these regional fares. For example, if you purchase an Eastern one-region ticket, you could travel North from New York City to Montréal, go South to New Orleans, and stop in Washington, DC on you way back to New York.

On a Western one-region pass, you might travel from Los Angeles to Denver, Salt Lake City, and San Francisco, all for one fare. Availability may be limited, so reserve early. If you think big enough, a flexible, inter-regional itinerary, can take you on a complete circle trip around the U.S.A. for a single fare!

Regional passes may be purchased year-round for Coach as well as Sleeper accommodations. Fares fluctuate with the seasons—Summer is the most expensive. One-region passes cost about $180 through mid-May; two-region trips are approximately $230; and three-region roundtrips, $260. One or two children between the ages of 2 and 15 accompanied by an adult travel for half-price.

Reservations are generally required for sleeper cars, custom cars, and long-distance coach seats. Most discount fares

# PASSPORT TO
# DISCOUNT TRAVEL

have advance purchase requirements similar to those of airlines. Purchase your tickets by a specific deadline, or risk losing your reservation.

Reserve sleepers or bedrooms three to four months in advance, because they fill up rapidly in Summer, Fall and on holidays. Trains are least crowded in Winter, so bargain fares are more plentiful. Call Amtrak for details at 1-800 USA-RAIL.

The following chart shows sample fares on some long-distance trains in the West. (All fares are approximate and subject to change without notice.)

**Sample Fares:**    **COAST STARLIGHT**

| | L.A.-Seattle (33 hours; 1,388 miles) | Oakland-Seattle (22 hours; 923 miles) |
|---|---|---|
| Coach (one-way) | $145 | $142 |
| Coach (roundtrip) | $152-$221 | $149-$221 |
| Economy BR (one-way) | $311-$380 | $269-$341 |
| Family BR (one-way) | $416-485 | $337-$409 |
| Deluxe BR (one-way) | $482-$551 | $391-$463 |

**Samples Fares:**    **CALIFORNIA ZEPHYR**

| | Chicago-Oakland (51 hours; 2,422 miles) | Denver-Oakland (33 hours; 1,384 miles) |
|---|---|---|
| Coach (one-way) | $196 | $145 |
| Coach (roundtrip) | $203-$298 | $152-$221 |

# TRAINS

| | | |
|---|---|---|
| Economy BR | | |
| (one-way) | $483-$578 | $361-$430 |
| Family BR | | |
| (one-way) | $595-$690 | $446-$515 |
| Deluxe BR | | |
| (one-way) | $792-$887 | $596-$665 |

## Other Discount Fares

Amtrak discounts one-way fares for a variety of travelers: senior citizens, military personnel, handicapped persons, and groups of 15 or more. Travelers over 62 years of age enjoy a 15% discount on lowest available fares—some date restrictions apply. Disabled passengers receive a 25% discount on all regular one-way coach fares year round, except on the Metroliner (between Washington, DC and New York) and on the Auto Train. Any number of youngsters, ages 2 through 11, accompanied by an adult pay half the adult fare. A limit of two children ages 12 through 15, may travel for half fare when accompanied by an adult.

All passengers are eligible for reduced rates on sleeper car accommodations during off-peak "value seasons" on specific routes. Check with Amtrak for details.

Under Amtrak's cancellation policy, unused sleeper accommodations, not canceled at least 2 days before departure, carry substantial penalties. Tour packages including accommodations must be canceled before the deadline or you may incur a penalty of at least one night's hotel charge. For specifics contact Amtrak or your tour operator.

For more information about fares and rail travel in the U.S., read RAIL VENTURES by Jack Swanson, Wayfinder Press.

# PASSPORT TO DISCOUNT TRAVEL

## Luggage

Amtrak allows two carry-on bags per coach passenger. Travelers in bedrooms or roomettes may take as much luggage as can fit safely into the room. Since large suitcases are cumbersome, consider checking them. Carry a small overnight bag with clothes, toiletries, medications, and personal items you may need during the trip. Always be careful of your belongings. Amtrak assumes no liability for lost or stolen carry-on luggage or possessions.

Each ticketed passenger may check, without charge, up to three bags not exceeding 75 lbs. per bag or 150 lbs. total; boxes or cartons should not exceed 50 lbs. Every item must be clearly labeled with your name and phone number. Amtrak accepts responsibility for checked baggage up to a certain dollar amount; call for details about coverage. Extra insurance may be purchased at check-in. Special handling charges may be assessed for items such as skis, bicycles, golf clubs, and musical instruments. Pets are not allowed, with the exception of guide animals such as seeing-eye dogs.

Most stations supply luggage handcarts free, or for a nominal fee. "Red Cap" luggage handlers are on hand to assist at most large stations. Although tipping is not mandatory, it's always a good idea to reward those who make your trip more enjoyable. Don't forget the porter—about $3 to $5 a night is appropriate.

Most Amtrak trains have at least one coach and sleeper car equipped for handicapped persons. Amtrak's Special Services Desk reserves wheelchairs for use at the terminal and on the train, and will also handle special meal requests for kosher, vegetarian, or restricted-diet food, if given at least 72 hours notice.

# TRAINS

## THE ROMANCE OF THE RAILS

To illustrate what sleeper cars are like, here's a story about an acquaintance's first overnight train trip.

He was a salesman from New York who had just completed his rounds in Miami. Since it was Friday, and he was not due back to work until Monday, he decided to take the train, rather than fly. The trip would take about 28 hours, so he reserved a roomette. He didn't know what to expect, but thought it would be more comfortable than sitting upright in a coach seat all night. He also liked the idea of having his own bedroom, toilet, and privacy.

When he arrived at the station he saw his train, *The Silver Meteor,* preparing to streak up the East Coast through large cities and small to the largest of all, New York. It had 21 cars: three engines, six baggage cars, six coaches, three sleepers, two lounges, and a dining car.

He was intrigued by the scene inside the train as the conductor escorted him to his sleeper. Walking through several coach cars with individual semi-reclining seats filled with soldiers, students, couples and kids, he congratulated himself for his wisdom in reserving a roomette.

Passing through the lounge car, he quickly glanced at the cocktail menu making a mental note to return later. Like intruders in the night, he and the conductor slipped through the baggage/mail car staffed by an armed guard. They entered the dining car, went through the kitchen where chefs were working, exited the restaurant area, and finally came to the first sleeper car. It was a long walk!

Entering the first sleeper, he felt as though he had found a home at last. Wrong! Two more cars remained. This one

# PASSPORT TO
# DISCOUNT TRAVEL

contained family suites, each with twin double bunk beds, sitting room, and shower. After seeing the hurly-burly of coach, he was impressed by the quiet and relative luxury of this part of the train and began to imagine how lovely his roomette would be.

He didn't have to fantasize for long. Arriving at his car– –#2202—"The Richmonder," he entered its hushed, darkened corridor, lined with curtain-covered doorways. Stopping in front of one of the doors, the conductor drew open the curtain, turned the key, and ushered him to his new world of Amtrak.

The roomette! He took one step forward— that was it. The room was so tiny, he couldn't take another step without hitting the opposite wall. The room was 3 1/2 feet wide and 6 1/2 feet long. Not exactly the spacious dimensions he had envisioned after seeing the large family rooms in the other sleeper cars.

Along the entire length of the outer wall and half the height of the room was a huge, tinted window with a pull-down shade. Glancing out at the flurry of preparation for the train's 1,500 mile journey to the Land of the Yankees (and the Mets), he was glad to be a part of it, if only for a day.

He then remembered leaving his suitcase out in the hallway. He grabbed it, brought it into the room only to discover there was no more room left. Something had to be done. He simply was not going to spend the next 28 hours with a suitcase in the middle of the floor.

Looking skyward in exasperation, he noticed hanging from the ceiling, a luggage rack sturdy enough to hold several suitcases. Putting his bag in its proper place, he then plopped down on the rather comfortable couchette—a small couch similar to a love seat—sat back and placed his feet on the black footstool conveniently located opposite the couchette.

"Where is the bed and the private toilet I paid for?" he

mused. There were lots of latches, catches, and hooks, but no signs of a bed or toilet. He unfastened one latch, and a small closet revealed itself, so he unpacked some clothes and hung them in it.

Turning back, he tripped over what looked like a tunafish can on the floor. Stepping on it, the little black "footstool" flushed! Upon closer inspection, he realized the "footstool" was actually his toilet, with the lid closed.

Relieved, he began exploring the roomette's other nooks and crannies. He found a tiny cabinet perfect for his razor and toothbrush; another one revealed the toilet paper, something he was glad to have found when he did rather than having to search for it later.

Spying a large handle on the wall next to the toilet, he reached up and turned it—the wall attacked him, nearly knocking him over. What had apparently been a wall had instantly turned into a full-size metal sink with all the trimmings—a chained rubber drain-stopper, tiny paper cups, mini-soap bars, and hot and cold running water.

So, he thought, what more could a man want in a sleeper, except a bed? But where was it? He was too embarrassed to ask. Exasperated, he slumped on the couch and looked heavenward for help, and once again, it arrived.

Noticing two latches at opposite ends of the couch, he unclasped first one, then the other, and down came a slender bed already made up with sheets, blankets and pillows. Barely 6 feet long and very narrow, it allowed little room for rolling over.

Now he was getting good at this! As he sat on the bed, he spotted the thermostat and a small ceiling fan. Finding everything he needed, except food and drink, he returned to the dining car for a relaxing meal, with a much needed glass of wine.

After dinner he dropped by the lounge for a nightcap. He

---

spied an attractive young lady sitting alone, and he struck up a conversation.

She mentioned the sad fact that she was going to have to spend the entire night in the noisy, uncomfortable coach compartment. Being the gentleman he was, he ordered some champagne and invited her to join him for an after-dinner drink in his roomette. She accepted.

Ah! The romance of the rails! According to my friend, they conversed while sipping champagne, and watched day turn into night. The sun set, the moon rose, and the stars came out as they were gently soothed by the sound of the wheels and the rhythmic swaying of the train. They talked for hours, enjoyed some laughs, and became good friends. Overall, a most pleasant evening.

The Amtrak commercial is right. There is something about a train!

## VIA: CANADA'S TRAINS

Oh, Canada! Majestic country of the north... land of Mounties and mountains, maples and Maritime Provinces, modern cities and magnificent vistas. What better way to experience the splendor of this mighty country than through Canada's marvelous network of rails?

VIA, The Canadian Passenger Rail System crosses the entire continent from the Atlantic shores of Nova Scotia to the Pacific coast of British Columbia, through vast plains, mountain

# TRAINS

ranges, and forests. By following some simple rules, you can view Canada's remarkable scenery and experience her incredible diversity with savings of up to 50% off regular coach fares. To obtain discounts on VIA when traveling through selected regions, go on off-peak days or use the Canrailpass.

## The Canadian Route System

Before learning more about how to get discounts, let's see where Canada's trains go.

### REGIONAL ROUTES –

#### • ATLANTIC CANADA.

Four full-service trains link the Maritime Provinces of Nova Scotia and New Brunswick to eastern and central Canada, with connections through Ottawa, Toronto and southwestern Ontario. Most trains have lounge and dining cars, coach, day-niter coach (with larger, more comfortable reclining seats), and sleeper accommodations. Some routes include cities in addition to those mentioned. All routes and services are subject to change without notice. For complete details, contact VIA (800-561-3949, from the continental U.S.). Consult local directories for VIA's phone numbers when calling in Canada, or use the applicable toll-free number in the Appendix.

**The Atlantic** – Halifax to Montréal via Saint John and Sherbrooke

# PASSPORT TO DISCOUNT TRAVEL

**The Ocean** – Halifax to Montréal, Mont-Joli, Campbellton and Moncton

**The Chaleur** – Montréal to Gaspé via Rivi'ere du-Loup and Matapédia

**The Corridor** – Québec City to Windsor via Montréal, Ottawa, Kingston, Toronto, and Kitchener, with connections to Hamilton and Niagara Falls

The Corridor's first class features express check-in and boarding through special "VIA 1" gates, more comfortable seats, hot meals with complimentary beverages and cocktails, and free newspapers and magazines.


• **WESTERN CANADA**

**The Canadian** –Toronto to Vancouver via Winnipeg, Saskatoon, Edmonton, Jasper and Kamloops

**The Skeena** – Jasper to Prince Rupert via Prince George with links to The Canadian

Reservations are required for all "VIA 1" first class seats, sleeper car accommodations, and dayniter seats between Ontario, Québec, and the Maritimes. Reservations are canceled if tickets are not paid for by a specified ticketing deadline. Coach seats are guaranteed, but not pre-assigned, when tickets are purchased. Reservations and ticket purchases can be made up to six months before departure. Smoking and non-smoking sections are provided.

# TRANS

Passengers needing wheelchairs or special assistance should call VIA at least 24 hours in advance; those needing special meals, or medical equipment should give 48 hours notice.

Pillows and blankets are not given to overnight passengers in coach, but are supplied to dayniter passengers. All necessary bedding is provided in sleeper cars.

For information about baggage restrictions, customs duties, immigration requirements, and other concerns, contact VIA through one of their toll-free numbers.

## Discount Fares

Passengers can save up to 40% on many VIA routes by traveling during off-peak times. Children up to 12 years old, senior citizens over 60, and students may save even more:

(1) Travel within the Maritime Provinces of Nova Scotia and New Brunswick, or along the Québec City to Windsor corridor any day except Friday and Sunday, and save 40% on regular coach fares. Seats are limited at this reduced rate, and tickets must be purchased at least five days in advance.

These fares are usually not valid during national holidays, such as Christmas, Easter, and Thanksgiving. (Canada's Thanksgiving is celebrated the second Sunday in October.) Other national holidays in Canada are: Victoria Day (3rd Monday in May), Canada Day (July 1), and Labour Day (1st Monday in September). The Christmas holiday ( from mid-December to early January) has the longest blackout period for the 40% discount fares.

(2) Travel any day on trains between the Maritime Provinces of Atlantic Canada and the eastern corridor cities or the

# PASSPORT TO DISCOUNT TRAVEL

Gaspé region, and save 40% on standard coach charges, if you buy your ticket at least seven days in advance. These discounts are not valid over the Christmas holidays, or during the summer (June 1 to early September). Blackout periods can vary, and may change at any time, so contact VIA before making your plans.

## Senior Citizen and Student Fares

Throughout the VIA system, full-time students, and senior citizens over 60, receive an extra 10% off fares, in addition to 40% savings, normal for advance purchase of "off-peak" travel in selected regions. Without advance purchase, seniors and students enjoy a straight 10% off full fares.

## Children's Fares

Children, 2 to 12, accompanied by an adult, can ride free in coach (one child per adult). Additional children of similar age traveling with an adult, as well as unaccompanied children 8 to 12 years of age, travel for half the lowest applicable adult fare. Children under 8 must travel with an adult. Dayniter, first-class, and sleeper car charges are extra. Consult VIA for restrictions concerning unaccompanied children.

## Canrailpass

The Canrailpass is economical, convenient, flexible, and reasonably priced. It is perfect for someone planning to stop at various cities in Canada. Compared to the cost of individual one-

# TRAINS

way or roundtrip fares, the pass is a bargain; travel during low season, and save even more.

For one price, you get unlimited coach class travel on Canadian passenger trains for up to 30 consecutive days. Purchase either a system-wide pass for coast to coast or western travel, or an Eastern Canada pass covering cities such as Montréal, Ottawa, Toronto, Halifax, and Niagara Falls. Set your own pace and make as many stops as you wish within the limit.

On most routes, advance reservations are a must, especially during peak seasons. Always reserve seats on the most popular routes, such as Montréal to Toronto, and Edmonton to Vancouver.

The chart on the next page shows approximate fares for the Canrailpass, quoted in U.S. dollars based on conversion rates from Canadian to U.S. currency as of presstime. Passes purchased in the U.S. at travel agencies or Canrail Outlets are generally less expensive than if purchased in Canada.

Prices and "high" and "low" seasons are subject to change. High season usually runs from June 1 through Sept. 30; low season, Oct. 1 through May 31.

Check VIA for current prices, seasonal variations, and any restrictions which may apply.

**CANRAILPASS SAMPLE PRICES:**

| System Wide | Youth (Under 25) | Adult |
| --- | --- | --- |
| High Season | $345 | $375 |
| Low Season | $216 | $256 |

# PASSPORT TO
# DISCOUNT TRAVEL

| Eastern | Youth (Under 25) | Adult |
|---------|------------------|-------|
| High Season | $187 | $230 |
| Low Season | $136 | $156 |

## EUROPEAN TRAINS

European trains have an excellent reputation for reliability, punctuality, and comfort. They feature tens of thousands of daily departures, using some of the fastest, most modern equipment anywhere.

Europe's efficient rail network covers thousands of miles, transporting people into the heart of many cities close to hotels, shops, and restaurants. The system also takes travelers to remote rural towns and secluded areas, some of which are only accessible by train.

There are hundreds of trains to choose from: rugged Alpine country rails, rapid commuter coaches, and luxurious intercity expresses, such as the nostalgic Orient Express, between London and Venice and The EuroCity network, linking 200 major European cities via state-of-the-art trains.

Traveling by train, plane, or automobile in Europe is a personal preference. Each mode of transportation has its advantages and disadvantages. Generally, going by train is the fastest way to cover medium distances (about 200 to 400 miles). For instance, the Geneva/Paris express covers the 391 miles in just three hours. It would take twice as long and be more exhausting to go by car. Flying may be quicker, but much more expensive. If cost is a consideration, there is no question you will save

# TRAINS

money traveling with a Eurailpass, or with a single-country railpass.

To promote tourism, many European cities offer bargains on their municipal transportation systems. They sell discount cards, which, for a specific number of days, provide unlimited access to local public transportation, and reduced admissions to some museums and popular tourist attractions.

These cards are a must if you plan to do a lot of sightseeing or traveling within a city. Some municipalities offer several types of cards depending on length of stay or distance covered. Consider your options carefully before purchasing. Some cards must be bought in the United States before departure, while others are sold only at the destination. For details, contact the tourist board representing the city or country you'll be visiting.

## The Train to the Top of Europe

One of those hard-to-reach places, accessible only by train, is the very top of Europe—the spectacular Oberland Mountain Range, in Switzerland's Bernese region. These mountainous peaks, running like a spine through the middle of the Continent, include most of Europe's highest summits: Eiger, Monch, Jungfrau, and Jungfraujoch, among others.

One train is not enough to reach the top of Europe—it takes three. The first train departs from Interlachen, a lovely lakefront town deep in an Alpine valley. It winds its way up along the base of the mountains through pastures and meadows of edelweiss to Grimelwald, a picture-postcard town facing Eiger Alp towering thousands of feet above.

# PASSPORT TO
# DISCOUNT TRAVEL

There, you transfer to a narrower-track train which climbs through steep passes, twists around thundering waterfalls, and finally stopping at a high plateau: the Eiger Station. This spot, halfway to the peaks, is a combination train depot, restaurant, and rescue shelter for skiers and climbers. The air is noticeably thinner here.

At Eiger Station, the third train awaits. This rugged mountain rail's sure-footedness on the steep face of Jungfraujoch comes from gears tightly clutching a cable under the track. The angle of climb approaches 45 degrees, so the floors of this cleverly-designed train are built at a sharp angle, allowing passengers and conductors to move about without leaning precipitously.

The entire multi-train journey to the top of Europe takes about two hours, and is worth every minute. If you reach the peak on a clear day, before the clouds build up, the view is both spectacular and humbling. The awesome, sweeping panorama of the Alps unfolds before you—in the distance to the south are Italy and France, and to the north, Germany and Austria. The farms and villages thousands of feet below appear minuscule.

At the summit, you may be greeted by friendly St. Bernard dogs. These playful lumbering animals, housed at a rescue center, await calls by the Swiss Ski Patrol to aid those clumsy less sure-footed animals ... humans!

If all the excitement, the cold (even in summer), and the thin air at these altitudes make you light-headed, you may relax and regain your equilibrium inside the summit building which houses a cafeteria, museum, movie theater, and a gourmet restaurant renowned for its fine food, wine, and appropriate name... the Restaurant At The Top Of Europe. From its windows, you can gaze upon an extremely rare sight: a massive mountain glacier—a mile-wide river of ice—slicing through the mountains towards the valley below.

# TRAINS

If you're lucky, you may catch a glimpse of several intrepid skiers off in the distance "shushing" down the face of the glacier. What a place, this top of Europe—the glare of pristine snow, the bite of crystal air, the dizzying view, the way the mountains kiss the sky—and it's all yours to enjoy, courtesy of European trains!

## The Eurailpass

When visiting the Continent, explore the advantages of a Eurailpass, or "national" railpasses. Whether touring one country or several, you can find a variety of passes designed to fit your budget, schedule, and length of stay. Trains, rental cars, hotels, sightseeing, shopping, and even insurance are included in many of these programs.

When visiting only one or two countries, consider purchasing country-specific railpasses such as those of Austria, Belgium, France, England, Germany, Ireland, Italy, Spain, Switzerland, the Netherlands, and the countries of Scandanavia— Denmark, Finland, Norway, and Sweden. Get full details from EURAILPASS, P.O. Box 325, Old Greenwich, CT 06870 (800-722-7151); RAIL EUROPE, whose American booking agent is George Ferguson and Company, 7215 Sawmill Rd., Suite 50, Dublin, OH 43017-5001 (614-793-7650); or THE EUROPEAN PLANNING AND RAIL GUIDE, 257 Meade Court, Ann Arbor, MI 48105 (800-441-2387, Ext. 80).

Eurailpasses provide unlimited travel on more than 100,000 miles of track through 17 countries. In addition to those mentioned previously, Greece, Hungary, Luxembourg and Portugal, but not Great Britain, are also included. Eurail and Britrail passes may be purchased before leaving the United

# PASSPORT TO
# DISCOUNT TRAVEL

States or at Eurail Aid offices in London as well as on the continent. Passes bought in Europe must be paid for in local currency and cost about 10% more. Single-country passes may be purchased in America, or in the country of use upon presentation of your passport and transatlantic return ticket.

The Eurailpass is the most complete and most expensive of all European train passes, consequently, it's best used for long distance travel. Regular train tickets are a better value if you are traveling short distances. Consider the Eurailpass if you intend to cover an average of about 100 miles a day, or about 1,500 miles in two weeks, 2,500 miles in three weeks, 3,000 miles in a month or 4,500 miles in three months.

For information about usual discounts and bargains contact the railways directly, or refer to SALTZMAN'S RAIL GUIDES, at your library or local bookstore.

## EURAIL PROGRAMS

(1) **The Eurailpass** is valid for unlimited first class travel throughout nearly 20 countries for a specified number of days. It allows free, or deeply discounted transportation on many bus lines; on "steamers" cruising the Rhine, the Danube, and several Swiss lakes; and on ferries between Finland and Sweden, Ireland and France, and Italy and Greece.

A Eurailpass is priced according to length of time, not amount of use. Examples of consecutive-day price options are listed below. Fares quoted are "per person." They are approximations only, and are not actual prices. (Exact fares must be obtained from your travel agent or Eurail). Children ages 4 through 11 pay half fare; kids under 4 travel free.

# TRAINS

15 Days =$400 / One Month = $620
21 Days= $500 / Two Months= $850
Three Months = $1,050

(2) **The Eurail Saverpass**, ideal for families or couples, discounts 15-days of first class transportation for two or more people. (At least three people must travel together on a Saverpass between April 1 and September 30.) This pass provides all the privileges of the regular Eurailpass, for about $100 less, or approximately $300 per person.

(3) **The Eurail Flexipass**, an even more economical way to travel by train, ferry and steamer, is intended for those who plan to stay in one location for a few days, rather than heading to a new destination every day.

On the Flexipass, you get the benefits of the Eurailpass and save money, because you pay for fewer days of travel. The Eurail Flexipass is used for transportation on a certain number of days over a specific length of time. For example:

- 5 days of rail travel within 15 days (approx. $230)
- 9 days of rail travel within 21 days (approx. $400)
- 14 days of rail travel within one month (approx. $500)

(4) **The Eurail Youthpass and Eurail Youth Flexipass**, for people under the age of 26, is perfect for students on vacation. Offering everything the Eurailpass does, except accommodations are in second class, where most Europeans sit. The Eurail Youthpass costs approximately $425 for one month of unlimited travel and $560 for two months.

The Eurail Youth Flexipass costs about $350 for 15 individual days of rail travel , and about $550 for 30 days of rail travel within three months.

# PASSPORT TO
# DISCOUNT TRAVEL

(5) **The EurailDrive Pass** offers the combined use of rail and rental cars in all of Eurail's participating countries except Hungary. The program allows four days of rail and three days of auto transportation. For two people traveling together, the per person rate starts at about $270 for a compact, $290 for a mid-size, and $300 for a full-size automobile. The car must be returned to the country from which it was rented. Each additional rail day beyond four, costs about $40, and each extra day of car rental costs between $50 to $75 depending on auto size. Solo travelers may purchase this pass at a slightly higher price.

Eurailpass does not guarantee a seat on a train, ferry, or steamer without reservations, a must for coach compartments, bedrooms, and roomettes. The price of a Eurailpass does not cover extra charges assessed for sleepers, couchettes (deluxe coach seats), food, beverages, luggage handling, port taxes and supplementary fees on steamers and ferries. Reservations for sleepers, costing approximately $100 more, must be made 24 hours in advance, but save the expense of a hotel room for the night.

Making reservations at busy train stations can be time-consuming; lines may be long and slow-moving. Unless you know exactly what you want, you may have to move to another line for information, because the ticket seller may not provide it. Sometimes you cannot book a European train by name or departure time only, you must know the designated number of the train. Plan ahead by checking train schedules, services and amenities in the THOMAS COOK EUROPEAN TIME-TABLE available in libraries and bookstores (about $20), or by calling 800-367-7984.

A free traveler's guide, with railroad maps and timetables, is available from EURAIL, Box 10383, Stamford, CT 06904-2383, or call 900-990-RAIL (about $2.00 a minute).

# TRAINS

To save time make your train reservation at a European travel agency; they can give you schedules, assign seats, and issue your ticket in just a few minutes—usually at no extra charge. Most U.S. travel agents are not equipped to handle European train bookings. Your local travel agent can, however, obtain a Eurail pass for you, which must be purchased in the United States or Canada before departing for Europe.

Eurail passes are strictly non-transferable. You may be asked by a conductor to show your pass along with your passport at any time, so keep them both handy. Make a copy of the validity dates and serial numbers of your Eurail pass and passport in case they get lost or stolen.

## NATIONAL RAIL PASSES

### France Railpass

Parlez-vous français? Tant mieux!

Whether you speak the language or not, the culture of France can be enjoyed in any language! Paris—the City of Lights—is a cosmopolitan capital where tourists converge year-round to experience its culture, cuisine, and architectural marvels. A few of its famous sites are the Cathedral of Notre Dame, the Arc de Triumph, the Eiffel Tower, and the Louvre—home of some of the world's finest art. Stroll past the fancy shops on the Champs-Élysées, or visit the nearby Palace of Versailles where Mozart, as a child, entertained the king of France. Don't forget Napoleon's tomb, the Rodin Museum, the

# PASSPORT TO
# DISCOUNT TRAVEL

Paris Opera House, the eerie underground catacombs, and the many other museums, cathedrals, restaurants, and shops which make Paris splendidly unique.

Equally enticing are the languid, watercolor landscapes of southern France, the rustic towns of the east, and the high-rolling resorts of the jet set strung like pearls along the French Riviera.

To get from Paris to the Riviera or almost anywhere else in the country, board any of the 15,000 daily departures using a **France Railpass.** For as little as $100 per person, you can zoom between major cities at nearly 300 miles an hour on one of the world's fastest trains, the famous TGV (Train 'a Grande Vitesse). A minimal reservation surcharge is assessed when using your **France Railpass** on the TGV. When exploring France's countryside or experiencing the charm of its cities, you can economize with a railpass' discounted fares and free extras, such as complimentary roundtrip transfers between Paris and either Orly or Poissy-Charles de Gaulle airport; one-day second class passes valid on the entire Parisian inner-city subway and bus system; 30% to 50% off scenic cruises on the Seine; 50% discounts on certain private touring railways; and savings on entrance fees at some museums.

The following options are available:

• **The France Rail Flexipass**, available in both first and second class, is good for any 4 days of transportation within 15 days, or any 9 days within 30. Prices start at about $100 for adults, and $60 for children, 4 through 11. Children under 4 ride free.

• **The France Rail and Drive Pass** provides visitors with virtually limitless flexibility. These tickets allow travel

# TRAINS

whenever and wherever you wish using a combination of trains and automobiles. Travel days need not be consecutive.

The **Rail and Drive Pass** offers two packages: seven days of transportation within two weeks, including four days of unlimited train travel and three days' use of a rental car; or 15 days of travel within a month, including nine days on the rails and six days in the car. Prices start at about $150 per person, based on two people traveling together. First class upgrades, larger cars, and single supplements are extra.

• **The France Rail, Drive, and Fly Pass** gives you maximum mobility with its two programs featuring three modes of transportation. The first includes four days of travel in either 1st or 2nd class on the entire French network, three days unlimited use of a  rental car, and one day flying within France on Air Inter, a domestic airline serving 30 cities. The second, for more extensive sightseeing provides a month of travel, including nine days on the train, three days in a car, and two days in the friendly skies of Air Inter. Travel days on any single mode of transportation need not be consecutive. Prices start at about $450 per person, based on two or more people traveling together.

With a **Rail, Drive, and Fly Pass** fly to a distant city in France, rent a car at the airport, explore the surroundings,  drop-off the car at a train station, then take the speedy TGV to a different city where another rental car awaits.

Or start by staying a few days in Paris, hop a train to a city such as Nice, Bordeaux or Strasbourg, drive a rental car to explore the outlying areas, then fly to northern France for a glimpse of the English Channel and a taste of real Belgian waffles. Or, as an alternative, fly to southern France for a view of the Mediterranean and a taste of the high-life on the Riviera. Use the final portion of the pass to fly back to Paris and connect with an international flight home.

# PASSPORT TO
# DISCOUNT TRAVEL

For guided tours, try the **Franceshrinkers'** sightseeing excursions from Paris, by rail and motorcoach. Led by knowledgeable English-speaking guides, tours are sold to **France Railpass** holders at discounts of 10% to 40%, and may be reserved when purchasing the pass. Lunch is usually served at an inn or restaurant along the way. Once confirmed by **Franceshrinkers**, tours are guaranteed to depart as scheduled, unless circumstances beyond their control cause a delay. This is a great way to see the highlights of France quickly and easily!

For more information, call your travel agent, or Abercrombie and Kent for a copy of the GREAT BRITAIN AND EUROPE EXPRESS brochure (800-323-7308), or contact FRANCE RAIL, 226 Westchester Ave., White Plains, NY 10604 (800-484-4000). The France Rail number handles calls from all over the United States. You may have to wait up to 15 minutes before speaking to an agent.

When planning to travel on French routes with frequent service, seats are usually available; you generally do not have to make reservations on those trains prior to leaving the United States, however, you should make reservations in France.

## Britrail Pass

Hail, Britannia! Former ruler of the seas and the master of an empire upon which the sun never set, Britain rules the rails with remarkable travel values throughout this enchanting island realm.

The beauty and stoic charm of England is legendary. London brims with history, royalty and hearty British cheer. Whether by its magnificent Buckingham Palace, Windsor Castle, the historic Tower of London or Westminster Abbey where world-famous poets, authors, and statesmen rest, or by the

# TRAINS

treasures contained in London's renown museums, England's capital continually captivates visitors' hearts. Its world famous theater, its friendly pubs and fascinating people are fun to know. Yet England's countryside, and the rest of the United Kingdom, are equally enticing. Enchanting castles, mysterious moors, magnificent mansions, defiant cliffs and rolling, idyllic meadows await the adventurous. Enjoy it all with the **BritRail Pass,** an excellent value for unlimited travel on virtually all the intercity trains and intracity buses in England, Scotland, and Wales.

There are a variety of BritRail passes, ranging from an 8-day **Youth Pass** (about $175) to a deluxe 30-day **Adult Pass** (approximately $700). Travelers over 60 get a special rate, while children, 5 to 15, ride at half-price. The Britrail Flexipass permits trail travel any four days in eight, any eight days in 15, or any 15 days in a month.

An exciting option is the two-country **BritFrance Pass,** a combination ticket, starting at about $250 standard, and $340 first class, for use on the transportation networks of both nations. For one fare travel the entire French and British rail systems, and cross the English Channel roundtrip on the famous high-speed hovercraft between Dover and Calais or Bologne. The pass offers unlimited rail travel any five days out of 15 in both countries for about $350 first class, and $250 standard. Young people, 12 through 24, pay around $200. Extended passes are offered for 10 days of transportation within 30, for about $500 first class, $400 standard, and $300 youth.

The **BritRail Pass** also discounts **Britainshrinkers'** rail and motorcoach tours to manor homes, museums, and memorable locations such as Stonehenge, the Cotswolds, and classic castles. A travel agent can give you more details, or call BRITRAIL (212-599-5400).

# PASSPORT TO
# DISCOUNT TRAVEL

## German Railpass

Consider the grandeur of Germany: history harking back to the Roman Empire; centuries-old walled cities; cosmopolitan Munich with its annual Oktoberfest; culturally-thriving Berlin; the Rhine River with its beautiful castles and lush vineyards; the majestic Alps; the mysterious Black Forest; terrific touring roads; timeless villages, and much more.

Germany's state-of-the-art rail system, known for its speed, convenience, and dependability, offers unlimited travel to most of these destinations. Prior to German reunification, this standard of excellence in the rail system was associated more with West Germany than East Germany. Efforts are being made to standardize the quality of all transportation services.

In Germany and throughout much of Europe, you'll notice that train stations are different from those in the U.S. Many European train stations are 19th-century architectural masterpieces playing a prominent role in the social life of their cities. Located in the heart of town, they are centers for shopping, dining, civic activities, and tourist information.

Among the many restaurants and shops clustered around stations, one invariably finds a tourist aid office, marked with the prominent "i" sign, indicating "information". Descriptions of nearby hotels, guesthouses, and eateries are posted outside, along with photos, phone numbers, and prices. This can be a lifesaver if you arrive when the tourist office is closed.

Beginning at $150, the **German Railpass** lets you cover more than 13,000 miles and visit nearly 6,000 cities and towns. The network features many modern, intercity expresses, local trains, and ferries connecting intercity bus lines to reach outlying towns and villages.

# TRAINS

The **German Railpass** and **Flexipass** provide all-inclusive travel for four, nine, or sixteen days including free transportation on Rhine steamers between Dusseldorf and Mainz, and on steamers cruising the Mainz and Moselle Rivers. They also provide discounts on various lake steamers and many city and castle tours. Travel free on certain major bus lines, including those on the historic "Castle Road" and the scenic "Romantic Road," which pass picturesque castles, medieval walled-cities, and Roman ruins.

Prices in second class start at about $130 for five days ($90 for Eurail Youth Pass holders), and $200 for 10 days ($120 for youths). With the reunification, a railpass becomes an even greater bargain, taking you well beyond its former limits in West Germany, and deep into the expanded nation. For the first time ever, unlimited travel in former East Germany is now possible with a charge added to the cost of either a **German Railpass**, or a **Eurailpass**. For GERMAN RAIL information, call 212-308-3103 or 800-223-6036.

## Swiss Pass

Spectacular Switzerland!—Europe's tallest mountains, massive glaciers, crystalline lakes, Alpine vistas, flower-filled meadows, picturesque farms, glamorous resorts, cosmopolitan cities, top-notch craftsmanship, superb cheeses, unsurpassed chocolates, and some of the world's richest banks.

See Switzerland by train to fully appreciate this magnificent country. In summer, swim or sail on freshwater lakes fed by graceful waterfalls cascading down surrounding snow-capped mountains. Flowers bloom everywhere—on mountainsides, along roadsides, and in windowboxes outside many buildings. In

# PASSPORT TO DISCOUNT TRAVEL

winter, ski a steep trail, skirt across a glacier, skate on a frozen lake, and slide in a horse-drawn sleigh before sitting by a warm fire in the evening sipping a fine wine and supping on a savory fondue.

**The Swiss Pass** takes you on fast, clean, efficient trains into the heart of Switzerland's famous cities, through breathtaking scenery ranging from the snow-covered Alps to picturesque pastures to palm trees along the southern border with Italy. Travel is unlimited on the entire Swiss Federated Railway, and on many private scenic railroads such as the "Glacier Express" and the "Panorama Express." Also included is passage on most ferries, buses, cable cars, and many lake steamers, as well as municipal transit systems in over 20 cities.

You receive 25% to 50% discounts on mountain railroads and aerial cars traversing otherwise inaccessible peaks— a most unforgettable way to travel. These safe, dependable gondolas are pulled up mountainsides on cables. Suspended thousands of feet in the air with the clouds above and the birds below, you enjoy incomparable views in every direction.

The **Swiss Pass** is available in first and second class for 8, 15, or 30 days. Prices start at about $160; children under 16, accompanied by a parent, travel free.

Some options are:

• **The Swiss Flexipass** provides all the amenities of a **Swiss Pass** and costs less, because it is valid only three days in 15. It allows freedom to spend extra time in favorite locations without feeling compelled to travel each day to get the most mileage out of your ticket. Prices are approximately $130 second class and $200 first class.

# TRAINS

• **The Swiss Card** is a variation of the railpass designed for even less extensive travels supplying roundtrip tickets between any Swiss airport or border town and any single destination within the country. You must complete each leg of your trip within a single day. The Swiss Card also slashes 50% off most Swiss national railroads, mountain trains, buses, and steamers. Valid for 30 days, the Swiss Card costs about $80 for second class or $110 for first.

• **The Swiss Rail 'N' Drive Pass** permits three days of train and two days of auto transportation during a 15-day period. Train privileges are the same as the **Swiss Pass**. The rental car comes with unlimited mileage and free drop-off at designated sites within the country. Prices begin at around $150 per person, for two or more traveling together; about $220 for singles. To learn more about Swiss Rail, contact EURAIL (800-722-7151).

## Scanrail Pass

Scandinavia—magical land of fjords, furs, and fairy tales, home of the legendary midnight sun and hypnotic northern lights. Explore the diverse lands, lakes, and cityscapes of northern Europe on the trains, buses, and ferries of Denmark, Finland, Norway, and Sweden. Enjoy this remarkable part of the world, encompassing several countries, on a **Scanrail Pass** integrating these transportation services, much as Mother Nature has combined the seas, sky, and shores to create Scandinavia's rugged beauty.

Discounts are offered on private scenic railroads, and free passage is included on many ferry crossings such as those between Sweden and Denmark or Finland and Germany. This **Scanrail Pass** offers 4, 9, and 14-day packages starting at about

# PASSPORT TO
# DISCOUNT TRAVEL

$140 for second class and $180 for first. Call EURAIL (800-722-7151) for details.


## Spain Railpass

Enjoy the vibrant textures that are España! Savor this land of light and love, artists and artisans! Visit towering Gothic churches and amazing Moorish castles, roam the beaches, attend bullfights, explore historic Madrid, sample the seafood and sip some sangria, take a trip to the Rock of Gibraltar, hop over to Morocco for a visit to exotic Tangiers or Casablanca—and save money with a railpass.

The low-priced **Spain Railpass** costs about $120 in second class, $160 in first, and permits travel any four days within 15. In comparison, one roundtrip fare between Madrid and Barcelona only, costs about $145 first class and $105 second class. Eight and 15-day travel passes are offered on all Spanish National Railroads (RENFE). Call EURAIL (800-722-7151).


## Benelux Tourail Pass

The **Benelux Tourail Pass** is valid for travel in Belgium, the Netherlands, and Luxembourg. See the medieval splendor of Brussels and Antwerp, where some of the finest diamonds in the world can be purchased; enjoy the charming Dutch people, savor their delicious chocolates and cheeses; visit Holland's windmill villages; and glide peacefully along the friendly canals of cosmopolitan Amsterdam. These are but a few of the pleasures awaiting you via the **Benelux Tourail Pass.**

# TRAINS

This is a flexipass valid for five days of travel within a 17-day period; first-class costs about $130; second-class $100. Passes may be purchased overseas or from the BELGIAN BOARD OF TOURISM, 355 Lexington Ave., New York, NY 10017 (212-370-7360).

## Emerald Isle Pass

**The Emerald Isle Pass** is a flexipass enabling you to frolic in the gorgeous green countryside of Limerick, view the River Shannon, cross the colorful Ring of Kerry, traverse the rugged coastline, sail the lovely lakes of Killarney, and enjoy magnificent mountain scenery on your way to Blarney Castle to kiss the famous stone.

This pass is valid on trains and long-distance buses in Ireland and Northern Ireland, and on municipal transportation in Dublin, Belfast, Limerick, Galway, Waterford and Cork. Eight and 15-day options are available. Passes may be obtained in Ireland, or at CIE TOURS, 108 Ridgedale Ave., Morristown, NJ 07960-4244.

## Austria's Rabbit Card

Austria, an oasis all its own, is home to world-class Olympic skiing, fine pastries, exquisite music, and some of the most breathtaking scenery anywhere. Crystal-clean air, azure skies and verdant meadows abound. It is a country known for its history, as well as its sights and sounds. Salzberg, Mozart's birthplace, is the site of one of the oldest and largest medieval castles in Europe and the location for the filming of "The Sound of Music." Vienna is a cultural magnet attracting some of the finest classical musicians in the world. Explore Austria's historic cities, its picture-perfect country and more, all on the **Rabbit Card.**

Austria's **Rabbit Card** is a flexipass good for unlimited travel on the entire rail system, any four days within ten. Prices range from about $128 for first class to $95 for second class, with discounts for persons under 25. Sold through GERMAN RAIL (212-308-3103).

## Italian State Railway Pass

"La Dolce Vita"—the good life—makes Italy justly famous. Renowned for its art and architecture, culture and cuisine, romantic cities and cosmopolitan flare, Italy is most fondly known for the warmth and passion of its people. Perhaps some of this Italian joy of life is engendered by the wondrous diversity of the land—from snow-capped Alps in the north to lush agricultural principalities in the south. Italy is a picture with ever-changing scenes: the vineyards of pastoral Piedmont foothills; the trend-setting metropolis of Milan; the breathtaking Mediterranean Sea; sensuous Venice; beautiful Florence; volcanic southern islands facing Africa; and of course, magnificent, eternal Rome.

The Italian State Railway offers a flexipass for those who wish to partake of Italy's charms in the comfort of a train, avoiding the confusion and potential hazards of Italian roads. Flexipass options are: travel 4 out of 9 days for approximately $135 first class, $100 second class; travel 8 out of 21 days for $185 first class, $130 second class; or travel 12 out of 30 days for $225 first class, $155 second class.

# TRAINS

For details contact CIT, 666 Fifth Ave., 6th Floor, New York, NY 10103 (212-397-9300).

## European East Pass

As various Eastern European nations struggle with revamped economies and open markets in their move toward independence and democracy, lapses in service may occur in some areas— the rail system is no exception.

The **European East Pass** permits easy access to several former Iron Curtain countries. Created by the railroads of Hungary, Poland and Czechoslovakia, in cooperation with Austria, this pass allows unlimited first-class travel on any train in those countries. Unlike first-class travel elsewhere on the continent, reservations are not required on most of these routes. Travel is valid any 5 days in 15 for about $160, or any 10 days in 30, approximately $260.

An especially good bargain is the single-country **Hungary Pass,** through the land of the mighty Magyars and the beautiful blue Danube: only $35 for five days of train travel within a 15-day period and $55 for any 10 days within a month. Passes must be obtained in North America. Contact FRANCERAIL (800-848-7245) for purchase.

Once again, please note all prices listed are approximations and not actual fares. Rates can and do change, so contact your travel agent, Eurail or the rail system in which you are interested for up-to-date information.

# PASSPORT TO DISCOUNT TRAVEL

# Chapter 9

# INSURE YOUR TRIP

**"Anything that can go wrong, will go wrong
... and at the worst possible time."**
Murphy's Law

## WHAT IF YOUR PLANS CHANGE?

You've been waiting a long time to take a much-antici-pated vacation. You booked and paid for your trip in advance to get a good deal. Now, you're all set to go. You're not worried that your airline tickets, hotel reservations and ground trans-portation arrangements may be non-changeable and non-refund-able— you're going, no matter what.

The morning of your vacation finally arrives! The car is packed, the dog is in the kennel, the mail has been stopped. You gulp down your last cup of coffee and head for the door to catch your early flight. Just as you are about to leave, the phone rings. Your mother, living in a distant city, has been rushed to a hos-pital in critical condition, and the rest of the family wants you there.

Of course you'll go to your family, but how can you change all your plans at the last minute and not lose the money paid for your trip?

# PASSPORT TO
# DISCOUNT TRAVEL

Not only could you be out that money, but now you also have to buy another airline ticket to be with your family. Your non-changeable and non-refundable vacation tickets were to the islands, not your mother's hometown. What's more, because of the short notice, the new ticket will more than likely be expensive. Walk-up fares invariably cost more, because you simply don't have enough time to qualify for a discount fare (usually 7 to 14 days before departure).

What to do?

Call the airline, tour operator or your travel agent and explain your situation. If you're lucky, they may refund some of your money, particularly the airfare. However, if you purchased a tour package or cruise, and the cancellation deadline has expired, you will probably not receive a refund or a voucher for future travel. On the other hand, if you purchased airline tickets independent of a tour package, you may be able to cancel them for a full refund, or use them at a later time, depending on the airline's policy.

Changing or refunding airline tickets without penalty because of a medical emergency is a relatively common practice, despite the rules governing non-refundable and non-changeable tickets. Most domestic airlines refer to this policy as an illness/death waiver. Some airlines will not charge extra for canceling or changing reservations due to the illness of yourself, or the death or illness of an immediate family member, or any travel companions. Some other airlines may charge a fee for emergency changes.

Present the airline with satisfactory proof of the emergency, including the name and phone number of the hospital or attending physician, or a copy of a death certificate. Normally, refunds are handled either in person at the airline ticket counter, by mail through the airline refund accounting department, or by your travel agency.

# INSURE YOUR TRIP

But, how do you fly to your mother's side without paying a costly walk-up fare? Request a compassion or medical/death emergency fare, which discounts normal short-notice rates, if someone in your family suddenly becomes seriously ill or dies. Proof of the emergency situation is usually required. (See **Compassion Fares** under AIRLINES for more details.)

In contrast to the airlines, getting refunds for last-minute cancellations from cruise or tour operators is usually impossible. Normally, cruise tickets, hotel rooms and tour packages are non-refundable after expiration of the cancellation deadline. If an emergency suddenly prevents you from going, kiss your money goodbye!

That's why travel insurance is so important. It insures your investment in the event of the cancellation or interruption of your trip, and reimburses you for a variety of mishaps you may encounter along the way.

## LIABILITY EXCLUSIONS

To determine the type of travel insurance you should buy, look at specific details in the travel brochure. If the tour or cruise operator includes basic travel insurance in the price, this may be all the coverage you need. Sometimes, the insurance included in the price of a tour or cruise may be insufficient to cover eventualities which may occur, so buy additional protection.

Read the waiver of responsibility disclaimers on all tickets and brochures. They explain whether or not the travel operator is liable for trip interruptions caused by something beyond their control, or is responsible for completing their obligation to you. It may also indicate whether a refund is possible.

# PASSPORT TO DISCOUNT TRAVEL

You'd be surprised how many people think they deserve reimbursement if their trip is affected by an act of God, such as a hurricane, by an act of civil unrest such as a war, or by an accident, such as a fire in the hotel. If you ever encounter these or similar circumstances shortly before or during your journey, unless you've purchased appropriate insurance, you're out of luck!

## TYPES OF TRAVEL INSURANCE

Before buying travel insurance, check your current medical, homeowner's, or renter's policies for coverage if something goes wrong. One of these policies may contain travel clauses only covering personal injury, and lost/stolen baggage or belongings. It may not reimburse you for any money paid if, for some reason, you do not complete your journey.

Review your policies or contact your insurance agent for details on the limits of your coverage. Examine the types of travel insurance available and purchase any additional protection necessary.

Travel agencies, cruise lines, and tour operators sell several types of insurance. Tailor your coverage to protect against practically all contingencies, or just a few. Consult your travel agent concerning adequate insurance.

Before you buy, make sure you know what you are getting. Travel insurance policies may differ only slightly in price, but greatly in coverage. Many policies have significant exclusions, so read the fine print to know the limits of your coverage.

# INSURE YOUR TRIP

An article in the August 1990 CONSUMER REPORTS TRAVEL LETTER compared the coverage, benefits, and costs of travel policies from several national insurance companies. It offered advice on acquiring travel insurance, including the reminder to first check your household and health policies for travel-related benefits before buying, and if possible, purchase directly from the insurance company. For a copy of the article, send $5 to CRTL, 256 Washington St., Mount Vernon, NY 10553.

Consider the following travel insurance options:

• **Trip cancellation and/or trip interruption insurance**, usually sold as a package, eliminates the loss of your travel investment due to an accident, illness, or death of a family member. Extra protection may be purchased against disruptions caused by weather, unannounced strikes, or lost or stolen passports. Some policies also cover jury duty or unforeseen circumstances, such as a fire at home, an accident on the way to the airport, or even the death of a business associate.

Available from travel agents, cruise companies, and tour operators, this insurance is normally added as an option to the cost of a trip. It's a wise investment because it protects your money should you have to postpone your journey, or return home before completion. But beware, some policies will not reimburse you if the travel company goes out of business before your departure, or if you elect to leave a trip after it has started.

In general, insurance against travel interruptions, delays or cancellations is relatively inexpensive compared to the total cost of a tour, cruise, or airline ticket. The average premium is about $5 to $15 for each $100 of coverage.

Choose a policy which covers the full cost of a one-way coach ticket home—not just the tour package airfare. Some policies pay for the full cost of a replacement ticket; others pay

# PASSPORT TO
# DISCOUNT TRAVEL

only the difference between the value of your unusable ticket and the cost of a new one.

Another option pays for a replacement ticket, or refunds your investment, if the airline or travel company ceases operations. However, this option is usually not valid if the carrier has already filed for bankruptcy before you buy or use your tickets. Once a travel vendor closes shop or declares bankruptcy, you will have difficulty getting any refunds due. Make sure the policy isn't limited to a formal declaration of bankruptcy, since some firms fail to do this publicly, even after closing shop.

Trip cancellation/interruption insurance has some drawbacks. Policies must usually be purchased several weeks before departure, making it virtually impossible to purchase coverage if you have to leave in a hurry. Conversely, it may be difficult to cancel your trip at the last minute without penalty, because written notice of your cancellation may be required at least 24 hours before scheduled departure. Policies may not be able to compensate for every expense and inconvenience resulting from a trip cancellation or disruption, therefore read the fine print carefully to know exactly what you are buying.

One of the best ways to protect your money is by paying for a ticket, cruise, or tour with a major credit or charge card. Most card companies go after a defaulting travel operator in order to get your refund. Even if you are not reimbursed, using a card at least lets you hold on to your money while the questionable charge is being investigated. If you pay by cash, you may have to go to court in an attempt to get your refund, which can be an expensive and time-consuming proposition.

• **Travel-medical insurance**, low-cost, optional coverage for illness-related expenses incurred while traveling may be purchased as primary medical protection or secondary protection to cover the deductible on personal health insurance. This could range from $100 to $1,000 depending on your policy.

Even if you have your own personal medical plan, trip-related medical coverage may be a good investment, especially when traveling in foreign countries where medical care and insurance claim processing may be radically different from here Numerous pre-existing conditions may be excluded from these policies, such as pregnancy, illnesses treated within 60 days prior to purchasing the insurance, and some sports activities including hang gliding and scuba diving. Medicare, as well as some individual and group health insurance plans are **not** valid outside the U.S. Check your health insurance provider for details.

• **Bad weather insurance**, another frequently selected, inexpensive option, protects your travel investment should you decide to cancel your trip because of dangerous conditions such as hurricanes, blizzards, and typhoons.

• **Baggage Loss/Delayed Insurance** pays for essential items if your bags do not arrive when you do, or if they never arrive at all. (Valuables such as jewelry, watches, furs, cameras, and important papers or documents are usually excluded.) Your personal insurance may cover most of your belongings lost, damaged, or stolen while traveling, provided you pay a minimum deductible. Check your policy for specifics. Baggage Loss/Delayed insurance pays this deductible for you. Some tour operators and travel wholesalers include this basic insurance in the price of a ticket.

Several domestic airlines insure the contents of a passenger's baggage for at least $1,000 per bag, others use that amount to cover all the passenger's luggage, regardless of how many pieces are lost. A few carriers cover the contents of each bag up to $1,250.

# PASSPORT TO DISCOUNT TRAVEL

• **Comprehensive insurance** covers items ranging from canceled flights and lost luggage to trip disruptions and medical emergencies. Because of its expanded coverage, comprehensive insurance is the most expensive, and has certain limitations. But, the extra cost may be worthwhile; added protection can mean the difference between disaster and mere annoyance if something goes awry on a trip.

• **Legal assistance insurance** covers most legal and bond fees which may arise.

• **War and terrorism insurance** is an option which may be added to some trip cancellation/interruption policies to guard against expenses incurred as the result of war or terrorism. A number of countries are excluded under these policies, even unexpected ones such as Great Britain. Some companies only cover incidents reported as terrorist events in the WALL STREET JOURNAL; most have strict time limits, so read the fine print!

## WHY BUY TRAVEL INSURANCE?

Since circumstance may prevent the start or completion of a trip, travelers should purchase trip cancellation/interruption insurance. If they cannot start or finish their pre-paid journey, the appropriate travel insurance will reimburse them. Wise travelers know that other mishaps may also occur along the way, such as accidents or lost luggage. Purchasing the proper insurance to protect against these potential possibilities produces peace of mind.

# INSURE YOUR TRIP

With the rapid changes in the world, such as the turmoil in the Middle East, the disappearance of the Iron Curtain in eastern Europe, and the upheavals in many nations, travelers may have to alter arrangements quickly. If you decide at the last minute not to travel because of safety concerns, hazardous weather, terrorist activities, or war, you are generally **not** entitled to a refund from the tour operator, cruise company, or airline. Therefore consider buying insurance.

If only using an airline ticket or planning a quick trip just a few weeks away, you probably don't need to buy extra insurance; but if taking an expensive tour or cruise or booking months in advance, obtain the additional protection.

Listed below are some of the largest suppliers of individual travel insurance.

• The AMERICAN AUTOMOBILE ASSOCIATION offers its members "TripAssist," which combines traditional travel protection with a 24-hour hotline for medical, legal, and travel assistance. In foreign countries multilingual representatives direct you to English-speaking doctors, dentists, or pharmacists, and make other emergency arrangements. Contact your local AAA for more details.

• AMERICAN EXPRESS TRAVEL PROTECTION PLAN (800-234-0375). In addition to trip cancellation/interruption, and baggage loss insurance, this plan provides medical and emergency assistance, document fees and legal aid. Costs vary depending on where you live and the coverage you buy. Call for enrollment and further details.

• TRAVEL ASSISTANCE INTERNATIONAL, underwritten by Transamerica (800-821-2828 or 202-347-2025), is one

# PASSPORT TO
# DISCOUNT TRAVEL

of the oldest travel insurance specialists. A one-time premium, based on the duration of the policy (which could be as short as one day or as long as one year), secures basic medical, legal, travel, and translation services in the U.S. and abroad. This coverage supplements any other personal medical, accidental death/injury, or baggage insurance you may have. For a small fee, accompanying family members are also protected.

Other features of the basic insurance program include replacement of lost prescriptions, payment of hospital bills up to $5,000, arrangements for return-home travel of dependent children under 16, and expenses-paid visits by a friend or relative after 10 days' hospitalization. Lawyer and interpreter referral is provided, plus aid in finding lost luggage or documents, assistance in foreign telephone usage, and message transmission to friends, relatives, or business associates. It also insures against cancellations due to terrorist acts between the time you purchase the insurance and your departure date. A number of countries are excluded such as Greece, Turkey, and some Middle Eastern nations. For more information, call Transamerica.

• TRAVEL GUARD INTERNATIONAL (800-826-1300) offers a wide variety of trip cancellation and baggage insurance, plus coverage for acts of war, normally excluded from most policies. The basic coverage costs about $70, and provides emergency assistance for injuries incurred resulting from war anywhere in the world. It pays up to $1 million for death and $200,000 for medical expenses.

# INSURE YOUR TRIP

• ACCESS AMERICA (800-284-8300) has policies covering trip interruption/cancellation, accidents, baggage loss/delay, legal help, medical aid, and emergency transportation. They do not cover war, but do cover acts of terrorism taking place within 30 days of your scheduled arrival—excluding countries such as Iran, Iraq, Lebanon, Libya, North Korea, and Yemen.

Two other companies offering travel-related policies are HEALTH CARE ABROAD, from Wallach and Co. (800-237-6615), and TRAVEL INSURANCE PAK, from the Travelers Companies (800-243-3174).

# PASSPORT TO
# DISCOUNT TRAVEL

# Chapter 10

# BEWARE OF TRAVEL
# RIP-OFFS

**"It's strange that men should take
up crime when there are so many
legal ways to be dishonest."**
Al Capone

Have you ever received postcards announcing unbelievable travel bargains, or naming you the winner of exciting unexpected vacations?

"Congratulations! You've just won a fabulous vacation for two!"

"Today is your lucky day! Your name has been selected for a deluxe dream vacation! This is our way of introducing you to a new wholesale travel club offering incredible savings ..."

"Fly round trip to Europe for only $99!"

If you receive such material, it's time to:

# PASSPORT TO
# DISCOUNT TRAVEL

(1) be skeptical

(2) drag out the magnifying glass for the fine print

(3) follow the advice of Michael Crichton, author of TRAVELS, who warns "be cautious of anyone who seems interested in your money."

These come-ons prove the old cliché, "Anything that sounds too good to be true, probably is."

If you are among the many consumers who have responded to similar postcards or telephone solicitations, you are not alone. Thousands of people have been victimized by these nationwide scams which have netted the operators millions of dollars. Most of those fooled, are probably considerably poorer, sadly disappointed, and perhaps a little wiser. They should have listened to Ralph Hodgen who said, "The handwriting on the wall may be a forgery."

You can avoid travel schemes by learning to differentiate between legitimate travel vendors offering real savings, and con-artists preying on naive and greedy individuals.

Always beware of direct advertising promoting exceptionally low-cost travel.

## VACATION SCAMS

There are thousands of vacation scams, but for the most part two predominate: **the vacation certificate** and **the travel club.**

Vacation certificates arriving by mail, or offered over the phone, usually feature free accommodations in resort areas. They may sometimes be given as free gifts for attending sales

# BEWARE OF
# TRAVEL RIP-OFFS

promotions which market time-shares, real estate, and even cars. Many of these certificates are also offered as prizes in some non-existent contest. You may be told that you've been chosen as winner of a fabulous vacation while, more than likely, your name, address, and phone number were probably obtained from commercial mailing lists.

Typically, these offers state that certificates for the free travel must be claimed by calling a 900 telephone number. Callers are told that the certificate only covers complimentary hotel lodging, however, in order to stay at the hotel, they must purchase roundtrip airplane tickets at full price, not discount rates. For this information, and possibly a brochure, callers may be charged as much as $35 for using the 900 number—a real surprise when the phone bill arrives!

Watch out for vendors who refuse to give hotel confirmation numbers or who require payment two to three months in advance. This gives shady operators an opportunity to skip town with your money. Be on your guard if you must call a 900 number in response to an offer, or if a large deposit is demanded up front.

Some certificates are legitimate values worth pursuing; others, aren't worth the paper they're printed on. The hidden charges may be so high that offer is no bargain at all. To use these vacation certificates, you may have to pay all transportation and meal costs; send a non-refundable payment to the promoter, not the hotel, when making the reservation; pay all taxes and other fees. Such offers should remind you of the proverb, "A half-truth is a whole lie."

When booking your vacation you may run into difficulty, because "the resort is sold out" or "is not available" at convenient times, or you may be only able to get a room at the free or discounted rate during the off-season when nobody else wants to go.

# PASSPORT TO
# DISCOUNT TRAVEL

If you do decide to take the trip, you may wish you hadn't. A few of the potential let-downs you may experience at the hotel on your so-called dream vacation are: tiny rooms, no view, churlish service, marginal cleanliness, or poor location miles away from attractions.

Also beware of some so-called, "travel clubs." These rip-off clubs are **not** to be confused with legitimate travel wholesalers, ticket consolidators, and last-minute travel clubs discussed in previous chapters. For one thing, scams operate differently. They come to you; you don't go to them. Because they want your money, they initiate the business. They usually contact you by phone or mail, and charge a membership fee ranging from $50 to $500, supposedly entitling you to one "free" round trip plane ticket, and a discounted room for two at some exciting locale. Legitimate wholesalers do not call you or pressure you to buy; they wait for you to contact them.

If involved in a travel rip-off, you're first suspicions should be aroused when you claim your vacation package. One "catch" you'll discover is that the fabulous offer you hoped for is normally valid "only if a companion comes along with you or an airline ticket is purchased through the club." The price of the requisite ticket is often so high that you could have saved money purchasing excursion tickets to the same destination yourself! The vacation "special" may also contain other unexpected negatives such as agency fees, limited availability, or questionable accommodations.

# BEWARE OF
# TRAVEL RIP-OFFS

## THE BOILER-ROOM

Most travel rip-offs run their business out of "boiler-rooms"—offices with numerous telephone banks manned by pushy sales people. The offices are temporary, and are vacated quickly when the authorities start closing in to shut them down. To make their operations appear legitimate, these scams often use names similar to reputable, well-known companies. For legal reasons, most of their presentations avoid using the word "free" to describe what you have won, which by now you know is anything but free. Their enticing sales pitches are nothing more than inducements to buy inferior vacations at inflated prices.

## IDENTIFYING TRAVEL SCHEMES

Four characteristics of most illegal travel schemes are:

(1)  High pressure salespeople urging immediate action.
(2)  Up-front payments or non-refundable deposits required to handle travel arrangements well in advance.
(3)  Emotional appeals emphasizing limited opportunities to participate.
(4) Hard-to-believe values offered through exaggerated claims, disguising true costs.

When considering a vacation package offered by phone or mail, keep an eye on the bottom line. Find out all you can about the actual costs involved.  Is free airfare included? Does

# PASSPORT TO
# DISCOUNT TRAVEL

another ticket have to be purchased, and if so, at what price? Is lodging included? If not, how much extra will it cost?

Obtain the name of the airline, cruise ship, or hotel to be used. Do your own research on prices, service, and accommodations to see if you are really getting a bargain. Travel agencies or vendors, not directly involved in the promotion, should give you insight into the typical costs of the services being offered and the reputation of the promoter.

Get the exact location of the hotel and determine if it is in a safe area close to attractions. How far is it from the beach or town? Are meals included, or do you have to purchase them separately or as part of a meal plan? Does the price include ground transportation between the airport and the hotel? Are there any extra charges, such as booking fees, departure taxes, hotel taxes, and gratuities? Do you have to pay membership fees or a redemption charge in order to use your vacation certificate?

Beware of other loopholes. When are you allowed to use your vacation vouchers? Are there blackout dates? Some schemes require traveling on a space available basis, or during very limited periods.

What about other restrictions? Are you required to pay for a travel companion? Can your children go with you, and for how much? Can you get a refund on your deposit? How much is the refund and what is the cancellation policy and deadline?

# BEWARE OF
# TRAVEL RIP-OFFS

## CREDIT CARD PRECAUTIONS

Be wary of the promoter who calls and pressures you to pay for your trip immediately by check or credit card. Some unscrupulous outfits even offer to send a courier to pick up your check, or will pay for overnight delivery service. When you give out your credit card number, your account will be charged immediately. Know the reputation of the travel vendor before revealing credit card information; a dishonest company could charge any amount it chooses. Get the cancellation deadline for obtaining a full refund without penalty in writing.

Never give your credit card number to anyone over the phone unless you have initiated the transaction. Be completely confident that you have all the facts necessary for making a safe and intelligent decision. Speaking to a persistent salesperson trying to close a fast deal is **not** the best way to get the details you need.

These con artists often process credit card charges using out-of-state merchant accounts with different company names than the ones mentioned over the phone. Your credit card statement may eventually show a charge from a business you've never heard of. This practice makes it harder to trace these unsavory operations should you seek a refund or other compensation.

If you are suspicious about any offer, call the Better Business Bureau or consumer protection agency near you, or near the company's location (if you know where it is). Ask them about the promoter's credibility **before** you pay any money. However, a record without previous complaints does not necessarily mean everything is legitimate. Many fraudulent operators simply collect their money, declare bankruptcy, and vanish before complaints can be lodged. They then set up similar operations in another state. Most fraud victims are reluctant to report a rip-off to authorities, because they are embarrassed to admit they were conned.

After accepting a travel offer solicitation, you will usually receive a package of information in the mail. Read it immediately. If the details of the trip do not seem right to you, cancel it at once, or at the most, within one week. Return the package, with a cancellation letter enclosed, by **Certified Mail,** with **return receipt requested**. Always communicate in writing, and keep copies of your letters and mail receipts.

Remember, a legitimate travel agency awaits **your** call; while a travel scam operator initiates the contact. You never go to con artists, they come to you.

To protect consumers, many full-service travel agencies belonging to the American Society of Travel Agents (ASTA), offer tour and cruise default programs, which reimburse you should an airline, cruise company, or tour operator go bankrupt or fail to deliver service as promised.

During recessionary times, people tend to be more susceptible to travel rip-offs while searching for bargains. Cost-conscious consumers may overlook possible unethical practices or potential pitfalls.

Perhaps the best advice before using any travel service is to ask for references from former customers. Word-of-mouth recommendations are the most trustworthy. Be sure to check with your local consumer protection agencies. Don't be fooled by slick advertising or sales gimmick promotion scams which could turn your dream vacation into a nightmare.

# Chapter 11

# SAFETY TIPS

**"Thieves can't help helping themselves."**
Henry Morgan

When traveling to new and exciting places, it easy to forget details which ensure safety and enjoyment. After embarking on a trip, one of the last things you want to hear your travel companion say is, "But I thought **you** locked the back door."

You plan on having fun, not becoming a victim. Having your money or possessions stolen will bring your idyllic vacation to a screeching halt. A helpful booklet, SAFE TRIP ABROAD, suggests ways to prevent theft and avoid acts of terrorism while traveling; available for one dollar from the Superintendent of Documents, U.S. Government Printing Office, Washington, DC 20402.

The following security precautions are suggested for domestic and international travelers.

## TRAVEL SAFETY CHECKLIST

(1) Tell your family or friends the details of your trip, and leave them a complete itinerary including all destinations

and side trips. Mention where you will be staying at each location, as well as a phone number and contact person. List the names and numbers of any people you will be visiting and include your transportation carrier(s). Always provide the names and numbers of persons to call in case of emergency.

(2) Know your existing balance and credit limit on credit cards you will be using. Individuals have been arrested in some countries for innocently exceeding their limits.

(3) Lock your luggage, and place your name and phone number (or the name and phone number of your travel agent) **inside and outside** each bag. Include the phone number of your destination hotel(s) as well. Obtain a claim receipt for each piece of luggage you check on board an airplane, train, bus, or cruise ship. Make sure the "destination" tags placed on bags indicate the correct city.

(4) While traveling abroad, use inconspicuous luggage tags that do not blatantly display your "USA" address or company affiliation.

(5) Blend in. Dress appropriately for each destination, and try not stand out as a tourist.

(6) Pack light. Lugging heavy, overstuffed suitcases makes you an easy target for thieves.

(7) Unless you will be dressing for a special occasion, leave your best clothes at home. Expensive jewelry and other important items should be left in a safe deposit box. If you don't have one, leave them with a trusted friend who does.

# SAFETY TIPS

(8) **Never** leave bags unattended in public places where someone could break into or steal them. Avoid areas where unattended bags are present in case one contains explosives.

(9) Protect your passport. Do **not** hand it over to unauthorized persons or pack it in your suitcase. Keep a record of your passport number with you, noting the date and place of issue. If your passport is lost or stolen, immediately notify local police and the nearest American embassy or consulate. You'll be issued a three-month temporary passport, have to fill out a detailed report, and follow the same procedure required to obtain your original passport.

(10) Bring two extra passport photos with you. Make photocopies of any visas, and the first two pages of your passport, and keep them in your luggage. U.S. embassies can issue new documents in about a day with these items on hand.

(11) Keep wallets in **front** pockets, which are harder to pick.

(12) Wear a money belt—it's inconvenient, but safe—or a jogger's "pouch" which can be strapped snugly around your waist.

(13) Carry binoculars, cameras, and shoulder bags with the strap diagonally over one shoulder and across your chest. Make sure camera bags and pocketbooks are buckled and/or zipped shut.

(14) Hold your purse or briefcase on your lap when seated; do not place it under a table or next to your chair. If it has a strap, wear it across your chest as mentioned above.

# PASSPORT TO DISCOUNT TRAVEL

(15)   Be observant, especially in crowded places. In airports and train stations, if traveling with a companion, designate one person to read signs and maps while the other keeps an eye on the luggage.

(16)   Curling irons, umbrellas, flashlights, portable radios, diving equipment, and anything else which could be mistaken for a weapon or explosive device should be placed in accessible areas of your luggage. Security guards will be able to inspect these items readily without tearing apart your bags.

(17)   Do not travel with  gift-wrapped parcels, because you may have to unwrap them for inspection at security checkpoints.

(18)   Carry all prescription medicines in their original, labeled containers. Keep them in your carry-on bags, not in checked luggage which may become lost or stolen. Bring copies of  prescriptions, should you need to replace medication.

(19)   Purchase traveler's checks before departing, and leave unnecessary credit cards at home. Keep a list of your traveler's check numbers separate from the checks themselves, so you can easily replace them if stolen. Never carry or stash all your money, credit cards and traveler's checks in one place.

(20)   Before departing, note any terrorist activity in areas you are visiting outside the U.S. Consult the State Department before leaving.

(21)   Don't linger near ticket counters, baggage check-in, or security screening areas. Be aware of exit locations, and always have an escape plan in mind should an emergency arise.

# SAFETY TIPS

(22) In airplanes, consider taking an aisle seat, preferably near an emergency exit. Try to sit close to the exit, but not necessarily right next to it in case the door becomes jammed and people push you in their attempt to get out.

(23) Hide your valuables and cash carefully in your hotel room, or better yet, store them in the hotel's safe or safe deposit boxes. The contents of those little safes provided in some hotel rooms are usually **not** insured by the hotel. Most hotels disclaim any responsibility for items left in the room or the room safe.

(24) Request a room between the third and seventh floors when making hotel reservations. This is high enough to prevent ready access to your room by an intruder, yet low enough for you to escape in case of a fire. Fire equipment can usually reach the seventh floor.

(25) Keep your hotel door closed and locked at all times.

(26) Before answering a knock at the door, be sure it is the maid or the room service you have requested. Call the front desk for confirmation, if uncertain.

(27) Never leave anything of value exposed or unattended in a car.

(28) Remove bumper stickers identifying your rental vehicle.

# PASSPORT TO DISCOUNT TRAVEL

## HOW THIEVES OPERATE

You've seen the TV commercials showing travelers losing their cash through carelessness or theft. Although somewhat exaggerated, these commercials do not overstate the risks of traveling with cash. No one wants their travel ruined by a rip-off; few things can dampen a business trip or a vacation faster than having cash or valuables stolen. Just as you should not leave home without traveler's checks, you should also not leave home without a thorough knowledge of how thieves operate.

Pickpockets prey on the unwary using various techniques.

### Purse Snatching

**Zip!** — Razor blades, knives and stilettos used by lightning-quick hands slash the straps of cameras, binoculars or purses; blades slit holes in pants or jacket pockets to let money fall out; hands snatch necklaces and bracelets. When ever traveling, always be on the alert.

**The Hook** — Beware of the dapper-looking gentleman strolling by with his "brolly." He may use that umbrella to trip you or swipe your shoulder bag as he passes. Look out for that apparently suave individual with a walking stick, which may be used to snare your purse or attache case from under a cafe table, museum bench, or subway seat.

# SAFETY TIPS

**The Cyclist** —Keep an eye on the many bicyclists, moped riders, and skaters passing by, not just for their safety and yours, but also for the safety of your belongings. One of these individuals may be a crook intent on snagging handbags, cameras or jewelry.

## Highway Robbery

**The Nail-In-The-Tire** — Thugs use this technique on victims parking at hotels, train stations, or restaurants. They push a nail into a tire creating a slow leak. The unsuspecting tourist returns, drives off, and is followed by the crooks. When the "mark" stops to check the flat, he is attacked and robbed by the bandits.

**The Window Smash** — Often attacking hatchback automobiles in which they've spotted suitcases, these highway pirates follow their prey on motorcycles until an opportunity arises to strike. They smash a side or rear window of a car, grab what they can, and speed off in a cloud of dust before the victims can respond.

**The Rental Car Rip-Off** — Crooks look for a rental company logo on parked cars, and break into them when the opportunity is right. **Never** leave anything valuable in your car, even in the trunk; thieves are able to pop open a locked trunk lid just as easily as a locked car door.

# PASSPORT TO
# DISCOUNT TRAVEL

## Pickpocket Piracy

**Bump And Run** — The pickpocket's classic move: bump into an unsuspecting person, create a distraction, grab their wallet or cash, and slip away.

**Kid Power** — Many cold-hearted, unscrupulous hoodlums prey on children forcing them to steal for a living. The youngsters usually operate in teams, swooping in on their targets, confusing them by persistently begging or pretending to sell magazines or food, which they shove into their victims' faces. The hapless tourists, like deer surrounded by wolves, may successfully drive off some tormentors, but are pounced on by others from the rear. These well-trained kids work fast. While looking at the sad-faced, pleading waifs, victims seldom notice their wallets or valuables have disappeared.

## Divert and Conquer

**Oops, I Dropped Some Money** — This is one of several sophisticated tricks used by teams of thieves who haunt airports or train stations. Using money as bait to lure their prey, one crook crosses in front of a target and nonchalantly drops some money on the floor. As the innocent dupe stoops to pick it up and return it to the culprit, his valise or suitcase is stolen by a second thief who promptly hands it off to a third partner-in-crime making a quick getaway.

**The Mustard Squirt** — While at a food counter, someone squirts mustard or ketchup, or spills a beverage on a traveler's clothes. The unsuspecting person's first instinct, of

# SAFETY TIPS

course, is to wipe it off. While doing so, his valuables are lifted by the "little squirt's" pal. The "spiller" helps clean up the mess, while his cohort cleans out the victim.

## HOME SECURITY

Some suggestions for safeguarding your home while you are traveling:

(1) Notify your local police, particularly officers you know and trust, about your vacation plans. Tell them when you will be gone so they can watch your house for signs of unexpected activity.

(2) Leave your house key with a relative or neighbor so they can look in on your home occasionally. Tell them about your travel plans and ask them to keep an eye on the place.

(3) Suspend all deliveries: mail, newspapers and any recurring home service, such as pest control and house cleaning.

(4) Arrange to have your lawn, garden and potted plants taken care of. Well-kept grounds give the impression of someone being home.

(5) Put your valuables in a safe deposit box at your bank. Place larger valuable items, such as furs, paintings, and coin or stamp collections in secured storage.

# PASSPORT TO
# DISCOUNT TRAVEL

(6)   Install a good home burglar alarm system and keep fresh batteries in your smoke alarms.

(7) Set up automatic timers to turn various lights on and off at different times during the day and night giving the appearance of normal occupancy. Do the same with a radio or TV so that it sounds as though someone is home.

(8)   Lock all windows and doors. Use dual locks on the windows and deadbolts on the doors. Your local police can advise you about effective locks for your home.

(9)   Unplug electric appliances such as televisions and computers, in case lightning strikes creating an electrical surge which can damage the equipment. Turn off the hot water heater; turn down the thermostat to between 55 and 63 degrees; empty and defrost the refrigerator and freezer if you will be gone for a while.

(10)  Have a friend or relative stay at your house while you are away, or hire a professional "house-sitter" to live in your home 24 hours a day to take care of your mail, plants, pets, etc. Check the yellow pages for listings of house-sitting services in your area. Obtain references and proof of bonding before hiring anyone.

A thorough discussion of personal and home security; baggage and monetary protection; terrorist activities; travel scams and theft techniques is presented in TRAVEL SAFETY, by Jack Adler and Thomas Tompkins, available at bookstores or from Hippocrene Books, 171 Madison Ave., New York, NY 10016 (718-454-2366).

# Chapter 12

# PACKING POINTERS

**"Thou shalt not travel with anything thou cannot carry at a dead run for half a mile and store under thy seat."**
Erma Bombeck

## KEEP IT LIGHT

When packing for a trip, the adage applies, "Bring half the clothes you think you'll need, and twice the amount of money." In most cases, you're better off traveling light—fewer bags or belongings to carry and worry about. Pack what you need; leave what you don't, and remember to bring the essentials. Follow Ken Kesey's advice, "Take what you can use and let the rest go by."

Be prepared for the possibility of losing your bags during a trip. Keep your money, jewelry, valuables, and important documents with you in carry-on bags. Don't pack hard-to-replace items in checked luggage which could get lost or stolen along the way. For safety, leave expensive jewelry, clothes, and furs at home or in secure storage. Take toiletries and prescription drugs with you in hand baggage, with copies of back-up prescriptions.

# PASSPORT TO DISCOUNT TRAVEL

As a final precaution, pack some of your clothes in your traveling companion's bag, and vice versa. This is especially important if you each have only one checked bag with all your belongings in it. This way, you will both have a change of clothes if one of the bags is lost or delayed.

• **Use the right bag**. For carry-on items, use soft-sided canvas, durable nylon or leather overnighter bags with lots of pockets. A size which will fit most on-board stowage areas is 10 x 14 x 23 inches. Versatile garment bags with straps and hangers are handy, because they can be checked or carried on board. Suitcases should be hard-sided, preferably with built-in combination locks, which are usually stronger than key-locks, and eliminate worrying about lost keys. If you prefer, a bag with wheels well-secured to the frame can be pulled with a handle or strap.

• **Prepare a checklist**. Write down what you need to take with you to minimize the chance of forgetting something.

Don't pack too much. Lay out everything you might want for the trip, then pack only what you really need. Walk around the room with your bags for a few minutes, if they feel too heavy, take out extraneous items.

• **Limit your luggage and make sure it is lightweight.** Since porters are not always available when you need them, you may have to fend for yourself. Muscle pulls and strained ligaments from carrying around heavy bags are no fun and contribute little to the enjoyment of the trip.

• **Mix and match color-coordinated clothes**. Color-coordinated separates—sportscoats, sweaters, slacks, skirts,

# PACKING POINTERS

shirts and blouses can be mixed and matched to create a variety of outfits, and can be layered depending on the weather. It's a good idea to take some clothing for unanticipated hot or cold temperatures.

• **Use every inch of luggage space.** Stuff socks into shoes, and roll up sweaters and underwear to fit into corners of suitcases. Pack bags full to keep the contents from sliding around, however, don't stuff them so full you can't easily close them. Place heavy items on the bottom, and layer your clothes with the least wrinkle-resistant items on top. To minimize wrinkling, place plastic dry cleaning bags between layers; button all shirts and dresses, fold them along the waist and seams, and unpack and hang them as soon as possible after your arrival

To press wrinkled clothing, bring a portable steam iron or steamer which is lightweight, compact and available with 120-240 voltage adaptors.

• **Label your bags inside and out.** As mentioned in former chapters, don't forget to clearly print your name and phone numbers, both home and work. Enclose a copy of your itinerary so if you lose your bags, someone will know where to return them. Remove old luggage tags and destination labels before departing.

• **Bring a first aid kit.** This should include: aspirin, cold tablets, antacids, diarrhea medicine, sunscreen, an antiseptic/ anesthetic cream, an elastic bandage, vitamins, and other necessities—toothbrush, toothpaste, mouthwash, shaver, brush or comb, and shampoo. A compact hairdryer, with an adapter to fit local electrical outlets is a good idea. Transfer liquids to plastic containers; don't fill them to the top. Seal with tape, and bring additional tape along to re-seal them later. Place containers in sealable plastic bags to minimize leaks.

# PASSPORT TO DISCOUNT TRAVEL

• **Take along a bag in which to carry souvenirs**. Pack a foldable fabric or vinyl bag in the bottom of your suitcase. When homeward bound, put your purchases in this bag to ease your way through airports and customs.

Take some plastic bags when going to the market. In many parts of Mexico, Europe, and elsewhere, food store customers are expected to supply their own bags. Carry a small pocket calculator for totaling prices and computing exchange rates.

• **Take duplicates of anything essential or difficult to replace**. Make at least three copies of all important prescriptions and travel documents such as passports, birth certificates, traveler's checks, credit cards, tickets and visas. Keep one set with you and deposit one in a safe place at the hotel. Leave the third set of copies at home or in a safe deposit box.

## TIPS FOR SENIORS

Pack your lens prescription and an extra pair of eyeglasses. Get your doctor's approval regarding your fitness to travel and obtain copies of medical records and prescriptions. Take these with you on your trip. The medical report should describe any specific health problems you may have and should include the items below:

- Name, address, and social security number
- Name and address of your insurance company
- Addresses and phone numbers of persons to notify in case of emergency

# PACKING POINTERS

- Blood type
- Medical history
- Current medications (generic names preferred), and dosages
- Causes of prior hospitalizations
- Allergies and adverse reactions to medications
- List of immunizations and dates

Know the generic names of your prescribed medications, especially overseas where trade names for pharmaceuticals may be different from those used in the United States.

Finally, don't leave home without your "medical alert" card or bracelet. These medical I.D. cards, bracelets, and necklaces state any life-threatening medical conditions or allergies you have, as well as your blood type. Wear it or carry it in your wallet or purse. If you don't have a medical alert ID, contact your pharmacy or physician to obtain one.

## PACKING FOR PICTURES

Experienced photographers know the folly of bringing all their expensive photo equipment with them on a pleasure trip—too much to pack, too heavy to carry, too easily stolen. Unless you are on a photographic assignment or safari, avoid encumbering yourself with excess lenses, camera bodies, flash-attachments and tripods. Plan your photo requirements and pack only the accessories you will need.

Take your cameras and lenses as carry-on baggage rather than checking them. This protects your equipment against damage and theft. Keep them by your side at all times. If you have too much equipment to carry with you, ship it ahead of time as freight and buy enough insurance to cover it (usually about $1 for every $100 of value). When filing a claim for lost or damaged equipment, you will probably need to present your original purchase receipts, as well as the receipts for any replacements.

In most cases, the carriers' liability for lost bags, normally a maximum of $1,000 to $1,250, does **not** extend to photographic equipment. No matter where you go or how you get there, be sure to adequately insure your equipment. Standard homeowner's or tenants' policies often cover most possessions while traveling, but may contain limitations on photographic items. Review your policy carefully, and if necessary, purchase a rider or additional insurance.

When taking foreign-made photographic equipment out of the country, register it with U.S. Customs before leaving to avoid being charged duty on it upon returning. Customs declaration forms are available at most international airline ticket counters.

Protect your camera lens with three simple items: a lens cap, a haze filter, and a shock-resistant case. Keep the lens cap on the camera when it's not in use. Put the filter over your lens and leave it on; it won't interfere with your photographs and will keep your expensive lens from getting scratched. Place delicate equipment in shock-absorbent material or cases, and keep a vigilant eye on it—one second is all it takes for unattended cameras to vanish.

Thieves are attracted by expensive-looking camera bags or photographic cases. Don't advertise your valuable photo gear. Tape over any brand-name logos on camera cases, or secure equipment in less conspicuous containers such as older camera bags, or used briefcases or back packs which appear less val-

# PACKING POINTERS

uable. These carriers can be fitted with foam inserts to protect your cameras and lenses.

Pack plenty of film and spare sets of batteries for your cameras and flash attachments. Take more film than you think you may need, in case you run out when stores are closed, or far away. Film is small and light, so why not take extra? Besides, in most of the world, film costs more than it does in the United States—at most tourist spots, you'll pay a premium for it.

Beware of airport X-ray machines. Repeated exposure to the X-rays produced by baggage security machines can blur the images and weaken the colors of your unexposed film. Once or twice through the machine probably won't hurt, but repeated exposure can be destructive. Although security personnel may tell you the X-ray is safe for film, why take a chance?

If you don't have a "film shield" protective bag, hand your film and camera, if loaded, to the security guard for manual inspection. If your bag has a lead-lined film shield, the security guards may decide to turn up the radiation to see through the protective case. To avoid this, simply open the bag away from the X-ray machine and show its contents to the guard; the same applies to video cassettes and computer disks. Give them to the guard away from the X-ray machine and metal detector.

To speed up the inspection process, pack your film in easy-access or see-through storage containers, or resealable plastic bags, so you can hand your film to the security guard without drawing attention to the fact that you are carrying expensive photo equipment. X-rays will not harm cameras, only film; it is OK to send the equipment through as part of your carry-on baggage. When flying internationally, your checked bags are also X-rayed, so don't pack any film in them.

Other alternatives are: have your film developed on location or mail the film back to your home or a film processing laboratory in the States. Take photo lab mailers with you.

# PASSPORT TO
# DISCOUNT TRAVEL

## CARRYING COMPUTERS

When traveling with a computer, whether carried-on or checked as baggage, you **must** have it manually inspected—**not** X-rayed. X-rays will destroy the memory hard drive disk information, as well as any memory chips; this also applies to computer disks you may be transporting. You may also be required to demonstrate to the security guard that it is a working computer not a shell possibly concealing explosives.

If not a lap-top, be sure you carry the power supply cord or other devices necessary to boot-up the machine readily available, not packed somewhere in your checked baggage.

Before using the computer enroute, always check the airline's policy regarding operation on a flight. Some computers can cause interference with the plane's on-board computer or navigational equipment.

# Chapter 13

# WHAT ABOUT MONEY?

**"The safest way to double your money
is to fold it over once and
put it in your pocket."**
Frank McKinney Hubbard

## CASH OVERSEAS

As part of your preparation, consider how much money to bring and the safest form in which to carry it. Take personal checks, traveler's checks, one or two major credit cards, and just enough cash in local currency to get by. Cashier's checks are not always instantly accepted at foreign banks. When cashing such checks overseas, you may have to wait two to three weeks until the check clears. Although personal checks drawn on American banks may not be accepted everywhere, many foreign stores will take them. You may even get a slightly better price on items purchased with a personal check than with a credit card, because the store may not have to add the fee it pays a credit card company.

Major credit cards are accepted at many locations worldwide, but if you use them for purchases abroad, you're gambling with the exchange rate. You are billed at the rate prevailing on the day the charge clears the United States, **not** at the rate in effect on the day you make your purchase. The difference may be large or small and it could work for or against you. You won't know until the bill arrives.

You can save some money by obtaining traveler's checks in U.S. Dollars from companies which do not charge a fee, such as Grand Circle Travel (clients), some banks (account holders), and automobile clubs (members). They offer traveler's checks issued by international financial institutions, which are accepted practically anywhere in the world, and are quickly replaced if lost or stolen. Bring traveler's checks in easily cashed denominations such as $20s and $50s. Cash traveler's checks for enough money to last you a short time, so if the funds are stolen or misplaced you will have less to lose.

When overseas, you may also want to take some travelers checks in stable currencies accepted worldwide, such as Swiss francs. Their rates may not fluctuate as much on the world market as the American dollar, and most large businesses will accept Swiss funds. Not all bank branches have foreign-exchange windows for cashing traveler's checks in other currencies, so before standing in line, ask a bank official if they exchange traveler's checks or dollars into local funds.

Before arriving in a foreign country, it's a good idea to exchange about $50 into local currency in small bills for initial miscellaneous expenses so you will not overpay by not having smaller change.

Always bring $20 to $30 in $1 bills. No matter where you are in the world, you can always find someone who will accept them; they are especially handy for tipping.

Exchange the bulk of your funds in the country you are visiting. The exchange rate is invariably better there than in the U.S. Local foreign banks usually offer the best exchange rates,

# WHAT ABOUT MONEY

much better than hotels, stores or money exchange booths. Never change money on the black market. You could get arrested, ripped off, or both.

Take the latest edition of RUESCH'S INTERNATIONAL CURRENCY GUIDE. This free booklet, updated three times a year, lists exchange rates for 24 countries, plus information on customs duties, import-export restrictions, and tipping. Send a stamped, self-addressed business-size envelope to Ruesch International, 1925 Century Park E., Suite 240, Los Angeles, CA 90067.

Ruesch also offers an inexpensive electronic calculator which automatically computes currency exchange rates and converts foreign currency amounts into the equivalent dollars and cents instantly and accurately (about $20). Several other exchange rate calculators, such as the Money X-Changer are available at department stores and travel specialty shops.

## FOREIGN CASH MACHINES

When overseas, why waste time at banks or hotel cashier desks changing dollars into local currency? Most major cities in Europe, Asia, and the Caribbean have automated teller machines (ATM's) which accept many American bank, charge, and credit cards. They frequently offer exchange rates better than those of foreign banks, hotels, and currency exchange companies. Conversions are based on bank-to-bank, or "wholesale" rates.

At the ATM, select the amount of foreign money desired, and instantly receive the cash in local currency. According to bank card companies, the conversion rate is the one in effect at the time of the transaction, but you won't know what that rate was until you receive your monthly statement, because most ATM's do not display current conversion rates.

A bank's "cash card," entitling you to withdraw cash from participating ATM's, differs from a "charge card" such as American Express, or a "credit card" such as VISA or Master-Card. A bank issues cash cards to customers who maintain an account with them. Cirrus, Plus, and Honor are three bank-affiliated card networks permitting Americans to receive foreign currency against dollars in their checking, or savings accounts.

When using cash cards, you are not charged interest on the money, however, you may be charged a small transaction fee. In comparison, when you use a credit card at an ATM to obtain foreign currency, you may receive two charges. Most credit cards charge transaction fees for foreign cash advances, as well as interest on the advance from the day the money is taken out.

American Express card members must have a Personal Identification Number (PIN) to use cash machines abroad. To apply for an American Express card or to find out which countries have ATM's accepting the AMEX card, call 800-227-4669. American Express' fees for cash advances range from $2 to $6 per transaction, plus a 1% charge on withdrawals.

Cirrus and Plus cardholders with four-digit PIN numbers can use their cards to activate many foreign ATM's. Cardholders having longer PIN numbers, or with letter combinations, must request new ones for foreign ATM's. Some transactions are free; others cost about $2 each. Check with your member bank for charges and a directory of ATM locations overseas. There are thousands of ATM's in America, but relatively few in some foreign countries. Without such a list it may be difficult to locate one.

# WHAT ABOUT MONEY

Many European ATM's accept MasterCard and VISA for cash advances in foreign currency. ATM fees for credit card advances cost a few dollars per transaction. In contrast, credit card cash advances from a bank teller, incur transaction fees of about 2% of the total advance with a maximum charge of $10. In most cases using the ATM is more economical. Since transaction fees may change at any time, contact your credit card company for more details before going abroad.

Credit card companies usually limit cash advances to $200-$500 at ATM's and restrict the number of cash advances per day (usually two or three). The conversion rate used is the one in effect at the time of withdrawal.

Remember, you are charged interest from the date of the transaction on credit card cash advances. Some interest rates may be as high as 21%. All fees and interest rates may change at any time, so consult your bank if you have questions.

A helpful leaflet, published by the BankCard Holders of America Association, reviews basics such as credit limits, exchange rates, and steps to make sure your credit card bill does not go unpaid while you are away. Members may obtain a free copy; others may get one for $1 from BANKCARD HOLDERS OF AMERICA, 560 Herndon Parkway, Herndon, VA 22070 (800-638-6407).

## AVOIDING THE DREADED "VAT"

When shopping in Europe, you can avoid paying the pervasive, expensive "value-added tax" (VAT). A fair amount of

# PASSPORT TO DISCOUNT TRAVEL

time and paperwork is involved to do so when paying by cash or check, but the effort is usually worth it. Using a credit card simplifies the process a little.

Value-added taxes are placed on a product's price based on the various stages of manufacture and distribution. These layered levies may raise the cost of some items as much as 30%, thus negating any savings you thought you'd achieve by shopping abroad. Avoid the VAT and obtain your anticipated savings by filling out the appropriate forms supplied by the store where the purchase is made, and the customs office in that country. Then wait for your VAT refund check to arrive in the mail.

Here's what you do. Before buying anything, ask the sales clerk whether the store will refund the VAT for export purchases. Most will, if you buy at least $100 worth of merchandise. Take your sales slip and passport to the store's special tax refund department where you will be given the necessary papers and a return envelope addressed to the store. If you have any questions, have the clerk help complete the forms.

When you are ready to leave the country, take your purchases and paperwork to the VAT refund department in the customs office, normally located near the passport control area at airports and train stations. Before flying out of the country, your purchases, no matter how large or cumbersome, will be examined with your luggage. The tax agent will provide VAT refund request forms. Have your receipts handy. There may be long lines at the customs office, so allow enough time to com-plete your paperwork before you depart. Mail the refund request in the pre-addressed envelope given to you by the sales clerk.

Your refund check should arrive a month or two later, and will probably be payable in foreign funds. Avoid paying the service charge assessed by many American banks to convert foreign currency into U.S. dollars by looking for a major bank which frequently exchanges foreign checks.

# WHAT ABOUT MONEY

Eliminate the hassle of cashing foreign checks by buying your overseas merchandise with a credit card. The store writes up two sales slips: one for the purchased item, the other for the VAT. The store holds on to your VAT charge slip until it receives all your completed refund request forms, then simply tears up the tax charge slip. The VAT never appears on your credit card bill.

## AVOIDING CANADIAN TAXES

Canada imposes a Goods and Services Tax (GST) of 7%on many purchases. Several of the provinces also assess a provincial tax as well, ranging from about 5% to 12%. For example: Québec's tax is about 9%; Ontario, about 8%. Some provinces will refund the provincial tax, others do not.

These taxes can take a hefty bite out of your budget, but if you are a non-Canadian, following the correct steps can avoid them. To claim refunds on these taxes, write to provincial tourist boards for instructions and forms. Usually, the federal GST refund must be processed first, because the Canadian government promises to return your purchase receipts which are needed to apply for Provincial tax refunds. Always keep a copy of all forms and receipts in case the originals are lost in the mail.

Whenever you stay at a hotel in Canada or purchase any other goods or services, have the merchant write his GST number on your receipt, and list the rebateable taxes **separately** instead of lumping them together on the bill. (NOTE: Taxes are **not** refundable on consumable items such as food, beverages, gasoline and dry cleaning. The taxes on trailer park and camping

299

# PASSPORT TO DISCOUNT TRAVEL

fees are not refundable, nor are taxes on tour packages. However, hotel taxes up to five dollars a night **are** refundable, if the rooms were not obtained through a tour operator.) Keep all your receipts in a safe place, and label them carefully.

When you are ready to leave the country, see the GST agent for your refund. Unfortunately, this may take a little work since GST offices are not always easily located at airports or train stations. Ask Customs employees or the personnel in Duty Free Shops, for the official in charge of refunding GST taxes. Lines may be long, so allow enough time to process the forms before leaving. To avoid delays when driving home, try to select a less traveled crossing point.

Present your receipts to the GST agent, and file the paperwork to receive a cash refund (in Canadian dollars) on the spot, if the total is not too high. You may also have to complete and mail additional forms to receive provincial tax refunds.

If the GST refund exceeds $500, mail your receipts, along with the completed refund request forms, to Ottawa. The Canadian Bureau of Revenue will return your money, by check payable in U.S. funds, within about two months.

Unless at least $100 in Canadian currency is spent on taxable goods and services, you will receive no rebate. Keep your receipts for a year, so that if you return to Canada and the taxes paid exceed the minimum limit, you can request your refund.

For an up-to-the minute explanation of how to claim Canadian tax refunds, write for a copy of the GST GOODS AND SERVICES TAX REBATE FOR VISITORS from the Canadian Embassy, 501 Pennsylvania Ave. N.W., Washington, DC 20001 (202-682-1740), or contact any of the 12 Canadian consulates located in major American cities. This booklet is also available in Canada at many hotels and duty free shops.

# WHAT ABOUT MONEY

## PHONING FROM OVERSEAS

Many foreign hotels assess a hefty surcharge for the convenience of permitting long-distance calls from your room. These surcharges are sometimes higher than the calls themselves! AT&T's USADirect Service helps reduce these costs. Dialing an access code immediately connects you to an AT&T English-speaking operator. To phone the U.S. from France, for instance, dial 19-0011 and then the number you wish to reach. Charge it on your calling card, or call collect, and avoid the hotel surcharge. It's simple and the savings can be substantial, especially when dialing from a hotel which normally adds a surcharge.

In some countries this service is available from any public phone; in others you must use specially marked AT&T phones located in tourist areas. If you charge your calling card, there is an initial fee of about $2.50 plus the per/minute long-distance costs. When calling collect, the initial fee is about $6, plus the per/minute charge, which is paid by the party accepting the call. Collect calls are higher because an operator is involved. For more information about overseas services, costs, and country access codes, call AT&T (800-874-4000).

AT&T also provides a full-time interpreter service for calls made to and from foreign countries. The LANGUAGE LINE PROGRAM has interpreters on duty seven days a week, 24 hours a day. AT&T can connect you, in a three-way conference call, with an interpreter and your party. Charges are about $3.50 per minute, plus the actual cost of the call. For complete details call 800-752-6096.

AT&T also sells TRAVEL TRANSLATORS, individual translation cards, organized by topics such as transportation, accommodations, entertainment, dining, and emergencies. The cards

# PASSPORT TO
# DISCOUNT TRAVEL

display English words and phrases next to their foreign equivalents. The user simply points to the phrases desired and says them in the appropriate language ($1.75 for one language; $6.95 for four and $9.95 for nine).

MCI (800-444-4444) and Sprint (800-877-4646) also provide direct-link dialing overseas and interpreter services. Call and compare prices and benefits to can get the best calling plan for your needs.

In addition to avoiding long distance surcharges, using direct-link phone services immediately accesses U.S. operators and saves time. In most countries, local and international operators cause bottlenecks in the communications system. Only a limited number of overseas operators are employed by local phone companies, so getting through may be time consuming. Difficulties in communicating with foreign operators may also slow the process. To an overseas operator, for example, "Place a call to Kalamazoo," may sound like "Please call to my zoo."

Most direct line services are reached by using special telephones installed in hotel lobbies, airports and train stations, or by dialing the specific access code from local phones. Such services are now offered in nearly every country, including those in Eastern Europe and Africa.

Occasionally, direct line services in a particular region may be temporarily suspended. If difficulties with foreign telephones arise, talk to your hotel's concierge—a concierge can do almost anything. In emergencies go to the U.S. Embassy or consulate; they will place calls for U.S. citizens, but only in the event of serious illness or death.

Anyone not possessing a direct-link calling card, or not wishing to call collect, may still avoid long-distance surcharges by billing their overseas calls to major credit cards, such as VISA, MasterCard, or American Express. CREDIT CARD CALLING

# WHAT ABOUT MONEY

SYSTEMS, enables callers to pay by plastic from public phones abroad. In dozens of countries they provide toll-free numbers which can be used to phone home, as well as call collect, person-to-person, or use directory assistance. For details, write CREDIT CARD CALLING SYSTEMS, Suite 2411, 67 Wall St., New York, NY 10005.

Similar services for international travelers are supplied by WORLD DIRECT and EXECUTIVE TELECARD (800-950-3800, for both). WORLD DIRECT connects the U.S. with over 50 countries and charges the call to any major credit card. It also offers conference calling, document translators, and language interpreters at a cost of approximately $3 per minute. EXECUTIVE TELECARD lets you charge your credit card for inter-country calls, such as England to Germany.

Many of the public phones in Europe use "telecards" to pay for local and long-distance calls. Resembling credit cards, they replace coins and tokens. In France and Italy, telecards are sold at tobacco shops, and in some post offices and cafes. The French "telecarte" generates a digital display on the telephone showing the user how much conversation time remains. The Italian phones give no warning and simply disconnect the call when the time is up. Therefore, in Italy it's better to pay for more time than you think you'll need.

In France, telecartes sell for about 40 francs ($8) for 50 "talk-units"—similar to message units in the U.S.—and 96 francs ($20) for 120 talk-units. France, by the way, offers a toll-free translation service by dialing 05-20-12-02. (The prefix 05 is the equivalent of our toll-free 800).

Similar to U.S. phone systems, the amount of time each talk-unit provides depends on the time of day and the distance called. Phoning from within the city of Paris to a nearby suburb on a Saturday evening would certainly cost fewer francs and use fewer talk-units than calling from Paris to Nice, hundreds of miles away, in the middle of a work day.

When calling the U.S., plan on using about 10 talk-units per minute. Of course, that will vary depending on where and when you call. In monetary terms, the cost of phoning home from Paris could range from a high of about 20 francs a minute during peak hours, to a low of 5 francs a minute during off-peak.

The Italian telecards are sold for about 5,000 lire and 10,000 lire, about $10 and $20 respectively. Actual prices depend on current exchange rates and/or changes in telephone company pricing policies.

# Chapter 14

# WORK IN THE WORLD
# OF TRAVEL

**"I am the master of my fate;
I am the captain of my soul."**
William E. Henley, "Invictus"

Would you like to travel extensively, but don't have a big bank account? Consider a career in travel. Many jobs in this field offer opportunities to see the world at wonderfully low prices.

Some occupations featuring excellent travel fringe-benefits are: airline employee, travel agent, tour/cruise representative, and air freight/express worker. These vocations offer a variety of positions. For instance, a travel agent may specialize in cruises, group tours, or work from home as an outside sales agent. An airline employee may work at any number of jobs, such as flight attendant, ticket agent, mechanic, secretary, pilot, or computer programmer, to name a few. Tour/cruise personnel may serve as tour guides, activity directors, food preparation specialists, or reservationists.

Virtually any of these careers permit you to travel the world at a fraction of full fare. Travel industry employees are eligible for special discounts from many airlines, hotels, rental car agencies, and similar services.

# PASSPORT TO
# DISCOUNT TRAVEL

Travel agents enjoy low-priced familiarization, or "fam" trips, designed to increase their knowledge of popular destinations. Fams are created by tourist boards, hotel chains, and tour operators to acquaint agents with the airports, hotels, services, and attractions of specific areas. These fabulously low priced trips usually include airfare, airport transfers, hotels, sightseeing and some meals. They typically go to luxurious resort areas in Europe, South America, the Caribbean, and the Orient. Lasting several days to a week, fams cost only a few hundred dollars or less!

In addition to being excellent bargains and highly informative, fams are fun. Meeting like-minded professionals in beautiful surroundings, far from the pressures of home and office, allows travel agents to make new friends and explore new places. Best of all, many agency managers encourage their employees to take fams because of their educational value.

Airline employees also benefit from generous industry discounts on hotels, rental cars, and literally thousands of domestic and international flights. Tour/cruise workers enjoy many reciprocal travel-industry discounts, as well.

Finding a job in the field of travel is not easy because competition is fierce and opportunities limited. In many cases, specialized training or experience is required to qualify. Entry-level positions are attainable without previous experience if vital job training is provided by the employer. Such jobs, however, are scarce, but do exist. Airlines train their new hires in necessary job skills; tour companies and cruise lines also educate new employees in the knowledge necessary to perform their duties.

But travel agencies usually do not provide training for beginners. Although a few agencies may occasionally hire novices, most prefer trained or experienced agents. Even knowledgeable agents must work to improve their skills and

# WORK IN THE WORLD OF TRAVEL

enhance their careers by taking specialty courses in computers, ticketing, and fare tariffs. No matter which travel field you enter, the most valuable and lasting knowledge typically comes from "OJT"—on-the-job-training. Even experienced pilots and mechanics must take refresher courses and advanced instruction.

Unable to work full time, but still want to travel? Consider working part-time for an airline, travel agency, tour/cruise operator, or overnight express company. They usually need people to fill-in during busy times.

Like being your own boss? Work out of your home as an "outside" sales agent for a local travel agency. Earn commissions by making travel arrangements and marketing cruises and tours. Set your own hours and sell to your own clientele. It's an easy way to get started in the business and requires little expertise beyond enthusiasm, energy, and a willingness to learn. But in the beginning, be prepared to make financial sacrifices—you won't get rich overnight.

For a realistic picture of what being a travel agent involves and the type of salaries to expect, send a stamped self-addressed business envelope to the INSTITUTE OF CERTIFIED TRAVEL AGENTS, 148 Linden Street, Wellesley, MA 02181 or call 800-542-4282.

Later, if you wish to increase your income, you will need to improve your skills. You will have to master: fares, fare rules, schedules, ticketing, reservations, refunds, deposits, miscellaneous charge orders, pre-paid tickets, cancellation penalties, hotel and cruise cabin classifications, aircraft types, seat assignments, commissions, travel vouchers, rental car requirements, insurance policies and numerous other details necessary to professionally handle and sell travel successfully.

To properly acquire all this knowledge you will either have to attend a travel training academy (look in the yellow

# PASSPORT TO DISCOUNT TRAVEL

pages or contact travel agencies for recommendations), or find a travel agent willing to train you.

The surest way to enter the business is to graduate from an accredited travel training school. In addition to complete and thorough instruction, academies provide job placement assistance. Travel training is expensive, so comparison shop to get your money's worth. Talk to recent grads who are currently working in the field about the quality of their training; check with the Better Business Bureau concerning the reputation and accreditation of schools in this field.

Another way to enter the profession is to work for a travel agency willing to train you. Although difficult to find successful agency managers with the time or desire to teach you, don't give up—they are out there. Sometimes a new agency, or an agency owned by a friend, relative, or acquaintance will work with you. Ask whether they are interested in taking on a trainee.

If the right opportunity comes along, and you are willing to earn very little money at first, you can master the tools of the trade without spending thousands of dollars for formal academy training. Your income will initially be meager—but hang in there. As time goes by, your skills, your clients, and your wages will increase.

No matter where you are taught, as a travel agent you must learn how to interpret both the domestic and the international versions of the OFFICIAL AIRLINE GUIDE (OAG), the certified commercial airlines schedule book. You must master city and airport codes, airline and aircraft codes, pricing and fare codes, minimum connecting times, taxes, departure fees, customs duties, valid routings, baggage handling agreements ,and acceptable forms of payment. You must also learn how to write airline and train tickets, issue cruise, hotel and rental car vouchers, generate boarding passes, and process refunds.

# WORK IN THE
# WORLD OF TRAVEL

Although, you may initially acquire these skills without any technical training, eventually, you will need to know how to operate a computer. Virtually all full-service travel agencies rely on computers. They simply could not function efficiently without them. As a fully qualified travel agent, you **must** become computer literate, and learn to operate one or more of the travel industry's major computer reservation systems.

The sophisticated computer programs used by agencies display schedules and fares for flights worldwide, log airline reservations and seat assignments, list special meals, book rental cars and hotel rooms, confirm tours and cruises, and indicate foreign entry requirements. Some even show current Broadway productions, celebrities appearing in Las Vegas and Atlantic City, the conditions at numerous ski resorts, and even titles of motion pictures shown on long-distance flights.

As a travel agent, the "product" you sell is the world: cities of culture, history and intrigue; resorts of pleasure and relaxation; exotic locales of natural beauty and grace; and cruises and tours to spectacular foreign destinations.

How do you learn about these products well enough to sell them? How do you become knowledgeable enough to advise others? Where do you acquire enough information to confidently recommend destinations, tours and travel services? You go there yourself! You personally experience as many cities, countries, hotels, restaurants, and historical sights as you can. And you do it at remarkably low prices!

To learn more about careers in travel, talk to travel professionals, ask how they got started, and find out which jobs may interest you. Search help wanted ads seeking travel agents, airline employees, cruise/tour representative, and overnight express personnel. Write to travel vendors asking if they are hiring. After you acquire the education and training needed for the job you want, the whole world of travel is open to you.

# PASSPORT TO
# DISCOUNT TRAVEL

# Chapter 15

# REMINDERS

**"We give advice, but we cannot
give the wisdom to profit by it."**
Duc de La Rochefoucauld

• Plan ahead...Remember the Boy Scout motto: "Be prepared."

• Do your homework. Learn about your destinations. Research the most economical ways to get there and the most affordable places to stay. Read travel books, brochures and literature. Seek the advice of an experienced travel agent. Talk to someone who has been there.

• Shop for bargains. Consult travel magazines, newspapers, guide books, and travel agencies for ideas.

• Try to find a hard-working, reliable travel agent who uses a "low fare finder" computer reservation system.

• Explore discounts offered by wholesalers, brokers, charter operators, and "last-minute" travel clubs.

# PASSPORT TO DISCOUNT TRAVEL

• Be flexible in your travel dates. Try to pick off-peak days and times to travel.

• Keep a sense of humor and maintain your perspective. The potentially troublesome trials and tribulations of travel will seem a lot funnier to you years from now. Several books illustrating this are:

WHEN YOU LOOK LIKE YOUR PASSPORT PHOTO, IT'S TIME TO GO HOME, by Erma Bombeck (Harper Collins)

TRAVELING THE WORLD, by Paul Theroux (Random House)

HOLIDAYS IN HELL, by P. J. O'Rourke (Vintage Press)

BAD TRIPS, edited by Keath Fraser (Vintage Press)

NEITHER HERE, NOR THERE by Bill Bryson (William Morrow)

• Bring back notes and photos from your trips in addition to memories. You then have material with which to write a story. Submit it to newspapers or magazines. If published, you may receive a small fee. Editors are often interested in well-written articles with photographs. However, first ask whether they want your article before sending it in.

• Think carefully before acting. Jet lag and the excitement of travel can muddle the senses and impair judgement. Don't do anything on the road that you wouldn't prudently do at home.

# REMINDERS

• Subscribe to travel newsletters. An especially helpful one is TRAVEL BOOKS WORLDWIDE, P. O. Box 162266, Sacramento, CA 95816-2266, which reviews a variety of publications ranging from travelogues and tales of adventure to guide books and maps. Only $36 per year for 10 issues, or $4 per single copy.

• Play it smart. Travel safely and wisely.

I sincerely hope the information contained in this book will, over the years, help you save hundreds, even thousands, of dollars in travel expenses.

May your many years of enjoyable, economical travel be filled with enough excitement, romance, and adventure to last a lifetime. As Erma Bombeck says, "Vacations aren't a shoe box full of slides that you store in the closet next to the bowling ball you haven't used in 20 years. They're moments in your memory."

If you have any questions, comments, or suggestions, write to World View Press, P.O. Box 620821, Orlando, FL 32862-0821.

# APPENDIX A

## AIRLINES

**Aer Lingus P.L.C.**
1-800-223-6537 (Cont. U.S. except N.Y.C.)

**Aerolineas Argentinas**
1-800-333-0276 (Cont. U.S., Canada)

**Aeromexico**
1-800-AEROMEX (Cont. U.S. [except Houston, TX.,] AK, HI, Puerto Rico, Canada

**Air Canada**
1-800-4- CANADA (Except ID, WA)
1-800-633-8370 (ID, WA)
1-800-387-2710 (MI, NY)

**Air France**
1-800-237-2747 (Cont. U.S., except N.Y.C.)

**Air India**
1-800-223-7776 (Cont. U.S.)

**Air Jamaica**
1-800-523-5585 (Cont. U.S., Puerto Rico, U.S. Virgin Islands)

**Alitalia**
1-800-223-5730 (Cont. U.S. except N.Y.)
1-800-442-5860 (New York except N.Y.C., Nassau and S. Westchester Counties)

# APPENDIX A

**All Nippon Airways**
1-800-235-9262 (Cont. U.S.)

**Aloha Airlines, Inc**
1-800-367-5250 (Cont. U.S.)

**American Airlines**
1-800-433-7300 (Cont. U.S., AK, HI, Canada)

**America West Airlines, Inc.**
1-800-247-5692 (Cont. U.S. AK, HI,
Puerto Rico, U.S. Virgin Isl.)

**Avianca**
1-800-284-2622 (Cont. U.S. except Miami, FL)

**Bahamasair**
1-800-222-4262

**British Airways**
1-800-AIRWAYS (Cont. U.S., AK, HI,
Puerto Rico)

**BWIA International**
1-800-327-7401 (Cont. U.S., [except FL], AK, HI
and Canada [except Toronto])

**Canadian Airlines International,Ltd.**
1-800-426-7000 (Cont. U.S. exc. WA)
1-800-552-7576 (WA)

# APPENDIX A

**Cathay Pacific Airways**
1-800-233-ASIA (Cont. U.S.)

**Cayman Airways**
1-800-422-9626 (Cont. U.S.)
1-800-441-3003 (Canada)

**Continental Airlines**
1-800-525-0280 (Cont. U.S., Honolulu,
HI, Canada)
1-800-231-0856 (AK, HI except Honolulu,
U.S. Virgin Isl., Caribbean)

**Delta Air Lines, Inc.**
1-800-221-1212 (Cont. U.S., AK, HI, Puerto Rico)

**Ecuatoriana**
1-800-ECUADOR (Cont. U.S. & Canada)

**Hawaiian Airlines**  367 - 5320
1-800-359-3220 (Cont. U.S. & Canada)
1-800-882-8811 (HI)

**Iberia Airlines of Spain**
1-800-772-4642 (Cont. U.S.)

**Icelandair**
1-800-223-5500 (Cont. U.S. [except N.Y.C.],
AK, HI, Puerto Rico, U.S. Virgin Isl., Canada)

# APPENDIX A

**Japan Airlines**
1-800-525-3663 (Cont. U.S.)
1-800-232-2517 (HI)

**K.L.M.-Royal Dutch Airlines**
1-800-777-5553 (Cont. U.S.)

**Korean Air**
1-800-421-8200 (Cont. U.S.)

**Lan Chile S.A.**
1-800-735-5526 (Cont. U.S.)

**Liat Airlines**
1-800-253-5011

**Lufthansa**
1-800-645-3880 (Cont. U.S. [except Nassau
County, NY & N.Y.C.], AK, HI, Puerto Rico,
U.S. Virgin Isl.)

**Mexicana**
1-800-531-7921 (Cont. U.S. except CA, TX)

**Quantas Airways**
1-800-227-4500 (Cont. U.S., HI, Canada)

**Royal Jordanian Airlines**
1-800-223-0470 (Cont. U.S. except N.Y.C.)

# APPENDIX A

**Sabena**
1-800-645-3790 (Cont. U.S. except NY)
1-800-541-4551 (NY)

**Scandinavian Airlines System**
1-800-221-2350 (Cont. U.S. [except N.Y.C.], HI)

**Singapore Airlines**
1-800-742-3333 (Cont. U.S.)

**Southwest Airlines**
1-800-531-5601 (Cont. U.S. except TX)
1-800-441-1616 (TX)

**Swissair**
1-800-221-4750 (Cont. U.S.-some cities excepted)

**Taca International Airlines**
1-800-535-8780 (Cont. U.S. except
New Orleans, LA)
1-800-452-7414 (New Orleans, LA)

**Tap Air Portugal**
1-800-221-7370 (Cont. U.S., HI, Puerto Rico,
U.S. Virgin Isl.)

**Thai Airways International**
1-800-426-5204 (Cont. U.S., AK, HI)

**Trans Brazil**
1-800-872-6773

# APPENDIX A

**Trans World Airlines, Inc.**
Domestic
1-800-221-2000 (Cont. U.S., AK, HI, Caribbean)
1-800-892-8466 (Puerto Rico, U.S. Virgin Isl.)
International
1-800-892-4141 (Cont. U.S., AK, HI)

**United Airlines**
1-800-241-6522 (Cont. U.S., AK, HI, Canada)

**USAir**
1-800-428-4322 (Cont. U.S., AK, HI, Canada)

**Varig Brazilian Airlines**
1-800-GO VARIG (Cont. U.S. [except N.Y.],
AK, HI, Puerto Rico, U.S. Virgin Isl.)
1-800-442-5938 (NY except Nassau County,
N.Y.C., & Southern Westchester County)

**Viasa-Venezuelan International Airways**
1-800-327-5454 (AL, AZ, AR, CA, CO, FL, GA,
ID, IA, KS, KY, LA, MN, MN, MO, MT, NE,
NV,NM, NY, NC, ND, OK, OR, SC, SD, TN, TX,
UT, WA, WY)
1-800-221-2150 (CT, DE, DC, IL, IN, ME, MD,
MA, MI, NH, NJ, OH, PA, RI, VT, VA, WV, WI)
1-800-432-9070 (FL)

**Virginia Atlantic Airways**
1-800-862-8621 (Cont. U.S.)

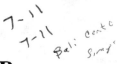

# APPENDIX B

## CAR RENTAL

**Agency Rent A Car**
1-800-321-1972 (Cont. U.S.)
1-800-362-1794 (Ohio)

**Airways Rent A Car**
1-800-952-9200

**Alamo Rent A Car**
1-800-327-9633 (Cont. U.S.)
1-800-732-3232 (Corporate )

**American International
Rent A Car**
1-800-527-0202

**Auto Host Rent A Car**
1-800-448-4678

**Avis Rent A Car**
1-800-331-1212 (Cont. U.S.)
1-800-228-0668 (Caribbean)
1-800-268-8900 (Canada)

**Budget Rent A Car**
1-800-527-0700 (Cont. U.S.)

**Dollar Rent A Car**
1-800-325-8007

**Entreprise Rent A Car**
1-800-421-6868

**General Rent A Car**
1-800-327-7607 (Cont. U.S.)

**Hertz Rent A Car**
1-800-227-3876 (International)
1-800-654-3131 (Cont. U.S.)
1-800-654-8200 (AK, HI)

**Inter American Car Rental**
1-800-327-1278

**National Car Rental**
1-800-CAR-RENT (Cont. U.S.)

**Payless Car Rental**
1-800-PAYLESS

**Rent A Wreck**
1-800-535-1391

**Snappy Car Rental**
1-800-669-4800

**Superior Rent A Car**
1-800-237-8106 (Cont. US)
1-800-551-9409 (Canada)

# APPENDIX B

**Thrifty Car Rental**
1-800-367-2277

**Value Rent A Car**
1-800-327-2501

*Handwritten notes:*

Dollar Rent - A CAR
1-800-800-4000

537.

MONDE 6.
179,06

6am 31 pm
24-

20%
4745
138,00
21,00

National
Canary
57.⁰⁰ RT 403653 3981
38 8:00

# 00016931USS
Budget

# APPENDIX C

**Admiral Cruises, Inc.**
1-800-327-0271 (Cont. U.S.)

**Bergen Line**
1-800-237-5361 (Cont. U.S.)

**Bermuda Star Line, Inc.**
1-800-237-5361 (Cont. U.S.)
Group Reservations
1-800-922-4262 (Cont. U.S.)

**Carnival Cruise Lines**
Group Reservations
1-800-327-5782 (Cont. U.S. except FL)
1-800-432-5424 (FL)
Hotline
1-800-327-2058 (Cont. U.S. except FL)
1-800-325-1216 (FL)
Air/Sea Reservations
1-800-321-6666 (Cont. U.S. except FL)

**Chandris Fantasy Cruises**
1-800-423-2100 (Cont. U.S. except FL)
1-800-621-3446 (Cont. U.S. except N.Y.C.)
1-800-432-4132 (FL)

**Commodore Cruise Lines**
1-800-327-5617 (Cont. U.S. except FL)
1-800-432-6793 (FL)

# APPENDIX C

**Costa Cruises**
1-800-462-6782 (Cont. U.S. except FL)
Group Reservations
1-800-447-6877 (Cont. U.S. except FL)

**Cunard**
(Cunard Countess, Cunard Princess, Queen Elizabeth 2,
Sagafjord and Vistafjord)
1-800-5-CUNARD (Cont. U.S., AK, HI)
1-800-228-6449 (AZ, CA [except Los Angeles], CO, ID,
MT, NV, NM, OR, UT, WA, WY)

**Delta Queen Steamboat Co.**
1-800-543-1949 (Cont. U.S.)

**Dolphin Cruise Line**
1-800-222-1003 (Cont. U.S.)
Group Reservations
1-800-843-5252 (Cont. U.S.)

**Epirotiki Lines**
1-800-221-2470 (Cont. U.S. [except New York], Canada

**Hapag-Lloyd Kreuzfahrten**
1-800-334-2724 (Cont. U.S. except New York)

**Holland America Line-Westours, Inc.**
1-800-426-0327 (Cont. U.S., AK, HI, Canada)
Group Reservations
1-800-426-0329 (Cont. U.S., AK, HI, Canada)

# APPENDIX C

**Norwegian Cruise Line**
1-800-327-7030 (Cont. U.S., Canada)
Group Reservations
1-800-327-7936 (Cont. U.S., Canada)

**Paquet Cruises, Inc.**
1-800-000-0555 (Cont. U.S.)

**Premier Cruise Lines**
1-800-327-7113 (Cont. U.S. except FL)
1-800-432-2545 (FL)
Group Reservations
1-800-327-9703 (Cont. U.S. except FL)
1-800-432-9923 (FL)

**Princess Cruises**
1-800-421-0522 (Cont. U.S., Canada)
Group Reservations
1-800-421-1700 (Cont. U.S., Canada)

**Royal Caribbean Cruise Lines, Inc.**
1-800-327-6700 (Cont. U.S. except FL)
1-800-432-6559 (FL)
Group Reservations
1-800-327-2055 (Cont. U.S. except FL)
1-800-423-3568 (FL)

**Royal Viking Line**
1-800-422-8000 (Cont. U.S.)
Group Reservations
1-800-423-1834

# APPENDIX C

**Seaescape Ltd.**
1-800-327-7400 (Cont. U.S. except FL)
1-800-432-0900 (FL)
Group Reservations
1-800-327-2005 (Cont. U.S. except FL)
1-800-432-4055 (FL)

**Sun Line Cruises**
1-800-872-6400 (Cont. U.S.)
1-800-468-6400 (Cont. U.S.)

**Windjammer Cruises, Inc.**
1-800-367-5000 (Cont. U.S., AK, HI)

# APPENDIX D

## HOTEL/MOTEL DIRECTORY

**Adam's Mark Hotels**
1-800-444-ADAM

**AMFAC Resorts**
(602) 527-2104

**Aston Hotels & Resorts**
1-800-922-7866
(808) 922-3368 (HI)

**Best Western International**
1-800-528-1234 (Cont. U.S., AK, HI, Canada)

**Budgetel Inns**
1-800-428-3438 (Cont. U.S., Canada)

**Budget Host Inns**
(817) 626-7064

**Chalet Susse**
1-800-258-1980 (Cont. U.S.)
1-800-572-1880 (NH)
1-800-858-5008 (Canada)

**Clarion Hotels & Resorts**
1-800-CLARION (Cont. U.S., AK, HI)
1-800-458-6262 Canada

# APPENDIX D

**Colony Hotels & Resorts, Inc.**
1-800-777-1700 (Cont. U.S., Canada)
1-800-367-6046 (HI)

**Comfort Inns International, Inc.**
1-800-228-5150 (Cont. U.S., HI, AK, Canada)

**Days Inns of America, Inc.**
1-800-325-2525 (Cont. U.S., AK, HI, Canada except Toronto)
(404) 320-2000 (Atlanta)
(416) 964-3434 (Toronto)

**Doral Hotels & Resorts**
1-800-327-6334 (Florida Hotels in Cont. U.S.)
1-800-FOR-A-TAN (Florida)
1-800-223-5823 (New York Hotels only Cont. U.S.)

**Econo Lodges of America, Inc.**
1-800-446-6900 (Cont. U.S., Canada)

**The Fairmont Hotels**
1-800-527-4727

**Four Seasons Hotels**
1-800-332-3442 (Cont. U.S.)
1-800-268-6282 (Canada)
(416) 445-5031 (Toronto)

**Guest Quarters Suite Hotels**
1-800-424-2900 (Cont. U.S. except D.C.)
(202) 861-6610 (DC)

# APPENDIX D

**Harley Hotels, Inc.**
1-800-321-2323 (Cont. U.S., Canada)

**Hawaiian Pacific Resorts**
1-800-367-5004 (Cont. U.S., AK, Canada)
1-800-272-5275 (HI)

**Helmsley Hotels**
1-800-334-3277 (Cont. U.S. except New York City, Canada)
(212) 888-1624 (New York)

**Hilton Hotels Corp.**
1-800-445-HILTONS (Cont. U.S., AK, HI)
1-800-268-9275 (Canada)
1-800-321-3232 (Group Reserverations of 10 rooms or more)

**Holiday Inns, Inc.**
1-800-465-4329 (Cont. U.S., AK, HI, Puerto Rico, U.S. Virgin Islands, Canada)

**Howard Johnson Franchise Systems Inc.**
1-800-654-2000 (Cont. U.S., Canada, Puerto Rico)
1-800-654-9122 (Group Reservations)
1-800-634-3464 (Senior Citizens Discount)

**Hyatt Hotels Corp.**
1-800-233-1234 (Cont. U.S., HI, Canada)
Group Reservations
(312) 641-1234 (Chicago, IL)
(808) 923-1234 (Hawaii)
(213) 670-4024 (Los Angeles)
(212) 490-6464 (New York)

# APPENDIX D

**Imperial Inns/Imperial Hotels Corp.**
(703) 524-4880

**Inter-Continental Hotels**
1-800-33-AGAIN (Cont. U.S., except Houston, TX)
(713) 931-1400 (Houston, TX)
1-800-327-0200 (Canada)

**The Leading Hotels of the World**
1-800-223-6800 (Cont. U.S., HI, Puerto Rico, U.S. Virgin Isl., Canada)
(212) 838-3110 (New York, N.Y.)
Group Reservations
1-800-223-1230 (Cont. U.S., HI, Puerto Rico, U.S. Virgin Isl.)
(212) 751-8915 (Canada)

**Lexington Hotel Suites**
1-800-537-8483 (Cont. U.S., Canada)

**Marriott Hotels & Resorts**
1-800-228-9290 (Cont. U.S. except NE, AK, HI, Puerto Rico, U.S. Virgin Isl., Canada)
1-800-642-8008 (NE)
(305) 643-2932 (Caribbean)
Group Reservations
(708) 318-0500 (Chicago, IL)
(213) 641-8702 (Los Angeles)
(212) 603-8200 (New York, N.Y.)
(703) 442-0440 (Wash., D.C.)

**Master Hosts Inns & Resorts**
1-800-251-1962 (Cont. U.S., Canada)

# APPENDIX D

**Meridien Hotels**
1-800-543-4300 (Cont. U.S., Canada)
<u>Group Reservations</u>
(404) 394-1240 (Atlanta, GA)
(312) 222-9200 (Chicago, IL)
(213) 854-0841 (Los Angeles, CA)
(212) 245-2920 (New York, N.Y.)
(202) 331-8856 (Washington, D.C.)

**Motel 6, Inc.**
(505) 891-6161

**Omni Hotels**
1-800-THE-OMNI (Cont. U.S., HI, Canada)

**Park Suites Hotels**
1-800-432-SARA (Cont. U.S.)
1-800-661-8363 (Canada)

**Penta Hotels, Inc.**
1-800-225-3456 (Cont. U.S. except N.Y.)
1-800-238-9877 (CA except Los Angeles)
(213) 622-2753 (Los Angeles)
(212) 239-8810 (New York, N.Y.)
1-800-634-3421 (Canada)

**Preferred Hotels Worldwide**
1-800-323-7500 (Cont. U.S., AK, HI, Puerto Rico, Canada)

# APPENDIX D

**Quality International, Inc.**
1-800-228-5151 (Cont. U.S., AK, HI, Canada)
Suite Reservations
1-800-221-2222 (Cont. U.S.)
Group Reservations
1-800-638-2657 (Cont. U.S., AK, HI, Canada, Mexico)
No Smoking Rooms
1-800-228-LUNG (Cont. U.S., HI, Canada)

**Ramada Hotel Group**
**Ramada Hotels**
1-800-228-2828 (Cont. U.S.)

**Ramada Renaissance Hotels**
1-800-228-9898 (Cont. U.S.)
(416) 485-2610 (Canada)
Group Reservations
(404) 843-8686 (Atlanta, GA)
(312) 372-5959 (Chicago, IL)
(213) 934-9341 (Los Angeles, CA)
(201) 587-1414 (New York, N.Y.)
(202) 429-0064 (Wash., D.C.)

**Red Carpet Inns**
1-800-251-1962 (Cont. U.S., Canada)

**Red Lion Hotels & Inns**
1-800-547-8010 (Cont. U.S., AK, HI, Puerto Rico, Canada)

**The Ritz-Carlton Hotel Company**
1-800-241-3333 (Cont. U.S., Canada)

# APPENDIX D

**Rodeway Inns International**
1-800-228-2000 (Cont. U.S., Canada, Bahamas)
Group Reservations
1-800-228-2660

**Shoney's Inns**
1-800-222-2222 (Cont. U.S.)
1-800-233-INNS (Canada)

**Sonesta International Hotels Corp.**
1-800-SONESTA (Cont. U.S., Canada)
Group Reservations
1-800-423-4740 (Cont. U.S. except IL)
(312) 787-8008 (IL)

**Stouffer Hotels and Resorts**
1-800-HOTELS-1 (Cont. U.S., Canada)
Meeting Express Service
1-800-USA-MEET (Cont. U.S.)

**Super 8 Motels, Inc.**
1-900-843-1991 (Cont. U.S., AK, HI, Canada)

**Swissotel**
1-800-63-SWISS (Cont. U.S.)

**Trusthouse Forte Hotels, Plc.**
1-800-CALLTHF (Cont. U.S., Canada)

# APPENDIX D

**The Vagabond Inns**
1-800-522-1555 (Cont. U.S., AK, HI, Puerto Rico,
U.S. Virgin Isl.)
1-800-468-2251 (Canada)

**Villas and Apartments Abroad**
1-800-433-3020

**Viscount Hotels**
1-800-CALLTHF (Cont. U.S., Canada)

**Walt Disney World Resorts**
1-800-647-7900 (Cont. U.S., Canada)

**Westin Hotels**
1-800-228-3000 (Cont. U.S., AK, HI, Canada)

**Wyndham Hotel Company**
1-800-822-4200 (Cont. U.S.)
1-800-631-4200 (Canada)
Group Reservations
1-800-327-8321 (Cont. U.S., AK, HI)

# APPENDIX E

## CANADA

**BC Rail Ltd.**
(604) 631-3500

**Via Rail Canada**
(514) 968-7805

## MEXICO

**National Railways of Mexico**
(312) 565-2778 (Chicago)
(213)203-8151 (Los Angeles)
(212) 755-7261 (New York)

## UNITED STATES

**Amtrak**
(800) USA-RAIL
(800) 4-AMTRAK (Canada)

**Alaska Railroad Corp.**
(800) 544-0552

## EUROPE

**Britrail**
(212) 599-5400

# APPENDIX E

**Benelux Tour Pass**
(212) 370-7360

**Eurail Pass**
(800) 722-7151

**European East Pass**
(800) 848-7245

**France Rail**
(800) 484-4000 or (800) 848-7245

**German Rail**
(800) 223-6036 or
(212) 308-3103

**Italian State Railway**
(212) 397-9300

**Spanish National Railroads**
**and Swiss Rail**
(800) 722-7151

# APPENDIX F

## STATE TOURISM OFFICES

Alabama
800-252-2262

Alaska
907-465-2010

Arizona
602-542-8687

Arkansas
800-NATURAL

California
800-862-2543

Colorado
800-433-2656

Connecticut
800-282-6863

Delaware
800-441-8846

Florida
904-487-1462

Georgia
800-847-4842

Hawaii
800-923-1811

Idaho
800-635-7820

Illinois
217-782-7139

Iowa
800-345-IOWA

Kansas
800-252-6727

Kentucky
800-225-8747

Louisiana
800-334-8626

Maine
800-533-9595

Maryland
800-543-1036

Massachusetts
800-447-6277

# APPENDIX F

Michigan
800-543-2937

Minnesota
800-657-3700

Mississippi
800-647-2290

Missouri
800-877-1234

Montana
800-541-1447

Nebraska
402-471-3111

Nevada
800-638-2328

New Hampshire
603-271-2343

New Jersey
800-537-7397

New Mexico
800-545-2040

New York
800-225-5697

North Carolina
800-847-4862

North Dakota
800-437-2077

Ohio
800-282-5393

Oklahoma
405-521-2409

Oregon
800-547-7842

Pennsylvania
800-847-4872

Rhode Island
800-556-2484

South Carolina
800-346-3643

South Dakota
800-843-1930

Tennessee
615-741-2158

Texas
800-888-8839

# APPENDIX F

Utah
801-538-1030

Vermont
802-828-3236

Virginia
800-248-4333

Washington
800-544-1800

West Virginia
800-225-5982

Wisconsin
800-432-8747

Wyoming
800-225-5996

# APPENDIX G

**Abercrombie & Kent International, Inc.**
800-323-7308

**Ameropa Travel**
800-221-9690

**Argosy Tours**
800-634-8105

**Arthur Frommer Holidays, Inc.**
800-221-9688
800-522-8860 (NY)

**ASTI Tours, Inc.**
800-223-7728
800-535-3711 (NY)

**Brendan Tours**
800-421-8446

**Chandris Tours**
800-223-0848

**CIE Tours International**
800-CIE-TOUR
800-522-5258 (NY)

**Creative Tours**
800-289-8687

**Cruise International Tours**
800-647-0009 or
800-222-3577

**Discovery Tours**
800-547-6310

**Domenico Tours**
800-554-TOUR

**Europa Tours**
800-523-9570

**Fantasy Holidays**
800-645-2555

**Funway Holidays**
800-558-3050

**Galaxy Tours**
800-523-7287

**Garber Magic Carpet Tours**
800-FLY-GARB

**Globus Gateway/ Cosmos**
800-221-0090 or
800-556-5454

# APPENDIX G

**Grand Circle Travel**
800-221-2610

**Great Connections Tours**
800-729-4567

**Great Escape Vacations**
800-223-2929

**Hawaiian Adventure**
800-248-9248

**Holiday Tours**
800-733-9011

**Ideal Vacations**
800-547-1464

**International Expeditions**
800-633-4734

**International Travel Planners**
800-223-7406

**Inter Tours Corp**
800-366-5458

**Jetset Tours**
800-453-8738 or
800-636-3273

**Jetway Tours**
800-421-8771

**Kemwel Group**
800-678-0678

**La Grand Tours**
800-327-2599
**Lifelong Learning Inc.**
800-854-4080

**Mackenzie Hawaii**
800-367-5190

**Magellan Tours**
800-445-3343

**Maiellano Tours**
800-223-1616

**Maupintour**
800-255-4266

**Olson-Travelworld**
800-421-2255
800-421-5785 (Calif.)

**Omega Tours**
800-645-1303

**Omni Tours**
800-962-0060

# APPENDIX G

Pacific Tours
800-843-1257

Perillo Tours
800-431-1515

Posh Hawaii
800-367-7674

Runaway Tours
800-622-0723

Scuba Ventures
Dive Tours
800-231-9707

Singleworld
Cruises and Tours
800-223-6490

Sobek Expeditions
800-777-7939

South America Reps.
800-423-2791 or
800-477-4470

Sportstalker
800-525-5520 or
800-332-5530

Student Travel International
800-525-0525

Supercities
800-556-5660

Tauck Tours
800-468-2825

Town and Country Tours
800-528-0421

Trafalgar Tours
800-854-0103

Travel Associates
800-452-0999

Trekamerica
800-221-0596

Unitravel
800-325-2222

Vacations Unlimited
800-284-0440

Villa Holidays
800-328-6262

# APPENDIX G

**Walt Disney Travel Co.**
800-327-2996 or 800-854-3104

**Wilderness Travel**
800-247-6700

**World Wide River Expeditions**
800-231-2769

# APPENDIX H

## TRAVEL INFORMATION HOTLINES

### AIR PASSENGER CONSUMER ADVOCACY GROUPS

**Aviation Consumer Action Project**
(202) 785-3704
A Ralph Nader consumer protection group.
Donations accepted for a copy of "Facts and
Advice for Airline Passengers."

**Airline Passengers Association of North America**
(703) 379-1152
Consumer rights group offering members legal
advice in disputes with airlines.

**Partnership for Improved Air Travel**
(800) 822-5210

### AIR TRAVEL COMPLAINTS & COMMENTS

**Dept. of Transportation**
(202) 366-2220
For your comments regarding commercial airline
service, schedules and fares

**Federal Aviation Administration**
(800) FAA-SURE
Consumer Information Hotline

# APPENDIX H

## FLIGHT SAFETY INFORMATION

### Federal Aviation Administration
(800) FAA-1111
Air safety and security updates

### The Aviation Safety Institute
(800) 848-7386
A private watchdog agency concerned with flight
 safety and security

### Consumer Affairs Office /Dept. of Transportation
(202) 366-2200
Publishes free fact sheets for flyers entitled:
"Tips for Defensive Flying;" "Tips on Avoiding Baggage
Problems;" "Public Charter Flights;" "Transporting Live
Animals;" "Frequent Flyer Programs"


## HEALTH QUESTIONS

### Center for Disease Control
(404) 332-4555  or (404) 639-1610
Advice on preventing serious illness
overseas, such as cholera and malaria

## PASSPORT INFORMATION

### U.S. State Department
(202) 647-0518
 24 hr. recorded passport information
(202) 326-6060
Additional passport information

# APPENDIX H

## TRAIN TRAVEL COMPLAINTS AND COMMENTS

**Amtrak Customer Relations**
(202) 906-2121

**National Assoc. of Railroad Passengers**
(202) 546-1550

## TRAVEL ADVISORY

**U.S. State Department**
(202) 647-5225
Visa and overseas health precautions,
trip-planning publications and updates on
dangerous or restricted areas for American
travelers

## TRAVEL AGENCY AND
## TOUR OPERATOR PROBLEMS

**American Society of Travel Agents (ASTA)**
(703) 739-2782

**National Tour Association (NTA)**
(800) 682-8886

**United States Tour Operators Assn. (USTOA)**
(212) 944-5727

# APPENDIX H

## WEATHER UPDATES

### American Express
(900) 932-8437
Weather reports for over 600 cities in
the U.S. and overseas

### American Automobile Assn.
(900) 884-AAA1
Weather updates, traffic reports and
road conditions

### Weather Trak
(900) 370-8728
Information and data on weather
conditions in over 750 cities
worldwide

# APPENDIX I

## TELEVISION TRAVEL DIRECTORY

*Check you local TV listings or cable guide for times & channels*

| NETWORK: | PROGRAM: |
|---|---|
| Arts & Entertainment | A Global Affair |
| Cable News Network | CNN Travel Guide |
| The Discovery Channel | The Adventurers<br>America Coast to Coast<br>Discovery on the Go |
| Nickelodeon | Kidsworld |
| Public Broadcasting System | Travels |
| The Travel Channel | American Road Trips<br>Arthur Frommer's Almanac<br>of Travel<br>Designs on Travel<br>The Great Escape<br>The Perfect Trip<br>Runaway with the Rich & Famous<br>Travel Bargains<br>Travel, Travel<br>United States |

# About The Author

Christopher Allen was born in Philadelphia, where he attended the Wharton School of Economics and graduated from the University of Pennsylvania.

He has worked in the travel industry for nearly 15 years, starting as a travel agent in Richmond, Virginia, then becoming director of marketing for two large travel agencies in the Washington, D.C. area.

He has served as a customer service representative for a domestic U.S. airline and as a supervisor with a major international carrier.

In this book, Mr. Allen shares his knowledge of the best values and discounts gleaned from his experiences of journeying nearly 1,000,000 miles and participating in numerous travel programs.

Hertz 640 Avis 189.00 - 378.00 7257695
Saint Barts July 31st to August 14 680.00